SUPER HOROSCOPE
LEO
2002
JULY 21–AUGUST 21

B

BERKLEY BOOKS, NEW YORK

A Berkley Book
Published by The Berkley Publishing Group
A division of Penguin Putnam Inc.
375 Hudson Street
New York, New York 10014

2002 SUPER HOROSCOPE LEO

The publishers regret that they cannot answer
individual letters requesting personal horoscope information.

PRINTING HISTORY
Berkley trade paperback edition / July 2001

Berkley trade paperback ISBN: 0-425-17974-5

The Penguin Putnam Inc. World Wide Web site address is
www.penguinputnam.com

PRINTED IN THE UNITED STATES OF AMERICA

10 9 8 7 6 5 4 3 2 1

CONTENTS

THE CUSP-BORN LEO

Are you *really* a Leo? If your birthday falls during the fourth week of July, at the beginning of Leo, will you still retain the traits of Cancer, the sign of the Zodiac before Leo? And what if you were born late in August—are you more Virgo than Leo? Many people born at the edge, or cusp, of a sign have difficulty determining exactly what sign they are. If you are one of these people, here's how you can figure it out, once and for all.

Consult the cusp table on the facing page, then locate the year of your birth. The table will tell you the precise days on which the Sun entered and left your sign for the year of your birth. In that way you can determine if you are a true Leo—or whether you are a Cancer or Virgo—according to the variations in cusp dates from year to year (see also page 17).

If you were born at the beginning or end of Leo, yours is a lifetime reflecting a process of subtle transformation. Your life on Earth will symbolize a significant change in consciousness, for you are either about to enter a whole new way of living or are leaving one behind.

If you are a Leo, born during the fourth week of July, you may want to read the horoscope book for Cancer as well as Leo. Cancer holds the keys to many of your secret uncertainties and deep-rooted problems, and your secret needs and wishes. You are the spirit of independence and creativity, or want to be. Yet through Cancer you reveal your deep, but often hidden, need to have strong ties. You may be trying to leave dependencies behind, yet you find yourself drawn again and again to the past or to family responsibilities.

You reflect the birth of a new sign, a ripe, whole person, fully able to tap and realize all your potentials for love and creativity.

If you were born after the third week of August, you may want to read the horoscope book for Virgo as well, for through Virgo you learn to put all your talents as a lover or creator to work. Your love for life is infectious, and your zest and sunny disposition are an inspiration to everyone around you. You are capable of seriousness, discipline, and great diligence.

You are a lover—ardent, passionate, and determined that love will not elude you. Though you may try to avoid it, you will find yourself in work, health, or duty situations that demand less emotion and more mind. You are not afraid of taking a gamble and are reluctant to give up your love of enjoyment for work or studies. You can blend professionalism and propriety in perfect amounts. You are the natural mixture of creativity and discipline, able to feel and to analyze. You symbolize the warmth and fullness of a late summer day, a natural ripeness and maturity that is mellow and comfortable to be near.

THE CUSPS OF LEO

DATES SUN ENTERS LEO (LEAVES CANCER)

July 23 every year from 1900 to 2010, except for the following:

July 22

1928	1953	1968	1981	1992	2001	2010
32	56	69	84	93	2002	
36	57	72	85	94	2004	
40	60	73	86	96	2005	
44	61	76	88	97	2006	
48	64	77	89	98	2008	
52	65	80	90	2000	2009	

DATES SUN LEAVES LEO (ENTERS VIRGO)

August 23 every year from 1900 to 2010, except for the following:

August 22				August 24	
1960	1980	1992	2001	1903	1919
64	84	93	2004	07	23
68	88	96	2005	11	27
72	89	97	2008	15	
76		2000	2009		

THE ASCENDANT: LEO RISING

Could you be a "double" Leo? That is, could you have Leo as your Rising sign as well as your Sun sign? The tables on pages 8–9 will tell you Leos what your Rising sign happens to be. Just find the hour of your birth, then find the day of your birth, and you will see which sign of the Zodiac is your Ascendant, as the Rising sign is called. The Ascendant is called that because it is the sign rising on the eastern horizon at the time of your birth. For a more detailed discussion of the Rising sign and the twelve houses of the Zodiac, see pages 17–20.

The Ascendant, or Rising sign, is placed on the 1st house in a horoscope, of which there are twelve houses. The 1st house represents your response to the environment—your unique response. Call it identity, personality, ego, self-image, facade, come-on, body-mind-spirit—whatever term best conveys to you the meaning of the you that acts and reacts in the world. It is a you that is always changing, discovering a new you. Your identity started with birth and early environment, over which you had little conscious control, and continues to experience, to adjust, to express itself. The 1st house also represents how others see you. Has anyone ever guessed your sign to be your Rising sign? People may respond to that personality, that facade, that body type governed by your Rising sign.

Your Ascendant, or Rising sign, modifies your basic Sun sign personality, and it affects the way you act out the daily predictions for your Sun sign. If your Rising sign indeed is Leo, what follows is a description of its effect on your horoscope. If your Rising sign is not Leo, but some other sign of the Zodiac, you may wish to read the horoscope book for that sign as well.

With Leo on the Ascendant, that is, in the 1st house, the planet that rules Leo is therefore in the 1st house. That planet is the Sun. Here it may give you a special robustness—in appearance, in health, in spirit, in action—that you can count on long after your normal energy reserves have dried up. On the negative side, the Sun here may give you an overdose of pride or insolence. Such pride could make you quick to resent or retaliate when reason instead should be the response.

Leo in the 1st house accentuates every Leo trait, for the Rising sign has a strong influence in your horoscope. A flair for the dramatic will be especially evident in the fabric of your life. You like managing people and events as long as you can play center stage, or at least weave a powerful character part, for much of the time. You could create intrigue if it provides an opportunity for you to take a leading role. However much you like pulling strings, though, your frank and generous disposition rises above petty disputes. You abhor superficial alliances or cliques of any sort.

There may also be drama in your personal appearance and in your possessions and surroundings. You have been known to adorn yourself and your environment as much, maybe sometimes more, for the effect it will create as for the comfort it will give you and others. Your appearance itself, whether natural or affected, may well run to the true Leo type: high coloring, proud head, bold stance. You can use physical gestures as signals to people—to lure, to persuade, to threaten. And because love, especially to be loved, is a fundament of your ego, your body language acts instinctively to attract people to you.

Your search for identity will never be a solitary, introspective one. Public appreciation and power are important to you. You need constant interaction with and approval from people. You are likely to find the most satisfying ties with groups whose goals are humanitarian and ideological, whether the groups are social or political or educational. But before you do, you may discover in youth and early adulthood many facets of yourself through creations that are not so tightly bound to an organized group. And it is imperative for you to create—a work of art, a child, an intrigue, a love affair, a partnership, a principle.

Your need for people may reflect an inner insecurity. That self-image, which you experience as constantly changing, may not be actualized until you see it mirrored in people's responses; a positive one reinforces your natural enthusiasm, a negative one may induce self-pity. Your need for creation may also be tied to the building of an ego. You seek success, and are very likely to get your lion's share of it in your lifetime, through what you do, not through what you are. For what you do allows you to know and then to be who you are. You expect your creations and your things to bestow honor upon you; they are not merely natural or spontaneous expressions.

Above all, love and loyalty are the key words through which you with Leo Rising seek to root yourself in your environment. Love and loyalty motivate your simplest act, your grandest attempt. They, too, can be the cause of pain and loss. You are happiest when you love and are loved in return.

RISING SIGNS FOR LEO

Hour of Birth*	Day of Birth		
	July 22–27	July 28– August 1	August 2–6
Midnight	Taurus	Taurus	Gemini
1 AM	Gemini	Gemini	Gemini
2 AM	Gemini	Gemini	Cancer
3 AM	Cancer	Cancer	Cancer
4 AM	Cancer	Cancer	Cancer
5 AM	Leo	Leo	Leo
6 AM	Leo	Leo	Leo
7 AM	Leo	Leo; Virgo 8/1	Virgo
8 AM	Virgo	Virgo	Virgo
9 AM	Virgo	Virgo	Virgo
10 AM	Libra	Libra	Libra
11 AM	Libra	Libra	Libra
Noon	Libra	Libra; Scorpio 7/30	Scorpio
1 PM	Scorpio	Scorpio	Scorpio
2 PM	Scorpio	Scorpio	Scorpio
3 PM	Sagittarius	Sagittarius	Sagittarius
4 PM	Sagittarius	Sagittarius	Sagittarius
5 PM	Sagittarius	Capricorn	Capricorn
6 PM	Capricorn	Capricorn	Capricorn
7 PM	Capricorn; Aquarius 7/26	Aquarius	Aquarius
8 PM	Aquarius	Aquarius	Aquarius; Pisces 8/3
9 PM	Pisces	Pisces	Pisces
10 PM	Aries	Aries	Aries
11 PM	Aries; Taurus 7/26	Taurus	Taurus

*Hour of birth given here is for Standard Time in any time zone. If your hour of birth was recorded in Daylight Saving Time, subtract one hour from it and consult that hour in the table above. For example, if you were born at 9 AM D.S.T., see 8 AM above.

Hour of Birth*	Day of Birth		
	August 7–11	August 12–17	August 18–24
Midnight	Gemini	Gemini	Gemini
1 AM	Gemini	Gemini	Cancer
2 AM	Cancer	Cancer	Cancer
3 AM	Cancer	Cancer	Cancer; Leo 8/22
4 AM	Leo	Leo	Leo
5 AM	Leo	Leo	Leo
6 AM	Leo	Leo; Virgo 8/16	Virgo
7 AM	Virgo	Virgo	Virgo
8 AM	Virgo	Virgo	Virgo; Libra 8/22
9 AM	Libra	Libra	Libra
10 AM	Libra	Libra	Libra
11 AM	Libra	Libra; Scorpio 8/14	Scorpio
Noon	Scorpio	Scorpio	Scorpio
1 PM	Scorpio	Scorpio	Scorpio; Sagittarius 8/22
2 PM	Sagittarius	Sagittarius	Sagittarius
3 PM	Sagittarius	Sagittarius	Sagittarius
4 PM	Sagittarius	Capricorn	Capricorn
5 PM	Capricorn	Capricorn	Capricorn
6 PM	Capricorn	Aquarius	Aquarius
7 PM	Aquarius	Aquarius	Pisces
8 PM	Pisces	Pisces	Pisces; Aries 8/21
9 PM	Aries	Aries	Aries
10 PM	Aries; Taurus 8/11	Taurus	Taurus
11 PM	Taurus	Taurus	Gemini

*See note on facing page.

THE PLACE OF ASTROLOGY IN TODAY'S WORLD

Does astrology have a place in the fast-moving, ultra-scientific world we live in today? Can it be justified in a sophisticated society whose outriders are already preparing to step off the moon into the deep space of the planets themselves? Or is it just a hangover of ancient superstition, a psychological dummy for neurotics and dreamers of every historical age?

These are the kind of questions that any inquiring person can be expected to ask when they approach a subject like astrology which goes beyond, but never excludes, the materialistic side of life.

The simple, single answer is that astrology works. It works for many millions of people in the western world alone. In the United States there are 10 million followers and in Europe, an estimated 25 million. America has more than 4000 practicing astrologers, Europe nearly three times as many. Even down-under Australia has its hundreds of thousands of adherents. In the eastern countries, astrology has enormous followings, again, because it has been proved to work. In India, for example, brides and grooms for centuries have been chosen on the basis of their astrological compatibility.

Astrology today is more vital than ever before, more practicable because all over the world the media devotes much space and time to it, more valid because science itself is confirming the precepts of astrological knowledge with every new exciting step. The ordinary person who daily applies astrology intelligently does not have to wonder whether it is true nor believe in it blindly. He can see it working for himself. And, if he can use it—and this book is designed to help the reader to do just that—he can make living a far richer experience, and become a more developed personality and a better person.

Astrology and Relationships

Astrology is the science of relationships. It is not just a study of planetary influences on man and his environment. It is the study of man himself.

We are at the center of our personal universe, of all our relationships. And our happiness or sadness depends on how we act, how we relate to the people and things that surround us. The emotions that we generate have a distinct effect—for better or worse—on the world around us. Our friends and our enemies will confirm this. Just look in the mirror the next time you are angry. In other words, each of us is a kind of sun or planet or star radiating our feelings on the environment around us. Our influence on our personal universe, whether loving, helpful, or destructive, varies with our changing moods, expressed through our individual character.

Our personal "radiations" are potent in the way they affect our moods and our ability to control them. But we usually are able to throw off our emotion in some sort of action—we have a good cry, walk it off, or tell someone our troubles—before it can build up too far and make us physically ill. Astrology helps us to understand the universal forces working on us, and through this understanding, we can become more properly adjusted to our surroundings so that we find ourselves coping where others may flounder.

The Challenge of Love

The challenge of love lies in recognizing the difference between infatuation, emotion, sex, and, sometimes, the intentional deceit of the other person. Mankind, with its record of broken marriages, despair, and disillusionment, is obviously not very good at making these distinctions.

Can astrology help?

Yes. In the same way that advance knowledge can usually help in any human situation. And there is probably no situation as human, as poignant, as pathetic and universal, as the failure of man's love.

Love, of course, is not just between man and woman. It involves love of children, parents, home, and friends. But the big problems usually involve the choice of partner.

Astrology has established degrees of compatibility that exist between people born under the various signs of the Zodiac. Because people are individuals, there are numerous variations and modifications. So the astrologer, when approached on mate and marriage matters, makes allowances for them. But the fact remains that some groups of people are suited for each other and some are not, and astrology has expressed this in terms of characteristics we all can study and use as a personal guide.

No matter how much enjoyment and pleasure we find in the different aspects of each other's character, if it is not an overall compatibility, the chances of our finding fulfillment or enduring happiness in each other are pretty hopeless. And astrology can help us to find someone compatible.

Astrology and Science

Closely related to our emotions is the "other side" of our personal universe, our physical welfare. Our body, of course, is largely influenced by things around us over which we have very little control. The phone rings, we hear it. The train runs late. We snag our stocking or cut our face shaving. Our body is under a constant bombardment of events that influence our daily lives to varying degrees.

The question that arises from all this is, what makes each of us act so that we have to involve other people and keep the ball of activity and evolution rolling? This is the question that both science and astrology are involved with. The scientists have attacked it from different angles: anthropology, the study of human evolution as body, mind and response to environment; anatomy, the study of bodily structure; psychology, the science of the human mind; and so on. These studies have produced very impressive classifications and valuable information, but because the approach to the problem is fragmented, so is the result. They remain "branches" of science. Science generally studies effects. It keeps turning up wonderful answers but no lasting solutions. Astrology, on the other hand, approaches the question from the broader viewpoint. Astrology began its inquiry with the totality of human experience and saw it as an effect. It then looked to find the cause, or at least the prime movers, and during thousands of years of observation of man and his *universal* environment came up with the extraordinary principle of planetary influence—or astrology, which, from the Greek, means the science of the stars.

Modern science, as we shall see, has confirmed much of astrology's foundations—most of it unintentionally, some of it reluctantly, but still, indisputably.

It is not difficult to imagine that there must be a connection between outer space and Earth. Even today, scientists are not too sure how our Earth was created, but it is generally agreed that it is only a tiny part of the universe. And as a part of the universe, people on Earth see and feel the influence of heavenly bodies in almost every aspect of our existence. There is no doubt that the Sun has the greatest influence on life on this planet. Without it there would be no life, for without it there would be no warmth, no division into day and night, no cycles of time or season at all. This is clear and easy to see. The influence of the Moon, on the other hand, is more subtle, though no less definite.

There are many ways in which the influence of the Moon manifests itself here on Earth, both on human and animal life. It is a well-known fact, for instance, that the large movements of water on our planet—that is the ebb and flow of the tides—are caused by the Moon's gravitational pull. Since this is so, it follows that these water movements do not occur only in the oceans, but that all bodies of water are affected, even down to the tiniest puddle.

The human body, too, which consists of about 70 percent water, falls within the scope of this lunar influence. For example the menstrual cycle of most women corresponds to the 28-day lunar month; the period of pregnancy in humans is 273 days, or equal to nine lunar months. Similarly, many illnesses reach a crisis at the change of the Moon, and statistics in many countries have shown that the crime rate is highest at the time of the Full Moon. Even human sexual desire has been associated with the phases of the Moon. But it is in the movement of the tides that we get the clearest demonstration of planetary influence, which leads to the irresistible correspondence between the so-called metaphysical and the physical.

Tide tables are prepared years in advance by calculating the future positions of the Moon. Science has known for a long time that the Moon is the main cause of tidal action. But only in the last few years has it begun to realize the possible extent of this influence on mankind. To begin with, the ocean tides do not rise and fall as we might imagine from our personal observations of them. The Moon as it orbits around Earth sets up a circular wave of attraction which pulls the oceans of the world after it, broadly in an east to west direction. This influence is like a phantom wave crest, a loop of power stretching from pole to pole which passes over and around the Earth like an invisible shadow. It travels with equal effect across the land masses and, as scientists were recently amazed to observe, caused oysters placed in the dark in the middle of the United States where there is no sea to open their shells to receive the nonexistent tide. If the land-locked oysters react to this invisible signal, what effect does it have on us who not so long ago in evolutionary time came out of the sea and still have its salt in our blood and sweat?

Less well known is the fact that the Moon is also the primary force behind the circulation of blood in human beings and animals, and the movement of sap in trees and plants. Agriculturists have established that the Moon has a distinct influence on crops, which explains why for centuries people have planted according to Moon cycles. The habits of many animals, too, are directed by the movement of the Moon. Migratory birds, for instance, depart only at or near the time of the Full Moon. And certain sea creatures, eels in particular, move only in accordance with certain phases of the Moon.

Know Thyself—Why?

In today's fast-changing world, everyone still longs to know what the future holds. It is the one thing that everyone has in common: rich and poor, famous and infamous, all are deeply concerned about tomorrow.

But the key to the future, as every historian knows, lies in the past. This is as true of individual people as it is of nations. You cannot understand your future without first understanding your past, which is simply another way of saying that you must first of all know yourself.

The motto "know thyself" seems obvious enough nowadays, but it was originally put forward as the foundation of wisdom by the ancient Greek philosophers. It was then adopted by the "mystery religions" of the ancient Middle East, Greece, Rome, and is still used in all genuine schools of mind training or mystical discipline, both in those of the East, based on yoga, and those of the West. So it is universally accepted now, and has been through the ages.

But how do you go about discovering what sort of person you are? The first step is usually classification into some sort of system of types. Astrology did this long before the birth of Christ. Psychology has also done it. So has modern medicine, in its way.

One system classifies people according to the source of the impulses they respond to most readily: the muscles, leading to direct bodily action; the digestive organs, resulting in emotion; or the brain and nerves, giving rise to thinking. Another such system says that character is determined by the endocrine glands, and gives us such labels as "pituitary," "thyroid," and "hyperthyroid" types. These different systems are neither contradictory nor mutually exclusive. In fact, they are very often different ways of saying the same thing.

Very popular, useful classifications were devised by Carl Jung, the eminent disciple of Freud. Jung observed among the different faculties of the mind, four which have a predominant influence on character. These four faculties exist in all of us without exception, but not in perfect balance. So when we say, for instance, that someone is a "thinking type," it means that in any situation he or she tries to be rational. Emotion, which may be the opposite of thinking, will be his or her weakest function. This thinking type can be sensible and reasonable, or calculating and unsympathetic. The emotional type, on the other hand, can often be recognized by exaggerated language—everything is either marvelous or terrible—and in extreme cases they even invent dramas and quarrels out of nothing just to make life more interesting.

The other two faculties are intuition and physical sensation. The sensation type does not only care for food and drink, nice clothes and furniture; he or she is also interested in all forms of physical experience. Many scientists are sensation types as are athletes and nature-lovers. Like sensation, intuition is a form of perception and we all possess it. But it works through that part of the mind which is not under conscious control—consequently it sees meanings and connections which are not obvious to thought or emotion. Inventors and original thinkers are always intuitive, but so, too, are superstitious people who see meanings where none exist.

Thus, sensation tells us what is going on in the world, feeling (that is, emotion) tells us how important it is to ourselves, thinking enables us to interpret it and work out what we should do about it, and intuition tells us what it means to ourselves and others. All four faculties are essential, and all are present in every one of us. But some people are guided chiefly by one, others by another. In addition, Jung also observed a division of the human personality into the extrovert and the introvert, which cuts across these four types.

A disadvantage of all these systems of classification is that one cannot tell very easily where to place oneself. Some people are reluctant to admit that they act to please their emotions. So they deceive themselves for years by trying to belong to whichever type they think is the "best." Of course, there is no best; each has its faults and each has its good points.

The advantage of the signs of the Zodiac is that they simplify classification. Not only that, but your date of birth is personal— it is unarguably yours. What better way to know yourself than by going back as far as possible to the very moment of your birth? And this is precisely what your horoscope is all about, as we shall see in the next section.

WHAT IS A HOROSCOPE?

If you had been able to take a picture of the skies at the moment of your birth, that photograph would be your horoscope. Lacking such a snapshot, it is still possible to recreate the picture—and this is at the basis of the astrologer's art. In other words, your horoscope is a representation of the skies with the planets in the exact positions they occupied at the time you were born.

The year of birth tells an astrologer the positions of the distant, slow-moving planets Jupiter, Saturn, Uranus, Neptune, and Pluto. The month of birth indicates the Sun sign, or birth sign as it is commonly called, as well as indicating the positions of the rapidly moving planets Venus, Mercury, and Mars. The day and time of birth will locate the position of our Moon. And the moment—the exact hour and minute—of birth determines the houses through what is called the Ascendant, or Rising sign.

With this information the astrologer consults various tables to calculate the specific positions of the Sun, Moon, and other planets relative to your birthplace at the moment you were born. Then he or she locates them by means of the Zodiac.

The Zodiac

The Zodiac is a band of stars (constellations) in the skies, centered on the Sun's apparent path around the Earth, and is divided into twelve equal segments, or signs. What we are actually dividing up is the Earth's path around the Sun. But from our point of view here on Earth, it seems as if the Sun is making a great circle around our planet in the sky, so we say it is the Sun's apparent path. This twelvefold division, the Zodiac, is a reference system for the astrologer. At any given moment the planets—and in astrology both the Sun and Moon are considered to be planets—can all be located at a specific point along this path.

Now where in all this are you, the subject of the horoscope? Your character is largely determined by the sign the Sun is in. So that is where the astrologer looks first in your horoscope, at your Sun sign.

The Sun Sign and the Cusp

There are twelve signs in the Zodiac, and the Sun spends approximately one month in each sign. But because of the motion of the Earth around the Sun—the Sun's apparent motion—the dates when the Sun enters and leaves each sign may change from year to year. Some people born near the cusp, or edge, of a sign have difficulty determining which is their Sun sign. But in this book a Table of Cusps is provided for the years 1900 to 2010 (page 5) so you can find out what your true Sun sign is.

Here are the twelve signs of the Zodiac, their ancient zodiacal symbol, and the dates when the Sun enters and leaves each sign for the year 2002. Remember, these dates may change from year to year.

ARIES	Ram	March 20–April 20
TAURUS	Bull	April 20–May 21
GEMINI	Twins	May 21–June 21
CANCER	Crab	June 21–July 22
LEO	Lion	July 22–August 23
VIRGO	Virgin	August 23–September 22
LIBRA	Scales	September 23–October 23
SCORPIO	Scorpion	October 23–November 22
SAGITTARIUS	Archer	November 22–December 21
CAPRICORN	Sea Goat	December 21–January 20
AQUARIUS	Water Bearer	January 20–February 18
PISCES	Fish	February 18–March 20

It is possible to draw significant conclusions and make meaningful predictions based simply on the Sun sign of a person. There are many people who have been amazed at the accuracy of the description of their own character based only on the Sun sign. But an astrologer needs more information than just your Sun sign to interpret the photograph that is your horoscope.

The Rising Sign and the Zodiacal Houses

An astrologer needs the exact time and place of your birth in order to construct and interpret your horoscope. The illustration on the next page shows the flat chart, or natural wheel, an astrologer uses. Note the inner circle of the wheel labeled 1 through 12. These 12 divisions are known as the houses of the Zodiac.

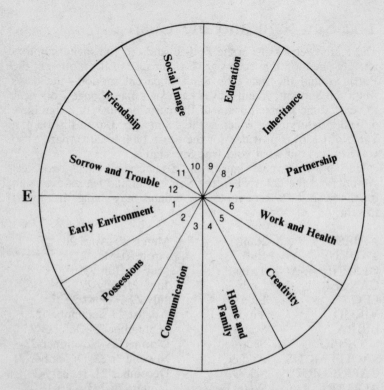

The 1st house always starts from the position marked E, which corresponds to the eastern horizon. The rest of the houses 2 through 12 follow around in a "counterclockwise" direction. The point where each house starts is known as a cusp, or edge.

The cusp, or edge, of the 1st house (point E) is where an astrologer would place your Rising sign, the Ascendant. And, as already noted, the exact time of your birth determines your Rising sign. Let's see how this works.

As the Earth rotates on its axis once every 24 hours, each one of the twelve signs of the Zodiac appears to be "rising" on the horizon, with a new one appearing about every 2 hours. Actually it is the turning of the Earth that exposes each sign to view, but in our astrological work we are discussing apparent motion. This Rising sign marks the Ascendant, and it colors the whole orientation of a horoscope. It indicates the sign governing the 1st house of the chart, and will thus determine which signs will govern all the other houses.

To visualize this idea, imagine two color wheels with twelve divisions superimposed upon each other. For just as the Zodiac is divided into twelve constellations that we identify as the signs, another twelvefold division is used to denote the houses. Now imagine one wheel (the signs) moving slowly while the other wheel (the houses) remains still. This analogy may help you see how the signs keep shifting the "color" of the houses as the Rising sign continues to change every two hours. To simplify things, a Table of Rising Signs has been provided (pages 8–9) for your specific Sun sign.

Once your Rising sign has been placed on the cusp of the 1st house, the signs that govern the rest of the 11 houses can be placed on the chart. In any individual's horoscope the signs do not necessarily correspond with the houses. For example, it could be that a sign covers part of two adjacent houses. It is the interpretation of such variations in an individual's horoscope that marks the professional astrologer.

But to gain a workable understanding of astrology, it is not necessary to go into great detail. In fact, we just need a description of the houses and their meanings, as is shown in the illustration above and in the table below.

THE 12 HOUSES OF THE ZODIAC

1st	Individuality, body appearance, general outlook on life	Personality house
2nd	Finance, possessions, ethical principles, gain or loss	Money house
3rd	Relatives, communication, short journeys, writing, education	Relatives house
4th	Family and home, parental ties, land and property, security	Home house
5th	Pleasure, children, creativity, entertainment, risk	Pleasure house
6th	Health, harvest, hygiene, work and service, employees	Health house
7th	Marriage and divorce, the law, partnerships and alliances	Marriage house
8th	Inheritance, secret deals, sex, death, regeneration	Inheritance house
9th	Travel, sports, study, philosophy and religion	Travel house
10th	Career, social standing, success and honor	Business house
11th	Friendship, social life, hopes and wishes	Friends house
12th	Troubles, illness, secret enemies, hidden agendas	Trouble house

The Planets in the Houses

An astrologer, knowing the exact time and place of your birth, will use tables of planetary motion in order to locate the planets in your horoscope chart. He or she will determine which planet or planets are in which sign and in which house. It is not uncommon, in an individual's horoscope, for there to be two or more planets in the same sign and in the same house.

The characteristics of the planets modify the influence of the Sun according to their natures and strengths.

Sun: Source of life. Basic temperament according to the Sun sign. The conscious will. Human potential.

Moon: Emotions. Moods. Customs. Habits. Changeable. Adaptive. Nurturing.

Mercury: Communication. Intellect. Reasoning power. Curiosity. Short travels.

Venus: Love. Delight. Charm. Harmony. Balance. Art. Beautiful possessions.

Mars: Energy. Initiative. War. Anger. Adventure. Courage. Daring. Impulse.

Jupiter: Luck. Optimism. Generous. Expansive. Opportunities. Protection.

Saturn: Pessimism. Privation. Obstacles. Delay. Hard work. Research. Lasting rewards after long struggle.

Uranus: Fashion. Electricity. Revolution. Independence. Freedom. Sudden changes. Modern science.

Neptune: Sensationalism. Theater. Dreams. Inspiration. Illusion. Deception.

Pluto: Creation and destruction. Total transformation. Lust for power. Strong obsessions.

Superimpose the characteristics of the planets on the functions of the house in which they appear. Express the result through the character of the Sun sign, and you will get the basic idea.

Of course, many other considerations have been taken into account in producing the carefully worked out predictions in this book: the aspects of the planets to each other; their strength according to position and sign; whether they are in a house of exaltation or decline; whether they are natural enemies or not; whether a planet occupies its own sign; the position of a planet in relation to its own house or sign; whether the sign is male or female; whether the sign is a fire, earth, water, or air sign. These are only a few of the colors on the astrologer's pallet which he or she must mix with the inspiration of the artist and the accuracy of the mathematician.

How To Use These Predictions

A person reading the predictions in this book should understand that they are produced from the daily position of the planets for a group of people and are not, of course, individually specialized. To get the full benefit of them our readers should relate the predictions to their own character and circumstances, coordinate them, and draw their own conclusions from them.

If you are a serious observer of your own life, you should find a definite pattern emerging that will be a helpful and reliable guide.

The point is that we always retain our free will. The stars indicate certain directional tendencies but we are not compelled to follow. We can do or not do, and wisdom must make the choice.

We all have our good and bad days. Sometimes they extend into cycles of weeks. It is therefore advisable to study daily predictions in a span ranging from the day before to several days ahead.

Daily predictions should be taken very generally. The word "difficult" does not necessarily indicate a whole day of obstruction or inconvenience. It is a warning to you to be cautious. Your caution will often see you around the difficulty before you are involved. This is the correct use of astrology.

In another section (pages 78–84), detailed information is given about the influence of the Moon as it passes through each of the twelve signs of the Zodiac. There are instructions on how to use the Moon Tables (pages 85–92), which provide Moon Sign Dates throughout the year as well as the Moon's role in health and daily affairs. This information should be used in conjunction with the daily forecasts to give a fuller picture of the astrological trends.

HISTORY OF ASTROLOGY

The origins of astrology have been lost far back in history, but we do know that reference is made to it as far back as the first written records of the human race. It is not hard to see why. Even in primitive times, people must have looked for an explanation for the various happenings in their lives. They must have wanted to know why people were different from one another. And in their search they turned to the regular movements of the Sun, Moon, and stars to see if they could provide an answer.

It is interesting to note that as soon as man learned to use his tools in any type of design, or his mind in any kind of calculation, he turned his attention to the heavens. Ancient cave dwellings reveal dim crescents and circles representative of the Sun and Moon, rulers of day and night. Mesopotamia and the civilization of Chaldea, in itself the foundation of those of Babylonia and Assyria, show a complete picture of astronomical observation and well-developed astrological interpretation.

Humanity has a natural instinct for order. The study of anthropology reveals that primitive people—even as far back as prehistoric times—were striving to achieve a certain order in their lives. They tried to organize the apparent chaos of the universe. They had the desire to attach meaning to things. This demand for order has persisted throughout the history of man. So that observing the regularity of the heavenly bodies made it logical that primitive peoples should turn heavenward in their search for an understanding of the world in which they found themselves so random and alone.

And they did find a significance in the movements of the stars. Shepherds tending their flocks, for instance, observed that when the cluster of stars now known as the constellation Aries was in sight, it was the time of fertility and they associated it with the Ram. And they noticed that the growth of plants and plant life corresponded with different phases of the Moon, so that certain times were favorable for the planting of crops, and other times were not. In this way, there grew up a tradition of seasons and causes connected with the passage of the Sun through the twelve signs of the Zodiac.

Astrology was valued so highly that the king was kept informed of the daily and monthly changes in the heavenly bodies, and the results of astrological studies regarding events of the future. Head astrologers were clearly men of great rank and position, and the office was said to be a hereditary one.

Omens were taken, not only from eclipses and conjunctions of the Moon or Sun with one of the planets, but also from storms and earthquakes. In the eastern civilizations, particularly, the reverence inspired by astrology appears to have remained unbroken since the very earliest days. In ancient China, astrology, astronomy, and religion went hand in hand. The astrologer, who was also an astronomer, was part of the official government service and had his own corner in the Imperial Palace. The duties of the Imperial astrologer, whose office was one of the most important in the land, were clearly defined, as this extract from early records shows:

> This exalted gentleman must concern himself with the stars in the heavens, keeping a record of the changes and movements of the Planets, the Sun and the Moon, in order to examine the movements of the terrestrial world with the object of prognosticating good and bad fortune. He divides the territories of the nine regions of the empire in accordance with their dependence on particular celestial bodies. All the fiefs and principalities are connected with the stars and from this their prosperity or misfortune should be ascertained. He makes prognostications according to the twelve years of the Jupiter cycle of good and evil of the terrestrial world. From the colors of the five kinds of clouds, he determines the coming of floods or droughts, abundance or famine. From the twelve winds, he draws conclusions about the state of harmony of heaven and earth, and takes note of good and bad signs that result from their accord or disaccord. In general, he concerns himself with five kinds of phenomena so as to warn the Emperor to come to the aid of the government and to allow for variations in the ceremonies according to their circumstances.

The Chinese were also keen observers of the fixed stars, giving them such unusual names as Ghost Vehicle, Sun of Imperial Concubine, Imperial Prince, Pivot of Heaven, Twinkling Brilliance, Weaving Girl. But, great astrologers though they may have been, the Chinese lacked one aspect of mathematics that the Greeks applied to astrology—deductive geometry. Deductive geometry was the basis of much classical astrology in and after the time of the Greeks, and this explains the different methods of prognostication used in the East and West.

Down through the ages the astrologer's art has depended, not so much on the uncovering of new facts, though this is important, as on the interpretation of the facts already known. This is the essence of the astrologer's skill.

But why should the signs of the Zodiac have any effect at all on the formation of human character? It is easy to see why people thought they did, and even now we constantly use astrological expressions in our everyday speech. The thoughts of "lucky star," "ill-fated," "star-crossed," "mooning around," are interwoven into the very structure of our language.

Wherever the concept of the Zodiac is understood and used, it could well appear to have an influence on the human character. Does this mean, then, that the human race, in whose civilization the idea of the twelve signs of the Zodiac has long been embedded, is divided into only twelve types? Can we honestly believe that it is really as simple as that? If so, there must be pretty wide ranges of variation within each type. And if, to explain the variation, we call in heredity and environment, experiences in early childhood, the thyroid and other glands, and also the four functions of the mind together with extroversion and introversion, then one begins to wonder if the original classification was worth making at all. No sensible person believes that his favorite system explains everything. But even so, he will not find the system much use at all if it does not even save him the trouble of bothering with the others.

In the same way, if we were to put every person under only one sign of the Zodiac, the system becomes too rigid and unlike life. Besides, it was never intended to be used like that. It may be convenient to have only twelve types, but we know that in practice there is every possible gradation between aggressiveness and timidity, or between conscientiousness and laziness. How, then, do we account for this?

A person born under any given Sun sign can be mainly influenced by one or two of the other signs that appear in their individual horoscope. For instance, famous persons born under the sign of Gemini include Henry VIII, whom nothing and no one could have induced to abdicate, and Edward VIII, who did just that. Obviously, then, the sign Gemini does not fully explain the complete character of either of them.

Again, under the opposite sign, Sagittarius, were both Stalin, who was totally consumed with the notion of power, and Charles V, who freely gave up an empire because he preferred to go into a monastery. And we find under Scorpio many uncompromising characters such as Luther, de Gaulle, Indira Gandhi, and Montgomery, but also Petain, a successful commander whose name later became synonymous with collaboration.

A single sign is therefore obviously inadequate to explain the differences between people; it can only explain resemblances, such as the combativeness of the Scorpio group, or the far-reaching devotion of Charles V and Stalin to their respective ideals—the Christian heaven and the Communist utopia.

But very few people have only one sign in their horoscope chart. In addition to the month of birth, the day and, even more, the hour to the nearest minute if possible, ought to be considered. Without this, it is impossible to have an actual horoscope, for the word horoscope literally means "a consideration of the hour."

The month of birth tells you only which sign of the Zodiac was occupied by the Sun. The day and hour tell you what sign was occupied by the Moon. And the minute tells you which sign was rising on the eastern horizon. This is called the Ascendant, and, as some astrologers believe, it is supposed to be the most important thing in the whole horoscope.

The Sun is said to signify one's heart, that is to say, one's deepest desires and inmost nature. This is quite different from the Moon, which signifies one's superficial way of behaving. When the ancient Romans referred to the Emperor Augustus as a Capricorn, they meant that he had the Moon in Capricorn. Or, to take another example, a modern astrologer would call Disraeli a Scorpion because he had Scorpio Rising, but most people would call him Sagittarius because he had the Sun there. The Romans would have called him Leo because his Moon was in Leo.

So if one does not seem to fit one's birth month, it is always worthwhile reading the other signs, for one may have been born at a time when any of them were rising or occupied by the Moon. It also seems to be the case that the influence of the Sun develops as life goes on, so that the month of birth is easier to guess in people over the age of forty. The young are supposed to be influenced mainly by their Ascendant, the Rising sign, which characterizes the body and physical personality as a whole.

It is nonsense to assume that all people born at a certain time will exhibit the same characteristics, or that they will even behave in the same manner. It is quite obvious that, from the very moment of its birth, a child is subject to the effects of its environment, and that this in turn will influence its character and heritage to a decisive extent. Also to be taken into account are education and economic conditions, which play a very important part in the formation of one's character as well.

People have, in general, certain character traits and qualities which, according to their environment, develop in either a positive or a negative manner. Therefore, selfishness (inherent selfishness, that is) might emerge as unselfishness; kindness and consideration as cruelty and lack of consideration toward others. In the same way, a naturally constructive person may, through frustration, become destructive, and so on. The latent characteristics with which people are born can, therefore, through environment and good or bad training, become something that would appear to be its opposite, and so give the lie to the astrologer's description of their character. But this is not the case. The true character is still there, but it is buried deep beneath these external superficialities.

Careful study of the character traits of various signs of the Zodiac are of immeasurable help, and can render beneficial service to the intelligent person. Undoubtedly, the reader will already have discovered that, while he is able to get on very well with some people, he just "cannot stand" others. The causes sometimes seem inexplicable. At times there is intense dislike, at other times immediate sympathy. And there is, too, the phenomenon of love at first sight, which is also apparently inexplicable. People appear to be either sympathetic or unsympathetic toward each other for no apparent reason.

Now if we look at this in the light of the Zodiac, we find that people born under different signs are either compatible or incompatible with each other. In other words, there are good and bad interrelating factors among the various signs. This does not, of course, mean that humanity can be divided into groups of hostile camps. It would be quite wrong to be hostile or indifferent toward people who happen to be born under an incompatible sign. There is no reason why everybody should not, or cannot, learn to control and adjust their feelings and actions, especially after they are aware of the positive qualities of other people by studying their character analyses, among other things.

Every person born under a certain sign has both positive and negative qualities, which are developed more or less according to our free will. Nobody is entirely good or entirely bad, and it is up to each of us to learn to control ourselves on the one hand and at the same time to endeavor to learn about ourselves and others.

It cannot be emphasized often enough that it is free will that determines whether we will make really good use of our talents and abilities. Using our free will, we can either overcome our failings or allow them to rule us. Our free will enables us to exert sufficient willpower to control our failings so that they do not harm ourselves or others.

Astrology can reveal our inclinations and tendencies. Astrology can tell us about ourselves so that we are able to use our free will to overcome our shortcomings. In this way astrology helps us do our best to become needed and valuable members of society as well as helpmates to our family and our friends. Astrology also can save us a great deal of unhappiness and remorse.

Yet it may seem absurd that an ancient philosophy could be a prop to modern men and women. But below the materialistic surface of modern life, there are hidden streams of feeling and thought. Symbology is reappearing as a study worthy of the scholar; the psychosomatic factor in illness has passed from the writings of the crank to those of the specialist; spiritual healing in all its forms is no longer a pious hope but an accepted phenomenon. And it is into this context that we consider astrology, in the sense that it is an analysis of human types.

Astrology and medicine had a long journey together, and only parted company a couple of centuries ago. There still remain in medical language such astrological terms as "saturnine," "choleric," and "mercurial," used in the diagnosis of physical tendencies. The herbalist, for long the handyman of the medical profession, has been dominated by astrology since the days of the Greeks. Certain herbs traditionally respond to certain planetary influences, and diseases must therefore be treated to ensure harmony between the medicine and the disease.

But the stars are expected to foretell and not only to diagnose.

Astrological forecasting has been remarkably accurate, but often it is wide of the mark. The brave person who cares to predict world events takes dangerous chances. Individual forecasting is less clear cut; it can be a help or a disillusionment. Then we come to the nagging question: if it is possible to foreknow, is it right to foretell? This is a point of ethics on which it is hard to pronounce judgment. The doctor faces the same dilemma if he finds that symptoms of a mortal disease are present in his patient and that he can only prognosticate a steady decline. How much to tell an individual in a crisis is a problem that has perplexed many distinguished scholars. Honest and conscientious astrologers in this modern world, where so many people are seeking guidance, face the same problem.

Five hundred years ago it was customary to call in a learned man who was an astrologer who was probably also a doctor and a philosopher. By his knowledge of astrology, his study of planetary influences, he felt himself qualified to guide those in distress. The world has moved forward at a fantastic rate since then, and yet people are still uncertain of themselves. At first sight it seems fantastic in the light of modern thinking that they turn to the most ancient of all studies, and get someone to calculate a horoscope for them. But is it *really* so fantastic if you take a second look? For astrology is concerned with tomorrow, with survival. And in a world such as ours, tomorrow and survival are the keywords for the twenty-first century.

ASTROLOGICAL BRIDGE TO THE 21st CENTURY

As the decade opens on a new century, indeed on a new millennium, the planets set the stage for change and challenge. Themes connecting past, present, and future are in play as new planetary cycles form the bridge to the twenty-first century and its broad horizons. The first few years of the new decade reveal hidden paths and personal hints for achieving your potential, for making the most of your message from the planets.

With the dawning of the twenty-first century look first to Jupiter, the planet of good fortune. Each new yearly Jupiter cycle follows the natural progression of the Zodiac. First is Jupiter in Aries and in Taurus through spring 2000, next Jupiter is in Gemini to summer 2001, then in Cancer to midsummer 2002, in Leo to late summer 2003, in Virgo to early autumn 2004, and so on through Jupiter in Pisces through June 2010. The beneficent planet Jupiter promotes your professional and educational goals while urging informed choice and deliberation. Jupiter sharpens your focus and hones your skills, providing a rich medium for creativity. Planet Jupiter's influence is protective, the generous helper that comes to the rescue just in the nick of time. And while safeguarding good luck, Jupiter can turn unusual risks into achievable aims.

In order to take advantage of luck and opportunity, to gain wisdom from experience, to persevere against adversity, look to beautiful planet Saturn. Saturn, planet of reason and responsibility, began a new cycle in earthy Taurus at the turn of the century. Saturn in Taurus until spring 2001 inspires industry and affection, blends practicality and imagination, all the while inviting caution and care. Persistence and planning can reverse setbacks and minimize risk. Saturn in Taurus lends beauty, order, and structure to your life. Then Saturn is in Gemini, the sign of mind and communication, until June 2003. Saturn in Gemini gives depth and inspiration to thought and feeling. Here, because of a lively intellectual capacity, the limits of creativity can be stretched and boundaries broken. Saturn in Gemini holds the promise of fruitful endeavor through sustained study, learning, and application.

Uranus, planet of innovation and surprise, started an important new cycle in January of 1996. At that time Uranus entered its natural home in airy Aquarius. Uranus in Aquarius into the year 2003 has a profound effect on your personality and the lens through which you see the world. A basic change in the way you project yourself is just one impact of Uranus in Aquarius. More significantly, a whole new consciousness is evolving. Winds of change blowing your way emphasize movement and freedom. Uranus in Aquarius poses involvement in the larger community beyond self, family, friends, lovers, associates. Radical ideas and progressive thought signal a journey of liberation. As the new century begins, follow Uranus on the path of humanitarianism. While you carve a prestigious niche in public life, while you preach social reform and justice, you will be striving to make the world a better place for all people.

Neptune, planet of vision and mystery, is enjoying a long cycle that excites creativity and imaginative thinking. Neptune is in airy Aquarius from November 1998 to February of 2012. Neptune in Aquarius, the sign of the Water Bearer, represents two sides of the coin of wisdom: inspiration and reason. Here Neptune stirs powerful currents bearing a rich and varied harvest, the fertile breeding ground for idealistic aims and practical considerations. Neptune's fine intuition tunes in to your dreams, your imagination, your spirituality. You can never turn your back on the mysteries of life. Uranus and Neptune, the planets of enlightenment and renewed idealism both in the sign of Aquarius, give you glimpses into the future, letting you peek through secret doorways opening into the twenty-first century.

Pluto, planet of beginnings and endings, began a new cycle of growth and learning late in 1995. Pluto entered fiery Sagittarius and remains there into the year 2008. Pluto in Sagittarius during its long stay over twelve years can create significant change. The great power of Pluto in Sagittarius is already starting its transformation of your character and lifestyle. Pluto in Sagittarius takes you on a new journey of exploration and learning. The awakening you experience on intellectual and artistic levels heralds a new cycle of growth. Uncompromising Pluto, seeker of truth, challenges your identity, persona, and self-expression. Uncovering the real you, Pluto holds the key to understanding and meaningful communication. Pluto in Sagittarius can be the guiding light illuminating the first decade of the twenty-first century. Good luck is riding on the waves of change.

THE SIGNS OF THE ZODIAC

Dominant Characteristics

Aries: March 21–April 20

The Positive Side of Aries

The Aries has many positive points to his character. People born under this first sign of the Zodiac are often quite strong and enthusiastic. On the whole, they are forward-looking people who are not easily discouraged by temporary setbacks. They know what they want out of life and they go out after it. Their personalities are strong. Others are usually quite impressed by the Ram's way of doing things. Quite often they are sources of inspiration for others traveling the same route. Aries men and women have a special zest for life that can be contagious; for others, they are a fine example of how life should be lived.

The Aries person usually has a quick and active mind. He is imaginative and inventive. He enjoys keeping busy and active. He generally gets along well with all kinds of people. He is interested in mankind, as a whole. He likes to be challenged. Some would say he thrives on opposition, for it is when he is set against that he often does his best. Getting over or around obstacles is a challenge he generally enjoys. All in all, Aries is quite positive and young-thinking. He likes to keep abreast of new things that are happening in the world. Aries are often fond of speed. They like things to be done quickly, and this sometimes aggravates their slower colleagues and associates.

The Aries man or woman always seems to remain young. Their whole approach to life is youthful and optimistic. They never say die, no matter what the odds. They may have an occasional setback, but it is not long before they are back on their feet again.

The Negative Side of Aries

Everybody has his less positive qualities—and Aries is no exception. Sometimes the Aries man or woman is not very tactful in communicating with others; in his hurry to get things done he is apt to be a little callous or inconsiderate. Sensitive people are likely to find him somewhat sharp-tongued in some situations. Often in his eagerness to get the show on the road, he misses the mark altogether and cannot achieve his aims.

At times Aries can be too impulsive. He can occasionally be stubborn and refuse to listen to reason. If things do not move quickly enough to suit the Aries man or woman, he or she is apt to become rather nervous or irritable. The uncultivated Aries is not unfamiliar with moments of doubt and fear. He is capable of being destructive if he does not get his way. He can overcome some of his emotional problems by steadily trying to express himself as he really is, but this requires effort.

Taurus: April 21–May 20

The Positive Side of Taurus

The Taurus person is known for his ability to concentrate and for his tenacity. These are perhaps his strongest qualities. The Taurus man or woman generally has very little trouble in getting along with others; it's his nature to be helpful toward people in need. He can always be depended on by his friends, especially those in trouble.

Taurus generally achieves what he wants through his ability to persevere. He never leaves anything unfinished but works on something until it has been completed. People can usually take him at his word; he is honest and forthright in most of his dealings. The Taurus person has a good chance to make a success of his life because of his many positive qualities. The Taurus who aims high seldom falls short of his mark. He learns well by experience. He is thorough and does not believe in shortcuts of any kind. The Bull's thoroughness pays off in the end, for through his deliberateness he learns how to rely on himself and what he has learned. The Taurus person tries to get along with others, as a rule. He is not overly critical and likes people to be themselves. He is a tolerant person and enjoys peace and harmony—especially in his home life.

Taurus is usually cautious in all that he does. He is not a person who believes in taking unnecessary risks. Before adopting any one line of action, he will weigh all of the pros and cons. The Taurus person is steadfast. Once his mind is made up it seldom changes. The person born under this sign usually is a good family person— reliable and loving.

The Negative Side of Taurus

Sometimes the Taurus man or woman is a bit too stubborn. He won't listen to other points of view if his mind is set on something. To others, this can be quite annoying. Taurus also does not like to be told what to do. He becomes rather angry if others think him not too bright. He does not like to be told he is wrong, even when he is. He dislikes being contradicted.

Some people who are born under this sign are very suspicious of others—even of those persons close to them. They find it difficult to trust people fully. They are often afraid of being deceived or taken advantage of. The Bull often finds it difficult to forget or forgive. His love of material things sometimes makes him rather avaricious and petty.

Gemini: May 21–June 20

The Positive Side of Gemini

The person born under this sign of the Heavenly Twins is usually quite bright and quick-witted. Some of them are capable of doing many different things. The Gemini person very often has many different interests. He keeps an open mind and is always anxious to learn new things.

Gemini is often an analytical person. He is a person who enjoys making use of his intellect. He is governed more by his mind than by his emotions. He is a person who is not confined to one view; he can often understand both sides to a problem or question. He knows how to reason, how to make rapid decisions if need be.

He is an adaptable person and can make himself at home almost anywhere. There are all kinds of situations he can adapt to. He is a person who seldom doubts himself; he is sure of his talents and his ability to think and reason. Gemini is generally most satisfied

when he is in a situation where he can make use of his intellect. Never short of imagination, he often has strong talents for invention. He is rather a modern person when it comes to life; Gemini almost always moves along with the times—perhaps that is why he remains so youthful throughout most of his life.

Literature and art appeal to the person born under this sign. Creativity in almost any form will interest and intrigue the Gemini man or woman.

The Gemini is often quite charming. A good talker, he often is the center of attraction at any gathering. People find it easy to like a person born under this sign because he can appear easygoing and usually has a good sense of humor.

The Negative Side of Gemini

Sometimes the Gemini person tries to do too many things at one time—and as a result, winds up finishing nothing. Some Twins are easily distracted and find it rather difficult to concentrate on one thing for too long a time. Sometimes they give in to trifling fancies and find it rather boring to become too serious about any one thing. Some of them are never dependable, no matter what they promise.

Although the Gemini man or woman often appears to be well-versed on many subjects, this is sometimes just a veneer. His knowledge may be only superficial, but because he speaks so well he gives people the impression of erudition. Some Geminis are sharp-tongued and inconsiderate; they think only of themselves and their own pleasure.

Cancer: June 21–July 20

The Positive Side of Cancer

The Moon Child's most positive point is his understanding nature. On the whole, he is a loving and sympathetic person. He would never go out of his way to hurt anyone. The Cancer man or woman is often very kind and tender; they give what they can to others. They hate to see others suffering and will do what they can to help someone in less fortunate circumstances than themselves. They are often very concerned about the world. Their interest in people generally goes beyond that of just their own families and close friends; they have a deep sense of community and respect humanitarian values. The Moon Child means what he says, as a rule; he is honest about his feelings.

The Cancer man or woman is a person who knows the art of patience. When something seems difficult, he is willing to wait until the situation becomes manageable again. He is a person who knows how to bide his time. Cancer knows how to concentrate on one thing at a time. When he has made his mind up he generally sticks with what he does, seeing it through to the end.

Cancer is a person who loves his home. He enjoys being surrounded by familiar things and the people he loves. Of all the signs, Cancer is the most maternal. Even the men born under this sign often have a motherly or protective quality about them. They like to take care of people in their family—to see that they are well loved and well provided for. They are usually loyal and faithful. Family ties mean a lot to the Cancer man or woman. Parents and in-laws are respected and loved. Young Cancer responds very well to adults who show faith in him. The Moon Child has a strong sense of tradition. He is very sensitive to the moods of others.

The Negative Side of Cancer

Sometimes Cancer finds it rather hard to face life. It becomes too much for him. He can be a little timid and retiring, when things don't go too well. When unfortunate things happen, he is apt to just shrug and say, "Whatever will be will be." He can be fatalistic to a fault. The uncultivated Cancer is a bit lazy. He doesn't have very much ambition. Anything that seems a bit difficult he'll gladly leave to others. He may be lacking in initiative. Too sensitive, when he feels he's been injured, he'll crawl back into his shell and nurse his imaginary wounds. The immature Moon Child often is given to crying when the smallest thing goes wrong.

Some Cancers find it difficult to enjoy themselves in environments outside their homes. They make heavy demands on others, and need to be constantly reassured that they are loved. Lacking such reassurance, they may resort to sulking in silence.

Leo: July 21–August 21

The Positive Side of Leo

Often Leos make good leaders. They seem to be good organizers and administrators. Usually they are quite popular with others. Whatever group it is that they belong to, the Leo man or woman is almost sure to be or become the leader. Loyalty, one of the Lion's noblest traits, enables him or her to maintain this leadership position.

Leo is generous most of the time. It is his best characteristic. He or she likes to give gifts and presents. In making others happy, the Leo person becomes happy himself. He likes to splurge when spending money on others. In some instances it may seem that the Lion's generosity knows no boundaries. A hospitable person, the Leo man or woman is very fond of welcoming people to his house and entertaining them. He is never short of company.

Leo has plenty of energy and drive. He enjoys working toward some specific goal. When he applies himself correctly, he gets what he wants most often. The Leo person is almost never unsure of himself. He has plenty of confidence and aplomb. He is a person who is direct in almost everything he does. He has a quick mind and can make a decision in a very short time.

He usually sets a good example for others because of his ambitious manner and positive ways. He knows how to stick to something once he's started. Although Leo may be good at making a joke, he is not superficial or glib. He is a loving person, kind and thoughtful.

There is generally nothing small or petty about the Leo man or woman. He does what he can for those who are deserving. He is a person others can rely upon at all times. He means what he says. An honest person, generally speaking, he is a friend who is valued and sought out.

The Negative Side of Leo

Leo, however, does have his faults. At times, he can be just a bit too arrogant. He thinks that no one deserves a leadership position except him. Only he is capable of doing things well. His opinion of himself is often much too high. Because of his conceit, he is

sometimes rather unpopular with a good many people. Some Leos are too materialistic; they can only think in terms of money and profit.

Some Leos enjoy lording it over others—at home or at their place of business. What is more, they feel they have the right to. Egocentric to an impossible degree, this sort of Leo cares little about how others think or feel. He can be rude and cutting.

Virgo: August 22–September 22

The Positive Side of Virgo

The person born under the sign of Virgo is generally a busy person. He knows how to arrange and organize things. He is a good planner. Above all, he is practical and is not afraid of hard work.

Often called the sign of the Harvester, Virgo knows how to attain what he desires. He sticks with something until it is finished. He never shirks his duties, and can always be depended upon. The Virgo person can be thoroughly trusted at all times.

The man or woman born under this sign tries to do everything to perfection. He doesn't believe in doing anything halfway. He always aims for the top. He is the sort of a person who is always learning and constantly striving to better himself—not because he wants more money or glory, but because it gives him a feeling of accomplishment.

The Virgo man or woman is a very observant person. He is sensitive to how others feel, and can see things below the surface of a situation. He usually puts this talent to constructive use.

It is not difficult for the Virgo to be open and earnest. He believes in putting his cards on the table. He is never secretive or underhanded. He's as good as his word. The Virgo person is generally plainspoken and down to earth. He has no trouble in expressing himself.

The Virgo person likes to keep up to date on new developments in his particular field. Well-informed, generally, he sometimes has a keen interest in the arts or literature. What he knows, he knows well. His ability to use his critical faculties is well-developed and sometimes startles others because of its accuracy.

Virgos adhere to a moderate way of life; they avoid excesses. Virgo is a responsible person and enjoys being of service.

The Negative Side of Virgo

Sometimes a Virgo person is too critical. He thinks that only he can do something the way it should be done. Whatever anyone else does is inferior. He can be rather annoying in the way he quibbles over insignificant details. In telling others how things should be done, he can be rather tactless and mean.

Some Virgos seem rather emotionless and cool. They feel emotional involvement is beneath them. They are sometimes too tidy, too neat. With money they can be rather miserly. Some Virgos try to force their opinions and ideas on others.

Libra: September 23–October 22

The Positive Side of Libra

Libras love harmony. It is one of their most outstanding character traits. They are interested in achieving balance; they admire beauty and grace in things as well as in people. Generally speaking, they are kind and considerate people. Libras are usually very sympathetic. They go out of their way not to hurt another person's feelings. They are outgoing and do what they can to help those in need.

People born under the sign of Libra almost always make good friends. They are loyal and amiable. They enjoy the company of others. Many of them are rather moderate in their views; they believe in keeping an open mind, however, and weighing both sides of an issue fairly before making a decision.

Alert and intelligent, Libra, often known as the Lawgiver, is always fair-minded and tries to put himself in the position of the other person. They are against injustice; quite often they take up for the underdog. In most of their social dealings, they try to be tactful and kind. They dislike discord and bickering, and most Libras strive for peace and harmony in all their relationships.

The Libra man or woman has a keen sense of beauty. They appreciate handsome furnishings and clothes. Many of them are artistically inclined. Their taste is usually impeccable. They know how to use color. Their homes are almost always attractively arranged and inviting. They enjoy entertaining people and see to it that their guests always feel at home and welcome.

Libra gets along with almost everyone. He is well-liked and socially much in demand.

The Negative Side of Libra

Some people born under this sign tend to be rather insincere. So eager are they to achieve harmony in all relationships that they will even go so far as to lie. Many of them are escapists. They find facing the truth an ordeal and prefer living in a world of make-believe.

In a serious argument, some Libras give in rather easily even when they know they are right. Arguing, even about something they believe in, is too unsettling for some of them.

Libras sometimes care too much for material things. They enjoy possessions and luxuries. Some are vain and tend to be jealous.

Scorpio: October 23–November 22

The Positive Side of Scorpio

The Scorpio man or woman generally knows what he or she wants out of life. He is a determined person. He sees something through to the end. Scorpio is quite sincere, and seldom says anything he doesn't mean. When he sets a goal for himself he tries to go about achieving it in a very direct way.

The Scorpion is brave and courageous. They are not afraid of hard work. Obstacles do not frighten them. They forge ahead until they achieve what they set out for. The Scorpio man or woman has a strong will.

Although Scorpio may seem rather fixed and determined, inside he is often quite tender and loving. He can care very much for others. He believes in sincerity in all relationships. His feelings about someone tend to last; they are profound and not superficial.

The Scorpio person is someone who adheres to his principles no matter what happens. He will not be deterred from a path he believes to be right.

Because of his many positive strengths, the Scorpion can often achieve happiness for himself and for those that he loves.

He is a constructive person by nature. He often has a deep understanding of people and of life, in general. He is perceptive and unafraid. Obstacles often seem to spur him on. He is a positive person who enjoys winning. He has many strengths and resources; challenge of any sort often brings out the best in him.

The Negative Side of Scorpio

The Scorpio person is sometimes hypersensitive. Often he imagines injury when there is none. He feels that others do not bother to recognize him for his true worth. Sometimes he is given to excessive boasting in order to compensate for what he feels is neglect.

Scorpio can be proud, arrogant, and competitive. They can be sly when they put their minds to it and they enjoy outwitting persons or institutions noted for their cleverness.

Their tactics for getting what they want are sometimes devious and ruthless. They don't care too much about what others may think. If they feel others have done them an injustice, they will do their best to seek revenge. The Scorpion often has a sudden, violent temper; and this person's interest in sex is sometimes quite unbalanced or excessive.

Sagittarius: November 23–December 20

The Positive Side of Sagittarius

People born under this sign are honest and forthright. Their approach to life is earnest and open. Sagittarius is often quite adult in his way of seeing things. They are broad-minded and tolerant people. When dealing with others the person born under the sign of the Archer is almost always open and forthright. He doesn't believe in deceit or pretension. His standards are high. People who associate with Sagittarius generally admire and respect his tolerant viewpoint.

The Archer trusts others easily and expects them to trust him. He is never suspicious or envious and almost always thinks well of others. People always enjoy his company because he is so friendly and easygoing. The Sagittarius man or woman is often good-humored. He can always be depended upon by his friends, family, and co-workers.

The person born under this sign of the Zodiac likes a good joke every now and then. Sagittarius is eager for fun and laughs, which makes him very popular with others.

A lively person, he enjoys sports and outdoor life. The Archer is fond of animals. Intelligent and interesting, he can begin an

animated conversation with ease. He likes exchanging ideas and discussing various views.

He is not selfish or proud. If someone proposes an idea or plan that is better than his, he will immediately adopt it. Imaginative yet practical, he knows how to put ideas into practice.

The Archer enjoys sport and games, and it doesn't matter if he wins or loses. He is a forgiving person, and never sulks over something that has not worked out in his favor.

He is seldom critical, and is almost always generous.

The Negative Side of Sagittarius

Some Sagittarius are restless. They take foolish risks and seldom learn from the mistakes they make. They don't have heads for money and are often mismanaging their finances. Some of them devote much of their time to gambling.

Some are too outspoken and tactless, always putting their feet in their mouths. They hurt others carelessly by being honest at the wrong time. Sometimes they make promises which they don't keep. They don't stick close enough to their plans and go from one failure to another. They are undisciplined and waste a lot of energy.

Capricorn: December 21–January 19

The Positive Side of Capricorn

The person born under the sign of Capricorn, known variously as the Mountain Goat or Sea Goat, is usually very stable and patient. He sticks to whatever tasks he has and sees them through. He can always be relied upon and he is not averse to work.

An honest person, Capricorn is generally serious about whatever he does. He does not take his duties lightly. He is a practical person and believes in keeping his feet on the ground.

Quite often the person born under this sign is ambitious and knows how to get what he wants out of life. The Goat forges ahead and never gives up his goal. When he is determined about something, he almost always wins. He is a good worker—a hard worker. Although things may not come easy to him, he will not complain, but continue working until his chores are finished.

He is usually good at business matters and knows the value of money. He is not a spendthrift and knows how to put something away for a rainy day; he dislikes waste and unnecessary loss.

Capricorn knows how to make use of his self-control. He can apply himself to almost anything once he puts his mind to it. His ability to concentrate sometimes astounds others. He is diligent and does well when involved in detail work.

The Capricorn man or woman is charitable, generally speaking, and will do what is possible to help others less fortunate. As a friend, he is loyal and trustworthy. He never shirks his duties or responsibilities. He is self-reliant and never expects too much of the other fellow. He does what he can on his own. If someone does him a good turn, then he will do his best to return the favor.

The Negative Side of Capricorn

Like everyone, Capricorn, too, has faults. At times, the Goat can be overcritical of others. He expects others to live up to his own high standards. He thinks highly of himself and tends to look down on others.

His interest in material things may be exaggerated. The Capricorn man or woman thinks too much about getting on in the world and having something to show for it. He may even be a little greedy.

He sometimes thinks he knows what's best for everyone. He is too bossy. He is always trying to organize and correct others. He may be a little narrow in his thinking.

Aquarius: January 20–February 18

The Positive Side of Aquarius

The Aquarius man or woman is usually very honest and forthright. These are his two greatest qualities. His standards for himself are generally very high. He can always be relied upon by others. His word is his bond.

Aquarius is perhaps the most tolerant of all the Zodiac personalities. He respects other people's beliefs and feels that everyone is entitled to his own approach to life.

He would never do anything to injure another's feelings. He is never unkind or cruel. Always considerate of others, the Water

Bearer is always willing to help a person in need. He feels a very strong tie between himself and all the other members of mankind.

The person born under this sign, called the Water Bearer, is almost always an individualist. He does not believe in teaming up with the masses, but prefers going his own way. His ideas about life and mankind are often quite advanced. There is a saying to the effect that the average Aquarius is fifty years ahead of his time.

Aquarius is community-minded. The problems of the world concern him greatly. He is interested in helping others no matter what part of the globe they live in. He is truly a humanitarian sort. He likes to be of service to others.

Giving, considerate, and without prejudice, Aquarius have no trouble getting along with others.

The Negative Side of Aquarius

Aquarius may be too much of a dreamer. He makes plans but seldom carries them out. He is rather unrealistic. His imagination has a tendency to run away with him. Because many of his plans are impractical, he is always in some sort of a dither.

Others may not approve of him at all times because of his unconventional behavior. He may be a bit eccentric. Sometimes he is so busy with his own thoughts that he loses touch with the realities of existence.

Some Aquarius feel they are more clever and intelligent than others. They seldom admit to their own faults, even when they are quite apparent. Some become rather fanatic in their views. Their criticism of others is sometimes destructive and negative.

Pisces: February 19–March 20

The Positive Side of Pisces

Known as the sign of the Fishes, Pisces has a sympathetic nature. Kindly, he is often dedicated in the way he goes about helping others. The sick and the troubled often turn to him for advice and assistance. Possessing keen intuition, Pisces can easily understand people's deepest problems.

He is very broad-minded and does not criticize others for their faults. He knows how to accept people for what they are. On the whole, he is a trustworthy and earnest person. He is loyal to his friends and will do what he can to help them in time of need. Generous and good-natured, he is a lover of peace; he is often willing to help others solve their differences. People who have taken a wrong turn in life often interest him and he will do what he can to persuade them to rehabilitate themselves.

He has a strong intuitive sense and most of the time he knows how to make it work for him. Pisces is unusually perceptive and often knows what is bothering someone before that person, himself, is aware of it. The Pisces man or woman is an idealistic person, basically, and is interested in making the world a better place in which to live. Pisces believes that everyone should help each other. He is willing to do more than his share in order to achieve cooperation with others.

The person born under this sign often is talented in music or art. He is a receptive person; he is able to take the ups and downs of life with philosophic calm.

The Negative Side of Pisces

Some Pisces are often depressed; their outlook on life is rather glum. They may feel that they have been given a bad deal in life and that others are always taking unfair advantage of them. Pisces sometimes feel that the world is a cold and cruel place. The Fishes can be easily discouraged. The Pisces man or woman may even withdraw from the harshness of reality into a secret shell of his own where he dreams and idles away a good deal of his time.

Pisces can be lazy. He lets things happen without giving the least bit of resistance. He drifts along, whether on the high road or on the low. He can be lacking in willpower.

Some Pisces people seek escape through drugs or alcohol. When temptation comes along they find it hard to resist. In matters of sex, they can be rather permissive.

Sun Sign Personalities

ARIES: Hans Christian Andersen, Pearl Bailey, Marlon Brando, Wernher Von Braun, Charlie Chaplin, Joan Crawford, Da Vinci, Bette Davis, Doris Day, W. C. Fields, Alec Guinness, Adolf Hitler, William Holden, Thomas Jefferson, Nikita Khrushchev, Elton John, Arturo Toscanini, J. P. Morgan, Paul Robeson, Gloria Steinem, Sarah Vaughn, Vincent van Gogh, Tennessee Williams

TAURUS: Fred Astaire, Charlotte Brontë, Carol Burnett, Irving Berlin, Bing Crosby, Salvador Dali, Tchaikovsky, Queen Elizabeth II, Duke Ellington, Ella Fitzgerald, Henry Fonda, Sigmund Freud, Orson Welles, Joe Louis, Lenin, Karl Marx, Golda Meir, Eva Peron, Bertrand Russell, Shakespeare, Kate Smith, Benjamin Spock, Barbra Streisand, Shirley Temple, Harry Truman

GEMINI: Ruth Benedict, Josephine Baker, Rachel Carson, Carlos Chavez, Walt Whitman, Bob Dylan, Ralph Waldo Emerson, Judy Garland, Paul Gauguin, Allen Ginsberg, Benny Goodman, Bob Hope, Burl Ives, John F. Kennedy, Peggy Lee, Marilyn Monroe, Joe Namath, Cole Porter, Laurence Olivier, Harriet Beecher Stowe, Queen Victoria, John Wayne, Frank Lloyd Wright

CANCER: "Dear Abby," Lizzie Borden, David Brinkley, Yul Brynner, Pearl Buck, Marc Chagall, Princess Diana, Babe Didrikson, Mary Baker Eddy, Henry VIII, John Glenn, Ernest Hemingway, Lena Horne, Oscar Hammerstein, Helen Keller, Ann Landers, George Orwell, Nancy Reagan, Rembrandt, Richard Rodgers, Ginger Rogers, Rubens, Jean-Paul Sartre, O. J. Simpson

LEO: Neil Armstrong, James Baldwin, Lucille Ball, Emily Brontë, Wilt Chamberlain, Julia Child, William J. Clinton, Cecil B. De Mille, Ogden Nash, Amelia Earhart, Edna Ferber, Arthur Goldberg, Alfred Hitchcock, Mick Jagger, George Meany, Annie Oakley, George Bernard Shaw, Napoleon, Jacqueline Onassis, Henry Ford, Francis Scott Key, Andy Warhol, Mae West, Orville Wright

VIRGO: Ingrid Bergman, Warren Burger, Maurice Chevalier, Agatha Christie, Sean Connery, Lafayette, Peter Falk, Greta Garbo, Althea Gibson, Arthur Godfrey, Goethe, Buddy Hackett, Michael Jackson, Lyndon Johnson, D. H. Lawrence, Sophia Loren, Grandma Moses, Arnold Palmer, Queen Elizabeth I, Walter Reuther, Peter Sellers, Lily Tomlin, George Wallace

LIBRA: Brigitte Bardot, Art Buchwald, Truman Capote, Dwight D. Eisenhower, William Faulkner, F. Scott Fitzgerald, Gandhi, George Gershwin, Micky Mantle, Helen Hayes, Vladimir Horowitz, Doris Lessing, Martina Navratalova, Eugene O'Neill, Luciano Pavarotti, Emily Post, Eleanor Roosevelt, Bruce Springsteen, Margaret Thatcher, Gore Vidal, Barbara Walters, Oscar Wilde

SCORPIO: Vivien Leigh, Richard Burton, Art Carney, Johnny Carson, Billy Graham, Grace Kelly, Walter Cronkite, Marie Curie, Charles de Gaulle, Linda Evans, Indira Gandhi, Theodore Roosevelt, Rock Hudson, Katherine Hepburn, Robert F. Kennedy, Billie Jean King, Martin Luther, Georgia O'Keeffe, Pablo Picasso, Jonas Salk, Alan Shepard, Robert Louis Stevenson

SAGITTARIUS: Jane Austen, Louisa May Alcott, Woody Allen, Beethoven, Willy Brandt, Mary Martin, William F. Buckley, Maria Callas, Winston Churchill, Noel Coward, Emily Dickinson, Walt Disney, Benjamin Disraeli, James Doolittle, Kirk Douglas, Chet Huntley, Jane Fonda, Chris Evert Lloyd, Margaret Mead, Charles Schulz, John Milton, Frank Sinatra, Steven Spielberg

CAPRICORN: Muhammad Ali, Isaac Asimov, Pablo Casals, Dizzy Dean, Marlene Dietrich, James Farmer, Ava Gardner, Barry Goldwater, Cary Grant, J. Edgar Hoover, Howard Hughes, Joan of Arc, Gypsy Rose Lee, Martin Luther King, Jr., Rudyard Kipling, Mao Tse-tung, Richard Nixon, Gamal Nasser, Louis Pasteur, Albert Schweitzer, Stalin, Benjamin Franklin, Elvis Presley

AQUARIUS: Marian Anderson, Susan B. Anthony, Jack Benny, John Barrymore, Mikhail Baryshnikov, Charles Darwin, Charles Dickens, Thomas Edison, , Clark Gable, Jascha Heifetz, Abraham Lincoln, Yehudi Menuhin, Mozart, Jack Nicklaus, Ronald Reagan, Jackie Robinson, Norman Rockwell, Franklin D. Roosevelt, Gertrude Stein, Charles Lindbergh, Margaret Truman

PISCES: Edward Albee, Harry Belafonte, Alexander Graham Bell, Chopin, Adelle Davis, Albert Einstein, Golda Meir, Jackie Gleason, Winslow Homer, Edward M. Kennedy, Victor Hugo, Mike Mansfield, Michelangelo, Edna St. Vincent Millay, Liza Minelli, John Steinbeck, Linus Pauling, Ravel, Renoir, Diana Ross, William Shirer, Elizabeth Taylor, George Washington

The Signs and Their Key Words

		POSITIVE	NEGATIVE
ARIES	self	courage, initiative, pioneer instinct	brash rudeness, selfish impetuosity
TAURUS	money	endurance, loyalty, wealth	obstinacy, gluttony
GEMINI	mind	versatility	capriciousness, unreliability
CANCER	family	sympathy, homing instinct	clannishness, childishness
LEO	children	love, authority, integrity	egotism, force
VIRGO	work	purity, industry, analysis	faultfinding, cynicism
LIBRA	marriage	harmony, justice	vacillation, superficiality
SCORPIO	sex	survival, regeneration	vengeance, discord
SAGITTARIUS	travel	optimism, higher learning	lawlessness
CAPRICORN	career	depth	narrowness, gloom
AQUARIUS	friends	human fellowship, genius	perverse unpredictability
PISCES	confinement	spiritual love, universality	diffusion, escapism

The Elements and Qualities of The Signs

Every sign has both an *element* and a *quality* associated with it. The element indicates the basic makeup of the sign, and the quality describes the kind of activity associated with each.

Element	Sign	Quality	Sign
FIRE	ARIES LEO SAGITTARIUS	CARDINAL	ARIES LIBRA CANCER CAPRICORN
EARTH	TAURUS VIRGO CAPRICORN	FIXED	TAURUS LEO SCORPIO AQUARIUS
AIR	GEMINI LIBRA AQUARIUS		
WATER	CANCER SCORPIO PISCES	MUTABLE	GEMINI VIRGO SAGITTARIUS PISCES

Signs can be grouped together according to their element and quality. Signs of the same element share many basic traits in common. They tend to form stable configurations and ultimately harmonious relationships. Signs of the same quality are often less harmonious, but they share many dynamic potentials for growth as well as profound fulfillment.

Further discussion of each of these sign groupings is provided on the following pages.

The Fire Signs

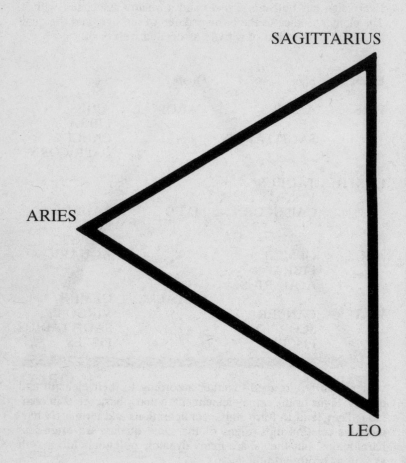

This is the fire group. On the whole these are emotional, volatile types, quick to anger, quick to forgive. They are adventurous, powerful people and act as a source of inspiration for everyone. They spark into action with immediate exuberant impulses. They are intelligent, self-involved, creative, and idealistic. They all share a certain vibrancy and glow that outwardly reflects an inner flame and passion for living.

The Earth Signs

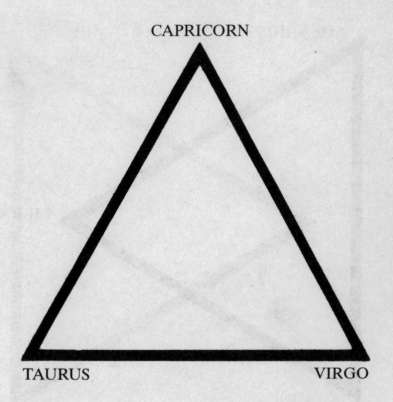

This is the earth group. They are in constant touch with the material world and tend to be conservative. Although they are all capable of spartan self-discipline, they are earthy, sensual people who are stimulated by the tangible, elegant, and luxurious. The thread of their lives is always practical, but they do fantasize and are often attracted to dark, mysterious, emotional people. They are like great cliffs overhanging the sea, forever married to the ocean but always resisting erosion from the dark, emotional forces that thunder at their feet.

The Air Signs

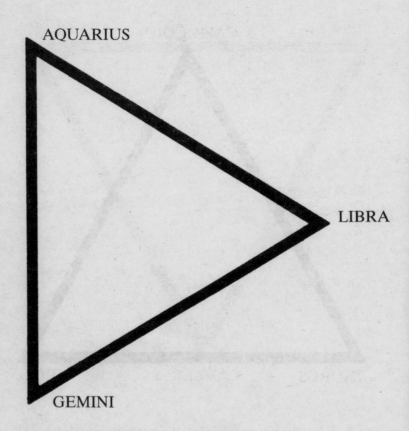

This is the air group. They are light, mental creatures desirous of contact, communication, and relationship. They are involved with people and the forming of ties on many levels. Original thinkers, they are the bearers of human news. Their language is their sense of word, color, style, and beauty. They provide an atmosphere suitable and pleasant for living. They add change and versatility to the scene, and it is through them that we can explore new territory of human intelligence and experience.

The Water Signs

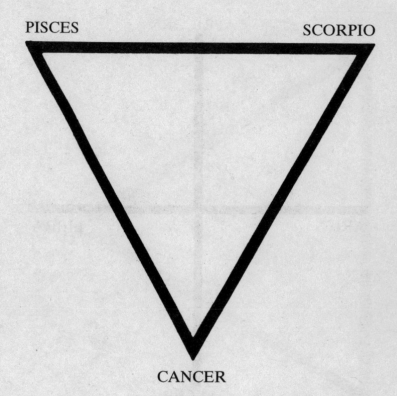

This is the water group. Through the water people, we are all joined together on emotional, nonverbal levels. They are silent, mysterious types whose magic hypnotizes even the most deter-mined realist. They have uncanny perceptions about people and are as rich as the oceans when it comes to feeling, emotion, or imagination. They are sensitive, mystical creatures with memories that go back beyond time. Through water, life is sustained. These people have the potential for the depths of darkness or the heights of mysticism and art.

The Cardinal Signs

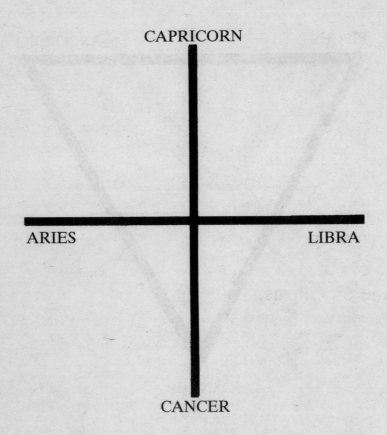

Put together, this is a clear-cut picture of dynamism, activity, tre-mendous stress, and remarkable achievement. These people know the meaning of great change since their lives are often character-ized by significant crises and major successes. This combination is like a simultaneous storm of summer, fall, winter, and spring. The danger is chaotic diffusion of energy; the potential is irrepressible growth and victory.

The Fixed Signs

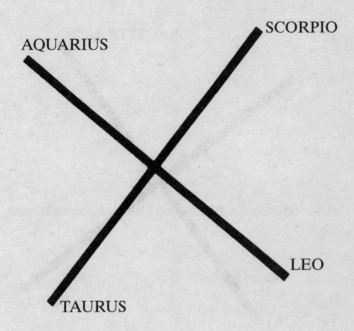

Fixed signs are always establishing themselves in a given place or area of experience. Like explorers who arrive and plant a flag, these people claim a position from which they do not enjoy being deposed. They are staunch, stalwart, upright, trusty, honorable people, although their obstinacy is well-known. Their contribution is fixity, and they are the angels who support our visible world.

The Mutable Signs

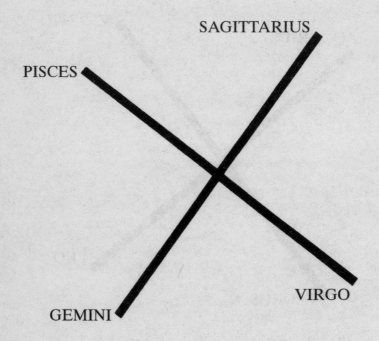

Mutable people are versatile, sensitive, intelligent, nervous, and deeply curious about life. They are the translators of all energy. They often carry out or complete tasks initiated by others. Combinations of these signs have highly developed minds; they are imaginative and jumpy and think and talk a lot. At worst their lives are a Tower of Babel. At best they are adaptable and ready creatures who can assimilate one kind of experience and enjoy it while anticipating coming changes.

THE PLANETS
OF THE SOLAR SYSTEM

This section describes the planets of the solar system. In astrology, both the Sun and the Moon are considered to be planets. Because of the Moon's influence in our day-to-day lives, the Moon is described in a separate section following this one.

The Planets and the Signs They Rule

The signs of the Zodiac are linked to the planets in the following way. Each sign is governed or ruled by one or more planets. No matter where the planets are located in the sky at any given moment, they still rule their respective signs, and when they travel through the signs they rule, they have special dignity and their effects are stronger.

Following is a list of the planets and the signs they rule. After looking at the list, read the definitions of the planets and see if you can determine how the planet ruling *your* Sun sign has affected your life.

SIGNS	RULING PLANETS
Aries	Mars, Pluto
Taurus	Venus
Gemini	Mercury
Cancer	Moon
Leo	Sun
Virgo	Mercury
Libra	Venus
Scorpio	Mars, Pluto
Sagittarius	Jupiter
Capricorn	Saturn
Aquarius	Saturn, Uranus
Pisces	Jupiter, Neptune

Characteristics of the Planets

The following pages give the meaning and characteristics of the planets of the solar system. They all travel around the Sun at different speeds and different distances. Taken with the Sun, they all distribute individual intelligence and ability throughout the entire chart.

The planets modify the influence of the Sun in a chart according to their own particular natures, strengths, and positions. Their positions must be calculated for each year and day, and their function and expression in a horoscope will change as they move from one area of the Zodiac to another.

We start with a description of the sun.

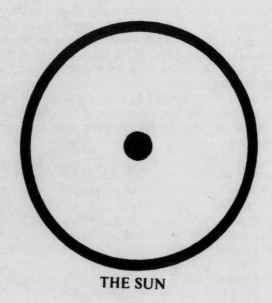

THE SUN

SUN

This is the center of existence. Around this flaming sphere all the planets revolve in endless orbits. Our star is constantly sending out its beams of light and energy without which no life on Earth would be possible. In astrology it symbolizes everything we are trying to become, the center around which all of our activity in life will always revolve. It is the symbol of our basic nature and describes the natural and constant thread that runs through everything that we do from birth to death on this planet.

To early astrologers, the Sun seemed to be another planet because it crossed the heavens every day, just like the rest of the bodies in the sky.

It is the only star near enough to be seen well—it is, in fact, a dwarf star. Approximately 860,000 miles in diameter, it is about ten times as wide as the giant planet Jupiter. The next nearest star is nearly 300,000 times as far away, and if the Sun were located as far away as most of the bright stars, it would be too faint to be seen without a telescope.

Everything in the horoscope ultimately revolves around this singular body. Although other forces may be prominent in the charts of some individuals, still the Sun is the total nucleus of being and symbolizes the complete potential of every human being alive. It is vitality and the life force. Your whole essence comes from the position of the Sun.

You are always trying to express the Sun according to its position by house and sign. Possibility for all development is found in the Sun, and it marks the fundamental character of your personal radiations all around you.

It is the symbol of strength, vigor, wisdom, dignity, ardor, and generosity, and the ability for a person to function as a mature individual. It is also a creative force in society. It is consciousness of the gift of life.

The underdeveloped solar nature is arrogant, pushy, undependable, and proud, and is constantly using force.

MERCURY

Mercury is the planet closest to the Sun. It races around our star, gathering information and translating it to the rest of the system. Mercury represents your capacity to understand the desires of your own will and to translate those desires into action.

In other words it is the planet of mind and the power of communication. Through Mercury we develop an ability to think, write, speak, and observe—to become aware of the world around us. It colors our attitudes and vision of the world, as well as our capacity to communicate our inner responses to the outside world. Some people who have serious disabilities in their power of verbal communication have often wrongly been described as people lacking intelligence.

Although this planet (and its position in the horoscope) indicates your power to communicate your thoughts and perceptions to the world, intelligence is something deeper. Intelligence is distributed throughout all the planets. It is the relationship of the planets to each other that truly describes what we call intelligence. Mercury rules speaking, language, mathematics, draft and design, students, messengers, young people, offices, teachers, and any pursuits where the mind of man has wings.

VENUS

Venus is beauty. It symbolizes the harmony and radiance of a rare and elusive quality: beauty itself. It is refinement and delicacy, softness and charm. In astrology it indicates grace, balance, and the aesthetic sense. Where Venus is we see beauty, a gentle drawing in of energy and the need for satisfaction and completion. It is a special touch that finishes off rough edges. It is sensitivity, and affection, and it is always the place for that other elusive phenomenon: love. Venus describes our sense of what is beautiful and loving. Poorly developed, it is vulgar, tasteless, and self-indulgent. But its ideal is the flame of spiritual love—Aphrodite, goddess of love, and the sweetness and power of personal beauty.

MARS

Mars is raw, crude energy. The planet next to Earth but outward from the Sun is a fiery red sphere that charges through the horoscope with force and fury. It represents the way you reach out for new adventure and new experience. It is energy and drive, initiative, courage, and daring. It is the power to start something and see it through. It can be thoughtless, cruel and wild, angry and hostile, causing cuts, burns, scalds, and wounds. It can stab its way through a chart, or it can be the symbol of healthy spirited adventure, well-channeled constructive power to begin and keep up the drive. If you have trouble starting things, if you lack the get-up-and-go to start the ball rolling, if you lack aggressiveness and self-confidence, chances are there's another planet influencing your Mars. Mars rules soldiers, butchers, surgeons, salesmen—any field that requires daring, bold skill, operational technique, or self-promotion.

JUPITER

This is the largest planet of the solar system. Scientists have recently learned that Jupiter reflects more light than it receives from the Sun. In a sense it is like a star itself. In astrology it rules good luck and good cheer, health, wealth, optimism, happiness, success, and joy. It is the symbol of opportunity and always opens the way for new possibilities in your life. It rules exuberance, enthusiasm, wisdom, knowledge, generosity, and all forms of expansion in general. It rules actors, statesmen, clerics, professional people, religion, publishing, and the distribution of many people over large areas.

Sometimes Jupiter makes you think you deserve everything, and you become sloppy, wasteful, careless and rude, prodigal and lawless, in the illusion that nothing can ever go wrong. Then there is the danger of overconfidence, exaggeration, undependability, and overindulgence.

Jupiter is the minimization of limitation and the emphasis on spirituality and potential. It is the thirst for knowledge and higher learning.

SATURN

Saturn circles our system in dark splendor with its mysterious rings, forcing us to be awakened to whatever we have neglected in the past. It will present real puzzles and problems to be solved, causing delays, obstacles, and hindrances. By doing so, Saturn stirs our own sensitivity to those areas where we are laziest.

Here we must patiently develop *method*, and only through painstaking effort can our ends be achieved. It brings order to a horoscope and imposes reason just where we are feeling least reasonable. By creating limitations and boundary, Saturn shows the consequences of being human and demands that we accept the changing cycles inevitable in human life. Saturn rules time, old age, and sobriety. It can bring depression, gloom, jealousy, and greed, or serious acceptance of responsibilities out of which success will develop. With Saturn there is nothing to do but face facts. It rules laborers, stones, granite, rocks, and crystals of all kinds.

THE OUTER PLANETS:
URANUS, NEPTUNE, PLUTO

Uranus, Neptune, Pluto are the outer planets. They liberate human beings from cultural conditioning, and in that sense are the lawbreakers. In early times it was thought that Saturn was the last planet of the system—the outer limit beyond which we could never go. The discovery of the next three planets ushered in new phases of human history, revolution, and technology.

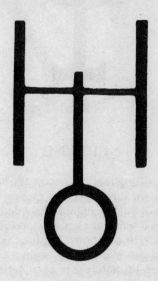

URANUS

Uranus rules unexpected change, upheaval, revolution. It is the symbol of total independence and asserts the freedom of an individual from all restriction and restraint. It is a breakthrough planet and indicates talent, originality, and genius in a horoscope. It usually causes last-minute reversals and changes of plan, unwanted separations, accidents, catastrophes, and eccentric behavior. It can add irrational rebelliousness and perverse bohemianism to a personality or a streak of unaffected brilliance in science and art. It rules technology, aviation, and all forms of electrical and electronic advancement. It governs great leaps forward and topsy-turvy situations, and *always* turns things around at the last minute. Its effects are difficult to predict, since it rules sudden last-minute decisions and events that come like lightning out of the blue.

NEPTUNE

Neptune dissolves existing reality the way the sea erodes the cliffs beside it. Its effects are subtle like the ringing of a buoy's bell in the fog. It suggests a reality higher than definition can usually describe. It awakens a sense of higher responsibility often causing guilt, worry, anxieties, or delusions. Neptune is associated with all forms of escape and can make things seem a certain way so convincingly that you are absolutely sure of something that eventually turns out to be quite different.

It is the planet of illusion and therefore governs the invisible realms that lie beyond our ordinary minds, beyond our simple factual ability to prove what is "real." Treachery, deceit, disillusionment, and disappointment are linked to Neptune. It describes a vague reality that promises eternity and the divine, yet in a manner so complex that we cannot really fathom it at all. At its worst Neptune is a cheap intoxicant; at its best it is the poetry, music, and inspiration of the higher planes of spiritual love. It has dominion over movies, photographs, and much of the arts.

PLUTO

Pluto lies at the outpost of our system and therefore rules finality in a horoscope—the final closing of chapters in your life, the passing of major milestones and points of development from which there is no return. It is a final wipeout, a closeout, an evacuation. It is a distant, subtle but powerful catalyst in all transformations that occur. It creates, destroys, then recreates. Sometimes Pluto starts its influence with a minor event or insignificant incident that might even go unnoticed. Slowly but surely, little by little, everything changes, until at last there has been a total transformation in the area of your life where Pluto has been operating. It rules mass thinking and the trends that society first rejects, then adopts, and finally outgrows.

Pluto rules the dead and the underworld—all the powerful forces of creation and destruction that go on all the time beneath, around, and above us. It can bring a lust for power with strong obsessions.

It is the planet that rules the metamorphosis of the caterpillar into a butterfly, for it symbolizes the capacity to change totally and forever a person's lifestyle, way of thought, and behavior.

THE MOON IN EACH SIGN

The Moon is the nearest planet to the Earth. It exerts more observable influence on us from day to day than any other planet. The effect is very personal, very intimate, and if we are not aware of how it works it can make us quite unstable in our ideas. And the annoying thing is that at these times we often see our own instability but can do nothing about it. A knowledge of what can be expected may help considerably. We can then be prepared to stand strong against the Moon's negative influences and use its positive ones to help us to get ahead. Who has not heard of going with the tide?

The Moon reflects, has no light of its own. It reflects the Sun—the life giver—in the form of vital movement. The Moon controls the tides, the blood rhythm, the movement of sap in trees and plants. Its nature is inconstancy and change so it signifies our moods, our superficial behavior—walking, talking, and especially thinking. Being a true reflector of other forces, the Moon is cold, watery like the surface of a still lake, brilliant and scintillating at times, but easily ruffled and disturbed by the winds of change.

The Moon takes about 27⅓ days to make a complete transit of the Zodiac. It spends just over 2¼ days in each sign. During that time it reflects the qualities, energies, and characteristics of the sign and, to a degree, the planet which rules the sign. When the Moon in its transit occupies a sign incompatible with our own birth sign, we can expect to feel a vague uneasiness, perhaps a touch of irritableness. We should not be discouraged nor let the feeling get us down, or, worse still, allow ourselves to take the discomfort out on others. Try to remember that the Moon has to change signs within 55 hours and, provided you are not physically ill, your mood will probably change with it. It is amazing how frequently depression lifts with the shift in the Moon's position. And, of course, when the Moon is transiting a sign compatible or sympathetic to yours, you will probably feel some sort of stimulation or just be plain happy to be alive.

In the horoscope, the Moon is such a powerful indicator that competent astrologers often use the sign it occupied at birth as the birth sign of the person. This is done particularly when the Sun is on the cusp, or edge, of two signs. Most experienced astrologers, however, coordinate both Sun and Moon signs by reading and confirming from one to the other and secure a far more accurate and personalized analysis.

For these reasons, the Moon tables which follow this section (see pages 86–92) are of great importance to the individual. They show the days and the exact times the Moon will enter each sign of the Zodiac for the year. Remember, you have to adjust the indicated times to local time. The corrections, already calculated for most of the main cities, are at the beginning of the tables. What follows now is a guide to the influences that will be reflected to the Earth by the Moon while it transits each of the twelve signs. The influence is at its peak about 26 hours after the Moon enters a sign. As you read the daily forecast, check the Moon sign for any given day and glance back at this guide.

MOON IN ARIES
This is a time for action, for reaching out beyond the usual self-imposed limitations and faint-hearted cautions. If you have plans in your head or on your desk, put them into practice. New ventures, applications, new jobs, new starts of any kind—all have a good chance of success. This is the period when original and dynamic impulses are being reflected onto Earth. Such energies are extremely vital and favor the pursuit of pleasure and adventure in practically every form. Sick people should feel an improvement. Those who are well will probably find themselves exuding confidence and optimism. People fond of physical exercise should find their bodies growing with tone and well-being. Boldness, strength, determination should characterize most of your activities with a readiness to face up to old challenges. Yesterday's problems may seem petty and exaggerated—so deal with them. Strike out alone. Self-reliance will attract others to you. This is a good time for making friends. Business and marriage partners are more likely to be impressed with the man and woman of action. Opposition will be overcome or thrown aside with much less effort than usual. CAUTION: Be dominant but not domineering.

MOON IN TAURUS
The spontaneous, action-packed person of yesterday gives way to the cautious, diligent, hardworking "thinker." In this period ideas will probably be concentrated on ways of improving finances. A great deal of time may be spent figuring out and going over

schemes and plans. It is the right time to be careful with detail. People will find themselves working longer than usual at their desks. Or devoting more time to serious thought about the future. A strong desire to put order into business and financial arrangements may cause extra work. Loved ones may complain of being neglected and may fail to appreciate that your efforts are for their ultimate benefit. Your desire for system may extend to criticism of arrangements in the home and lead to minor upsets. Health may be affected through overwork. Try to secure a reasonable amount of rest and relaxation, although the tendency will be to "keep going" despite good advice. Work done conscientiously in this period should result in a solid contribution to your future security. CAUTION: Try not to be as serious with people as the work you are engaged in.

MOON IN GEMINI
The humdrum of routine and too much work should suddenly end. You are likely to find yourself in an expansive, quicksilver world of change and self-expression. Urges to write, to paint, to experience the freedom of some sort of artistic outpouring, may be very strong. Take full advantage of them. You may find yourself finishing something you began and put aside long ago. Or embarking on something new which could easily be prompted by a chance meeting, a new acquaintance, or even an advertisement. There may be a yearning for a change of scenery, the feeling to visit another country (not too far away), or at least to get away for a few days. This may result in short, quick journeys. Or, if you are planning a single visit, there may be some unexpected changes or detours on the way. Familiar activities will seem to give little satisfaction unless they contain a fresh element of excitement or expectation. The inclination will be toward untried pursuits, particularly those that allow you to express your inner nature. The accent is on new faces, new places. CAUTION: Do not be too quick to commit yourself emotionally.

MOON IN CANCER
Feelings of uncertainty and vague insecurity are likely to cause problems while the Moon is in Cancer. Thoughts may turn frequently to the warmth of the home and the comfort of loved ones. Nostalgic impulses could cause you to bring out old photographs and letters and reflect on the days when your life seemed to be much more rewarding and less demanding. The love and understanding of parents and family may be important, and, if it is not forthcoming, you may have to fight against bouts of self-pity. The cordiality of friends and the thought of good times with them that

are sure to be repeated will help to restore you to a happier frame of mind. The desire to be alone may follow minor setbacks or rebuffs at this time, but solitude is unlikely to help. Better to get on the telephone or visit someone. This period often causes peculiar dreams and upsurges of imaginative thinking which can be helpful to authors of occult and mystical works. Preoccupation with the personal world of simple human needs can overshadow any material strivings. CAUTION: Do not spend too much time thinking—seek the company of loved ones or close friends.

MOON IN LEO

New horizons of exciting and rather extravagant activity open up. This is the time for exhilarating entertainment, glamorous and lavish parties, and expensive shopping sprees. Any merrymaking that relies upon your generosity as a host has every chance of being a spectacular success. You should find yourself right in the center of the fun, either as the life of the party or simply as a person whom happy people like to be with. Romance thrives in this heady atmosphere and friendships are likely to explode unexpectedly into serious attachments. Children and younger people should be attracted to you and you may find yourself organizing a picnic or a visit to a fun-fair, the movies, or the beach. The sunny company and vitality of youthful companions should help you to find some unsuspected energy. In career, you could find an opening for promotion or advancement. This should be the time to make a direct approach. The period favors those engaged in original research. CAUTION: Bask in popularity, not in flattery.

MOON IN VIRGO

Off comes the party cap and out steps the busy, practical worker. He wants to get his personal affairs straight, to rearrange them, if necessary, for more efficiency, so he will have more time for more work. He clears up his correspondence, pays outstanding bills, makes numerous phone calls. He is likely to make inquiries, or sign up for some new insurance and put money into gilt-edged investment. Thoughts probably revolve around the need for future security—to tie up loose ends and clear the decks. There may be a tendency to be "finicky," to interfere in the routine of others, particularly friends and family members. The motive may be a genuine desire to help with suggestions for updating or streamlining their affairs, but these will probably not be welcomed. Sympathy may be felt for less fortunate sections of the community and a flurry of some sort of voluntary service is likely. This may be accompanied by strong feelings of responsibility on several fronts and health may suffer from extra efforts made. CAUTION: Everyone may not want your help or advice.

MOON IN LIBRA
These are days of harmony and agreement and you should find yourself at peace with most others. Relationships tend to be smooth and sweet-flowing. Friends may become closer and bonds deepen in mutual understanding. Hopes will be shared. Progress by cooperation could be the secret of success in every sphere. In business, established partnerships may flourish and new ones get off to a good start. Acquaintances could discover similar interests that lead to congenial discussions and rewarding exchanges of some sort. Love, as a unifying force, reaches its optimum. Marriage partners should find accord. Those who wed at this time face the prospect of a happy union. Cooperation and tolerance are felt to be stronger than dissension and impatience. The argumentative are not quite so loud in their bellowings, nor as inflexible in their attitudes. In the home, there should be a greater recognition of the other point of view and a readiness to put the wishes of the group before selfish insistence. This is a favorable time to join an art group. CAUTION: Do not be too independent—let others help you if they want to.

MOON IN SCORPIO
Driving impulses to make money and to economize are likely to cause upsets all around. No area of expenditure is likely to be spared the ax, including the household budget. This is a time when the desire to cut down on extravagance can become near fanatical. Care must be exercised to try to keep the aim in reasonable perspective. Others may not feel the same urgent need to save and may retaliate. There is a danger that possessions of sentimental value will be sold to realize cash for investment. Buying and selling of stock for quick profit is also likely. The attention turns to organizing, reorganizing, tidying up at home and at work. Neglected jobs could suddenly be done with great bursts of energy. The desire for solitude may intervene. Self-searching thoughts could disturb. The sense of invisible and mysterious energies in play could cause some excitability. The reassurance of loves ones may help. CAUTION: Be kind to the people you love.

MOON IN SAGITTARIUS
These are days when you are likely to be stirred and elevated by discussions and reflections of a religious and philosophical nature. Ideas of faraway places may cause unusual response and excitement. A decision may be made to visit someone overseas, perhaps a person whose influence was important to your earlier character development. There could be a strong resolution to get away from present intellectual patterns, to learn new subjects, and to meet

more interesting people. The superficial may be rejected in all its forms. An impatience with old ideas and unimaginative contacts could lead to a change of companions and interests. There may be an upsurge of religious feeling and metaphysical inquiry. Even a new insight into the significance of astrology and other occult studies is likely under the curious stimulus of the Moon in Sagittarius. Physically, you may express this need for fundamental change by spending more time outdoors: sports, gardening, long walks appeal. CAUTION: Try to channel any restlessness into worthwhile study.

MOON IN CAPRICORN

Life in these hours may seem to pivot around the importance of gaining prestige and honor in the career, as well as maintaining a spotless reputation. Ambitious urges may be excessive and could be accompanied by quite acquisitive drives for money. Effort should be directed along strictly ethical lines where there is no possibility of reproach or scandal. All endeavors are likely to be characterized by great earnestness, and an air of authority and purpose which should impress those who are looking for leadership or reliability. The desire to conform to accepted standards may extend to sharp criticism of family members. Frivolity and unconventional actions are unlikely to amuse while the Moon is in Capricorn. Moderation and seriousness are the orders of the day. Achievement and recognition in this period could come through community work or organizing for the benefit of some amateur group. CAUTION: Dignity and esteem are not always self-awarded.

MOON IN AQUARIUS

Moon in Aquarius is in the second last sign of the Zodiac where ideas can become disturbingly fine and subtle. The result is often a mental "no-man's land" where imagination cannot be trusted with the same certitude as other times. The dangers for the individual are the extremes of optimism and pessimism. Unless the imagination is held in check, situations are likely to be misread, and rosy conclusions drawn where they do not exist. Consequences for the unwary can be costly in career and business. Best to think twice and not speak or act until you think again. Pessimism can be a cruel self-inflicted penalty for delusion at this time. Between the two extremes are strange areas of self-deception which, for example, can make the selfish person think he is actually being generous. Eerie dreams which resemble the reality and even seem to continue into the waking state are also possible. CAUTION: Look for the fact and not just for the image in your mind.

MOON IN PISCES

Everything seems to come to the surface now. Memory may be crystal clear, throwing up long-forgotten information which could be valuable in the career or business. Flashes of clairvoyance and intuition are possible along with sudden realizations of one's own nature, which may be used for self-improvement. A talent, never before suspected, may be discovered. Qualities not evident before in friends and marriage partners are likely to be noticed. As this is a period in which the truth seems to emerge, the discovery of false characteristics is likely to lead to disenchantment or a shift in attachments. However, when qualities are accepted, it should lead to happiness and deeper feeling. Surprise solutions could bob up for old problems. There may be a public announcement of the solving of a crime or mystery. People with secrets may find someone has "guessed" correctly. The secrets of the soul or the inner self also tend to reveal themselves. Religious and philosophical groups may make some interesting discoveries. CAUTION: Not a time for activities that depend on secrecy.

NOTE: When you read your daily forecasts, use the Moon Sign Dates that are provided in the following section of Moon Tables. Then you may want to glance back here for the Moon's influence in a given sign.

MOON TABLES

Atlanta, Boston, Detroit, Miami, Washington, Montreal,
Ottawa, Quebec, Bogota, Havana, Lima, Santiago..Same time
Chicago, New Orleans, Houston, Winnipeg, Churchill,
Mexico City... Deduct 1 hour
Albuquerque, Denver, Phoenix, El Paso, Edmonton,
Helena .... Deduct 2 hours
Los Angeles, San Francisco, Reno, Portland,
Seattle, Vancouver .... Deduct 3 hours
Honolulu, Anchorage, Fairbanks, Kodiak .... Deduct 5 hours
Nome, Samoa, Tonga, Midway..................... Deduct 6 hours
Halifax, Bermuda, San Juan, Caracas, La Paz,
Barbados...Add 1 hour
St. John's, Brasilia, Rio de Janeiro, Sao Paulo,
Buenos Aires, Montevideo...........................Add 2 hours
Azores, Cape Verde Islands...........................Add 3 hours
Canary Islands, Madeira, Reykjavik ....Add 4 hours
London, Paris, Amsterdam, Madrid, Lisbon,
Gibraltar, Belfast, Rabat ....Add 5 hours
Frankfurt, Rome, Oslo, Stockholm, Prague,
Belgrade..Add 6 hours
Bucharest, Beirut, Tel Aviv, Athens, Istanbul, Cairo,
Alexandria, Cape Town, Johannesburg ....Add 7 hours
Moscow, Leningrad, Baghdad, Dhahran,
Addis Ababa, Nairobi, Teheran, Zanzibar.........Add 8 hours
Bombay, Calcutta, Sri Lanka..................... Add 10 ½ hours
Hong Kong, Shanghai, Manila, Peking, Perth...... Add 13 hours
Tokyo, Okinawa, Darwin, Pusan.................... Add 14 hours
Sydney, Melbourne, Port Moresby, Guam.......... Add 15 hours
Auckland, Wellington, Suva, Wake................. Add 17 hours

2002 MOON SIGN DATES— NEW YORK TIME

JANUARY		FEBRUARY		MARCH	
Day Moon Enters		**Day Moon Enters**		**Day Moon Enters**	
1. Leo		1. Libra	3:45 am	1. Libra	
2. Virgo	6:35 pm	2. Libra		2. Scorp.	1:52 pm
3. Virgo		3. Scorp.	5:36 am	3. Scorp.	
4. Libra	8:25 pm	4. Scorp.		4. Sagitt.	4:56 pm
5. Libra		5. Sagitt.	10:22 am	5. Sagitt.	
6. Scorp.	11:42 pm	6. Sagitt.		6. Capric.	11:49 pm
7. Scorp.		7. Capric.	6:09 pm	7. Capric.	
8. Scorp.		8. Capric.		8. Capric.	
9. Sagitt.	4:58 am	9. Capric.		9. Aquar.	9:57 am
10. Sagitt.		10. Aquar.	4:16 am	10. Aquar.	
11. Capric.	12:19 pm	11. Aquar.		11. Pisces	9:57 pm
12. Capric.		12. Pisces	3:54 pm	12. Pisces	
13. Aquar.	9:42 pm	13. Pisces		13. Pisces	
14. Aquar.		14. Pisces		14. Aries	10:35 am
15. Aquar.		15. Aries	4:27 am	15. Aries	
16. Pisces	9:01 am	16. Aries		16. Taurus	11:02 am
17. Pisces		17. Taurus	4:59 pm	17. Taurus	
18. Aries	9:36 pm	18. Taurus		18. Taurus	
19. Aries		19. Taurus		19. Gemini	10:21 am
20. Aries		20. Gemini	3:51 am	20. Gemini	
21. Taurus	9:48 am	21. Gemini		21. Cancer	7:07 pm
22. Taurus		22. Cancer	11:17 am	22. Cancer	
23. Gemini	7:29 pm	23. Cancer		23. Cancer	
24. Gemini		24. Leo	2:37 pm	24. Leo	0:14 am
25. Gemini		25. Leo		25. Leo	
26. Cancer	1:18 am	26. Virgo	2:48 pm	26. Virgo	1:45 am
27. Cancer		27. Virgo		27. Virgo	
28. Leo	3:32 am	28. Libra	1:48 pm	28. Libra	1:05 am
29. Leo				29. Libra	
30. Virgo	3:41 am			30. Scorp.	0:22 am
31. Virgo				31. Scorp.	

Summer time to be considered where applicable.

2002 MOON SIGN DATES—
NEW YORK TIME

APRIL		MAY		JUNE	
Day Moon Enters		**Day Moon Enters**		**Day Moon Enters**	
1. Sagitt.	1:49 am	1. Capric.		1. Pisces	6:38 pm
2. Sagitt.		2. Aquar.	11:45 pm	2. Pisces	
3. Capric.	6:59 am	3. Aquar.		3. Pisces	
4. Capric.		4. Aquar.		4. Aries	6:52 am
5. Aquar.	4:08 pm	5. Pisces	10:47 am	5. Aries	
6. Aquar.		6. Pisces		6. Taurus	7:08 pm
7. Aquar.		7. Aries	11:23 pm	7. Taurus	
8. Pisces	3:59 am	8. Aries		8. Taurus	
9. Pisces		9. Aries		9. Gemini	5:30 am
10. Aries	4:42 pm	10. Taurus	11:33 am	10. Gemini	
11. Aries		11. Taurus		11. Cancer	1:16 pm
12. Aries		12. Gemini	10:05 pm	12. Cancer	
13. Taurus	4:56 am	13. Gemini		13. Leo	6:40 pm
14. Taurus		14. Gemini		14. Leo	
15. Gemini	3:57 pm	15. Cancer	6:34 am	15. Virgo	10:25 pm
16. Gemini		16. Cancer		16. Virgo	
17. Gemini		17. Leo	12:53 pm	17. Virgo	
18. Cancer	1:02 am	18. Leo		18. Libra	1:12 am
19. Cancer		19. Virgo	5:01 pm	19. Libra	
20. Leo	7:22 am	20. Virgo		20. Scorp.	3:43 am
21. Leo		21. Libra	7:20 pm	21. Scorp.	
22. Virgo	10:36 am	22. Libra		22. Sagitt.	6:43 am
23. Virgo		23. Scorp.	8:39 pm	23. Sagitt.	
24. Libra	11:23 am	24. Scorp.		24. Capric.	11:02 am
25. Libra		25. Sagitt.	10:21 pm	25. Capric.	
26. Scorp.	11:16 am	26. Sagitt.		26. Aquar.	5:37 pm
27. Scorp.		27. Sagitt.		27. Aquar.	
28. Sagitt.	12:14 pm	28. Capric.	1:55 am	28. Aquar.	
29. Sagitt.		29. Capric.		29. Pisces	3:02 am
30. Capric.	4:04 pm	30. Aquar.	8:36 am	30. Pisces	
		31. Aquar.			

Summer time to be considered where applicable.

2002 MOON SIGN DATES—
NEW YORK TIME

JULY Day Moon Enters		AUGUST Day Moon Enters		SEPTEMBER Day Moon Enters	
1. Aries	2:50 pm	1. Taurus		1. Cancer	4:15 pm
2. Aries		2. Gemini	10:48 pm	2. Cancer	
3. Aries		3. Gemini		3. Leo	9:38 pm
4. Taurus	3:17 am	4. Gemini		4. Leo	
5. Taurus		5. Cancer	7:03 am	5. Virgo	11:17 pm
6. Gemini	2:02 pm	6. Cancer		6. Virgo	
7. Gemini		7. Leo	11:28 am	7. Libra	10:58 pm
8. Cancer	9:38 pm	8. Leo		8. Libra	
9. Cancer		9. Virgo	1:04 pm	9. Scorp.	10:49 pm
10. Cancer		10. Virgo		10. Scorp.	
11. Leo	2:09 am	11. Libra	1:39 pm	11. Scorp.	
12. Leo		12. Libra		12. Sagitt.	0:45 am
13. Virgo	4:42 am	13. Scorp.	3:02 pm	13. Sagitt.	
14. Virgo		14. Scorp.		14. Capric.	5:49 am
15. Libra	6:40 am	15. Sagitt.	6:26 pm	15. Capric.	
16. Libra		16. Sagitt.		16. Aquar.	1:55 pm
17. Scorp.	9:14 am	17. Sagitt.		17. Aquar.	
18. Scorp.		18. Capric.	0:16 am	18. Aquar.	
19. Sagitt.	1:03 pm	19. Capric.		19. Pisces	0:19 am
20. Sagitt.		20. Aquar.	8:18 am	20. Pisces	
21. Capric.	6:27 pm	21. Aquar.		21. Aries	12:12 pm
22. Capric.		22. Pisces	6:12 pm	22. Aries	
23. Capric.		23. Pisces		23. Aries	
24. Aquar.	1:41 am	24. Pisces		24. Taurus	0:56 am
25. Aquar.		25. Aries	5:49 am	25. Taurus	
26. Pisces	11:05 am	26. Aries		26. Gemini	1:28 pm
27. Pisces		27. Taurus	6:33 pm	27. Gemini	
28. Aries	10:40 pm	28. Taurus		28. Gemini	
29. Aries		29. Taurus		29. Cancer	0:03 am
30. Aries		30. Gemini	6:46 am	30. Cancer	
31. Taurus	11:18 am	31. Gemini			

Summer time to be considered where applicable.

2002 MOON SIGN DATES—
NEW YORK TIME

OCTOBER		NOVEMBER		DECEMBER	
Day Moon Enters		**Day Moon Enters**		**Day Moon Enters**	
1. Leo	6:59 am	1. Libra	8:29 pm	1. Scorp.	6:16 am
2. Leo		2. Libra		2. Scorp.	
3. Virgo	9:53 am	3. Scorp.	8:11 pm	3. Sagitt.	6:59 am
4. Virgo		4. Scorp.		4. Sagitt.	
5. Libra	9:52 am	5. Sagitt.	8:02 pm	5. Capric.	8:40 am
6. Libra		6. Sagitt.		6. Capric.	
7. Scorp.	8:58 am	7. Capric.	10:00 pm	7. Aquar.	12:55 pm
8. Scorp.		8. Capric.		8. Aquar.	
9. Sagitt.	9:22 am	9. Capric.		9. Pisces	8:47 pm
10. Sagitt.		10. Aquar.	3:28 am	10. Pisces	
11. Capric.	12:46 pm	11. Aquar.		11. Pisces	
12. Capric.		12. Pisces	12:43 pm	12. Aries	7:59 am
13. Aquar.	7:52 pm	13. Pisces		13. Aries	
14. Aquar.		14. Pisces		14. Taurus	8:44 pm
15. Aquar.		15. Aries	0:39 am	15. Taurus	
16. Pisces	6:08 am	16. Aries		16. Taurus	
17. Pisces		17. Taurus	1:25 pm	17. Gemini	8:44 am
18. Aries	6:15 pm	18. Taurus		18. Gemini	
19. Aries		19. Taurus		19. Cancer	6:31 pm
20. Aries		20. Gemini	1:26 am	20. Cancer	
21. Taurus	6:58 am	21. Gemini		21. Cancer	
22. Taurus		22. Cancer	11:49 am	22. Leo	1:49 am
23. Gemini	7:18 pm	23. Cancer		23. Leo	
24. Gemini		24. Leo	8:01 pm	24. Virgo	7:06 am
25. Gemini		25. Leo		25. Virgo	
26. Cancer	6:11 am	26. Leo		26. Libra	10:54 am
27. Cancer		27. Virgo	1:43 am	27. Libra	
28. Leo	2:21 pm	28. Virgo		28. Scorp.	1:42 pm
29. Leo		29. Libra	4:55 am	29. Scorp.	
30. Virgo	7:00 pm	30. Libra		30. Sagitt.	4:02 pm
31. Virgo				31. Sagitt.	

Summer time to be considered where applicable.

2002 PHASES OF THE MOON— NEW YORK TIME

New Moon	First Quarter	Full Moon	Last Quarter
Dec. 14 ('01)	Dec. 22 ('01)	Dec. 30 ('01)	Jan. 5
Jan. 13	Jan. 21	Jan. 28	Feb. 4
Feb. 12	Feb. 19	Feb. 27	March 5
March 13	March 21	March 28	April 3
April 12	April 20	April 26	May 4
May 12	May 19	May 26	June 3
June 10	June 18	June 24	July 2
July 10	July 16	July 24	August 1
Aug. 8	Aug. 15	Aug. 22	Aug. 30
Sept. 6	Sept. 13	Sept. 21	Sept. 29
Oct. 6	Oct. 13	Oct. 21	Oct. 29
Nov. 4	Nov. 11	Nov. 19	Nov. 27
Dec. 4	Dec. 11	Dec. 19	Dec. 26

Each phase of the Moon lasts approximately seven to eight days, during which the Moon's shape gradually changes as it comes out of one phase and goes into the next.

There will be a solar eclipse during the New Moon phase on June 10 and December 4.

There will be a lunar eclipse during the Full Moon phase on May 26, June 24, and November 19.

2002 FISHING GUIDE

	Good	Best
January	1-2-21-25-28-29-30-31	6-13-26-27
February	12-20-24-25-26-27-28	4
March	6-14-25-26-27	1-2-22-28-29-30-31
April	12-20-24-28-29-30	4-25-26-27
May	4-19-26-27	12-23-24-25-28-29
June	10-22-23-24-27	3-18-21-25-26
July	2-21-24-25-26	10-17-22-23-27
August	8-20-21-22-25-31	1-15-19-23-24
September	7-13-18-21-22-23	19-20-24-29
October	19-20-21-24-29	6-13-18-22-23
November	11-17-20-21-22-27	4-18-19-23
December	4-17-18-19-22	11-16-20-21-27

2002 PLANTING GUIDE

	Aboveground Crops	Root Crops
January	17-18-22-23-26-27	5-6-7-8-12
February	13-14-18-19-23	1-2-3-4-8-9
March	17-18-22-23-26-27	1-2-3-7-8-12-13-29-30-31
April	13-14-18-19-25-26	4-8-9-27
May	16-22-23-24-25	1-2-6-7-11-28-29
June	12-13-18-19-20-21	2-3-7-8-25-26-29-30
July	16-17-18-22-23	4-5-9-27-28
August	12-13-14-15-18-19	1-2-6-23-24-28-29
September	8-9-10-11-15-19-20	2-3-24-25-29-30
October	7-8-12-13-17-18	22-23-27
November	5-8-9-13-14-18-19	2-3-23-24-29-30
December	6-10-11-15-16	1-2-20-21-27-28-29

	Pruning	Weeds and Pests
January	7-8	1-2-3-4-9-10-29-30-31
February	4	6-7-10-11-27
March	3-12-13-30-31	5-6-10-11
April	8-9-27	1-2-6-7-11-29
May	6-7	3-4-8-9-27-31
June	2-3-29-30	5-6-10-27-28
July	9-27-28	2-3-7-8-24-25-29-30
August	6-23-24	3-4-26-27-31
September	23-29-30	4-5-6-22-23-27-28
October	27	2-3-4-24-25-29-30-31
November	23-24	1-20-21-25-26-27-28
December	2-20-21-29	22-23-24-25-31

MOON'S INFLUENCE OVER PLANTS

Centuries ago it was established that seeds planted when the Moon is in signs and phases called Fruitful will produce more growth than seeds planted when the Moon is in a Barren sign.

Fruitful Signs: Taurus, Cancer, Libra, Scorpio, Capricorn, Pisces
Barren Signs: Aries, Gemini, Leo, Virgo, Sagittarius, Aquarius
Dry Signs: Aries, Gemini, Sagittarius, Aquarius

Activity	Moon In
Mow lawn, trim plants	**Fruitful sign:** 1st & 2nd quarter
Plant flowers	**Fruitful sign:** 2nd quarter; best in Cancer and Libra
Prune	**Fruitful sign:** 3rd & 4th quarter
Destroy pests; spray	**Barren sign:** 4th quarter
Harvest potatoes, root crops	**Dry sign:** 3rd & 4th quarter; Taurus, Leo, and Aquarius

MOON'S INFLUENCE OVER YOUR HEALTH

ARIES   Head, brain, face, upper jaw
TAURUS   Throat, neck, lower jaw
GEMINI   Hands, arms, lungs, shoulders, nervous system
CANCER   Esophagus, stomach, breasts, womb, liver
LEO   Heart, spine
VIRGO   Intestines, liver
LIBRA   Kidneys, lower back
SCORPIO   Sex and eliminative organs
SAGITTARIUS   Hips, thighs, liver
CAPRICORN   Skin, bones, teeth, knees
AQUARIUS   Circulatory system, lower legs
PISCES   Feet, tone of being

Try to avoid work being done on that part of the body when the
Moon is in the sign governing that part.

MOON'S INFLUENCE OVER DAILY AFFAIRS

The Moon makes a complete transit of the Zodiac every 27 days
7 hours and 43 minutes. In making this transit the Moon forms
different aspects with the planets and consequently has favorable
or unfavorable bearings on affairs and events for persons according to the sign of the Zodiac under which they were born.

When the Moon is in conjunction with the Sun it is called a
New Moon; when the Moon and Sun are in opposition it is called
a Full Moon. From New Moon to Full Moon, first and second
quarter—which takes about two weeks—the Moon is increasing
or waxing. From Full Moon to New Moon, third and fourth quarter, the Moon is decreasing or waning.

Activity	Moon In
Business: buying and selling new, requiring public support	Sagittarius, Aries, Gemini, Virgo 1st and 2nd quarter
meant to be kept quiet	3rd and 4th quarter
Investigation	3rd and 4th quarter
Signing documents	1st & 2nd quarter, Cancer, Scorpio, Pisces
Advertising	2nd quarter, Sagittarius
Journeys and trips	1st & 2nd quarter, Gemini, Virgo
Renting offices, etc.	Taurus, Leo, Scorpio, Aquarius
Painting of house/apartment	3rd & 4th quarter, Taurus, Scorpio, Aquarius
Decorating	Gemini, Libra, Aquarius
Buying clothes and accessories	Taurus, Virgo
Beauty salon or barber shop visit	1st & 2nd quarter, Taurus, Leo, Libra, Scorpio, Aquarius
Weddings	1st & 2nd quarter

Leo

LEO

Character Analysis

The person born under the sign of Leo usually knows how to handle a position of authority well. Others have a deep respect for the decisions he makes. The Leo man or woman generally has something aristocratic about him that commands respect. The person born under this fifth sign of the Zodiac generally knows how to stand on his own two feet. He is independent in many things that he does. He knows how to direct his energies so that he will be able to achieve his ends. He seldom wastes time; he is to the point. In love matters, the Leo is quite passionate. He doesn't stint when it comes to romance and is capable of deep emotions. The Leo is a stable person; he has the ability to see things through to the end without wavering on his standpoint.

Leo people are quite generous in all that they do. They give themselves fully to every situation. To others they often appear quite lordly; they are often at the helm of organizations, running things.

The Leo person does not believe in being petty or small. Quite often he goes out of his way to make others happy. He would never stoop to doing anything which he felt was beneath his dignity. He has a deep feeling of self-respect. He would never treat others badly. He is kindhearted, sometimes to a fault. Although he does his best not to hurt others, he is apt to have his moments of irritation when he feels that it is better to speak outright than to give a false impression of his attitudes.

Leo people generally learn to shoulder certain responsibilities at an early age. They have an understanding of life that others sometimes never attain. They do not shy away from conflict or troubles. They believe in dealing with opposition directly. They are quite active in their approach to problems. Life, to them, should be attacked with zest and vigor. There is nothing lazy or retiring about a person born under this sign. He is outgoing, often fond of strenuous sports, keenly interested in having a good time. Everything about his attitudes is likely to be king-sized.

When the Leo man or woman knows what he wants in life, he goes out after it. He is not a person who gives up easily. He perseveres until he wins. He is not interested in occupying a position where he has to be told what to do. He is too independent for that sort of thing. He wants to be the person who runs things and he seems almost naturally suited for an authoritative position. His bearing is that of someone who expects others to listen to him when he speaks. He is a forceful person; he knows how to command respect. He is seldom unsure of himself, but when he is, he sees to it that others do not notice. He is quite clever at organizing things. He is a person who likes order. He knows how to channel his creative talents in such a way that the results of whatever he does are always constructive and original. Leadership positions bring out the best in a person born under this sign.

The Leo person is generally quite tolerant and open-minded. He believes in live-and-let-live as long as the other person does not infringe on what he believes to be his natural rights. In most things, he is fair. He believes in being frank and open. On the whole, the Leo person is active and high-strung. If something irritates him or runs against his grain, he will let it be known. He can be short-tempered if the occasion calls for it.

He is a person who believes in sticking to his principles. He is not interested in making compromises—especially if he feels that his standpoint is the correct one. He can become angry if opposed. But, all in all, his bad temper does not last for a long time. He is the kind of person who does not hold grudges.

The Leo person often has a flair for acting. Some of the best actors in the world have been people born under the sign of the Lion. Their dramatic talents are often considerable. Even as children Leo people have a strong understanding of drama. There is also something poetic about them. They can be quite romantic at times. They have a deep love and appreciation of beauty. They are fond of display and have a love of luxury that often startles modest people.

On the whole, Lion or Lioness is a proud person. His head is easily turned by a compliment. The cultivated Leo, however, knows how to take flattery in his stride. Others may try to get around him by flattering him. They generally succeed with the weaker Leos, for they are quite caught up with themselves and feel that no compliment is too great. This should not be interpreted as pure vanity. The Leo person has a clear understanding of his own superiority and worth.

In spite of the fact that he is generous in most things, the person born under Leo may not appreciate others making demands of him. He may not mind offering favors, but he does not like them to be asked of him.

Leo men and women feel that it is important to be your own boss. He does not like others to tell him what to do. He is quite capable, he feels, of handling his own affairs—and quite well. If he has to work with others, he may become impatient, especially if they are somewhat slow or unsure. He does not like to be kept waiting. Teamwork for the Lion is sometimes a very frustrating experience. He likes to be on his own.

Health

The Leo person is generally well built. He is a sturdy person, capable of taking a lot of stress and strain if necessary. Still, he may take on more than he can manage from time to time, and this is likely to exhaust him physically. He enjoys challenge, however, and finds it difficult to turn down a proposition which gives him a chance to demonstrate his worth—even if it is beyond his real capabilities.

Although he is basically an active person, he does have his limits. If he refuses to recognize them, he may become the victim of a nervous disorder. Some people born under this sign are fond of keeping late hours, especially in pursuit of pleasure or of fame. They can keep this up for some time, but in the end it does have a telling effect on their health. People born under this sign often wear themselves out by going from one extreme to the other.

The weak parts of the Leo are his spine and heart. He should see to it that he does nothing that might affect these areas of his body. In many instances, the Leo has to restrain himself in order to protect his health. Heart disease or rheumatic fever sometimes strikes people born under this sign. In spite of this, the Leo generally has a strong resistance to disease. His constitution is good. Whenever he does fall ill, he generally recovers rather quickly. The Leo man or woman cannot stand being sick. He has to be up and around; lying in bed is quite bothersome for him.

On the whole, Leo is a brave person. However, he may have to learn the art of being physically courageous. This is generally not one of his natural attributes. When physical dangers threaten, he may be somewhat paralyzed by fear. But intellectually Leo is fearless. If ideas or principles are at stake he is not afraid to stand up and let others know his opinion.

The Leo man or woman has a deep love of life. He can be quite pleasure-oriented. He likes the good things that life has to offer. Sometimes he is overenthusiastic in his approach to things, and as a result accidents occur. Under certain conditions he may take chances that others wouldn't. It is important that the person born as a Lion or Lioness learn how to curb impulsiveness, as often it works against him.

Even when they become older, Leo people remain energetic. Their zest for life never dies. They can prolong their lives by avoiding excesses in drinking or by adopting a balanced and moderate lifestyle.

Occupation

Leo seems to gravitate to jobs where he will have a chance to exercise his ability to manage. He is best suited to positions of authority; people respect the decisions he makes. He seems to be a natural-born leader. He knows how to take command of any situation in which he finds himself. The decisions he makes are usually just. He is direct in the way he handles his business affairs. When dealing with others he is open. He says what he means—even if he runs the danger of being blunt or offensive. He is the kind of person who believes that honesty is the best policy. Lies don't go down well with him. The truth—even if it is painful—is better than a kind lie.

In spite of the fact that the Leo man or woman is sometimes critical to a fault, the people who work under him generally respect him and try to understand him. They seldom have reason to question his authority.

In work situations, Leo always tries to do his best. His interest in being the top person has considerable motivational force. He is not interested in second place; only the top position is good enough for him. He will strive until he gets the position he feels is his due. The Leo individual generally has a good understanding of the way things work and how to improve work situations so that better results can be obtained. He knows how to handle people—how they think and how they behave. His understanding of human nature is considerable. He is not the kind of person to rest on his laurels. He is always in search of ways to better an existing situation. He knows how to move along with the times and always tries to keep abreast of new developments in his field.

Leo is proud. In every struggle—be it physical or intellectual—he fights to win. Failure is something he finds difficult to accept. He seldom considers the possibility; success is the only thing he keeps in mind as he works. He coordinates all of his energies and efforts so that success is almost guaranteed. Dull, routine work he is glad to leave to others. His interest lies in the decision-making area of business. He wants to discuss important issues and have a hand in making policies.

Leo leads things well; there can be no question of that. He or she is deeply interested in people's welfare. Leo would never abuse his position as supervisor or manager, but would use it to help those working under him.

On the whole, Leo is a responsible person. He handles his duties capably. He does not, however, enjoy being told what to do. When others try to lord it over him, he is likely to resent it—sometimes quite violently. He feels that no one is in a position to lead him. He often finds fault with the way others try to run things; sometimes he is quite just in his criticism.

The person born under this fifth sign of the Zodiac usually does well in a position where he has to deal with the public. He knows how to be persuasive in his argument. Others seldom have reason to doubt his word, for he is usually sure of what he has to say. A Leo person is likely to do well in any kind of business where he is given an opportunity to make use of his managerial skills. Politics is another area where the man or woman born under the sign of the Lion is apt to do quite well.

As was mentioned before, many Leos seem to be natural-born actors. They have convincing ease when on the stage. They know how to immerse themselves completely in a dramatic role. They do well in almost any kind of creative work. They have the soul of an artist or poet. In whatever field he enters—theater, art, politics, advertising, or industrial management—the Lion or Lioness will do what they can to occupy the top position. If they do not have it in the beginning, you can be sure they are working toward it.

The Leo person is far from being stingy. He loves entertaining his friends and relatives in a royal manner. Generous, sometimes to a fault, he is far from being careless with his money. He has a deep-hidden fear of being poor. He'll do what he can to protect his interests. The Leo man or woman is generally fortunate enough to occupy a position that pays well. If he earns a lot, he is apt to spend a lot. He does not like to have to count pennies. Luxurious surroundings give him the feeling of success. Money is seldom a problem to the wise Leo man or woman. Some of them wind up considerably well-off early in life. They usually don't mind taking chances with their finances. Quite often they are lucky in speculation or gambling.

If Leo feels that someone is in serious financial trouble, he does not mind helping out. He is generous and good-hearted when it comes to lending money. But he doesn't like to be taken advantage of. If someone makes unnecessary demands of him financially, he is apt to become disagreeable.

Leo likes to treat the people he cares for and to give them presents. The gifts he gives are usually expensive and in good taste. He likes to please others—to make them grateful for the gifts he has given them. He likes others to think well of him and that is perhaps why he is eager to give presents. He likes to be the one others turn to when in trouble or lean on for support.

A show of wealth makes Leo men or women feel important. The cultivated Leo sees to it that their extravagance never becomes unreasonable or unbearable.

Home and Family

The Leo man or woman needs a place where he can relax in peace and quiet. His home is his castle. He likes to live in a place that radiates comfort and harmony. Home life is important to the Leo person. He likes to feel that his family needs him—financially as well as emotionally. He likes to be the one who runs things at home. He expects his standards to be upheld by the other members of his family. He is generally a good provider.

The Leo individual makes an excellent host. He knows how to make his guests feel at home. He likes to entertain his close friends quite often. The Leo woman does everything she can to make her guests feel they are liked and cared for. She is usually a very attentive hostess.

When the Leo person spends money, it is often to show that he is capable of spending it. For him it is a display of power or success. It lets others know what he is worth. He sees to it that his home has all of the latest appliances and luxuries. He enjoys impressing others by his clothes and furnishings, even though this may encourage them to envy him.

The woman born under this sign usually enjoys dressing well. Her wardrobe is apt to be large. If she is able, she may not wear the same thing more than once or twice. She is very conscious of being in style. If her husband is not a big earner, she may be quite a burden, for her extravagance is sometimes boundless. If she is married to a man who is not in a top earning position, she will do what she can to help him achieve it.

The Leo person is fond of children. Leos enjoy taking care of them and seeing them grow up. Sometimes, however, they are too forceful as parents and don't give their children a chance to develop their own potential. They like to be proud of their children and appreciate it when others pay them compliments about their children's behavior.

Some Leo parents love their children so much that they are blind to their faults. They become angry if others should accuse them of spoiling their children. They are anxious to see their children succeed and sometimes expect too much of them too soon. When the children reach adulthood and assert their own will, the Leo parent is apt to feel that his children are not appreciative of all that he has done for them. He may resent the youngsters' show of independence.

Social Relationships

Leo people have no trouble making friends. People seem to gravitate to them. It is unusual for someone born under this sign not to be popular. They are warm, friendly, and considerate. People like them because of their sure, authoritative ways. Leo people know how to keep the friends they make. They are outgoing, open, and helpful. They never refuse someone in real need.

They usually have what is popularly known as "personality". They are never dull or retiring people. They are always out front where they can easily be seen. They like having a rich and active social life. Sometimes they make considerable gains in their business affairs through social activities. For them, business and pleasure can mix. They are never short of important contacts.

Those who love Leos accept their leadership without having any qualms. They trust Leos' good judgment and their ability to regulate things.

Leo is tremendously loyal to true friends, so firm friendships may last a lifetime. But a problem can arise in finding true friends. Because Leos believe everyone is as noble as they are, a naive belief at best, they often immediately claim an associate or casual acquaintance as a friend. The trouble begins when the person does not live up to Leo's expectations of what a friend should be.

Such disappointing experiences prove to be useful lessons for the young Lion. As they mature, and as a defense against hurt or betrayal, Leos will maintain a measure of aloofness in many of their personal relationships. For that reason, many Leo men and women have few really intimate friends or close confidantes. Leo likes to mix with people, but he or she may feel it necessary to keep some distance.

The Lion's desire to win in any situation makes for a very competitive personality. This basic competitive nature sometimes interferes with an ability to get along with teammates. Also, many people who are peers and might become good friends may be regarded as rivals on any playing field. Of course, Leos are just as likely to compliment a worthy rival as to criticize a weak and undeserving one.

But Leo is all heart. Leo is deeply sympathetic with anyone who is perceived to lack the advantages. Leos go out of their way to nurture, aid, and lead this person to a richer, fuller life. Some of Leo's friends are those unfortunates who need a helping hand. Family members or associates may pick on Leo for such unconventional choices. But a generosity of spirit rises above what Leos consider to be petty considerations of wealth, class, and rank.

Love and Marriage

Leo is the sign of life and love of life. Leo is also the sign of pleasure and of children. Love together with love of life linked in the union of two loving individuals is the basis for pleasure and children. The supreme force of love motivates the Lion or Lioness in every aspect of living. But Leo's love is not strictly sexual nor earthily sensual nor purely mental. Leo's love embraces each kind yet extends to the romantic, idealistic, unrestrained, universal love that sustains all of humankind.

Because of love's impelling force, it can hardly be said that Leo men and women are cool, easygoing lovers. Quite the contrary! Most Lions are incredibly impulsive, even unpredictable, in affairs of the heart—and as a result Leos are very vulnerable.

With their intense emotionality, Leos are apt to get carried away in love. They throw caution to the winds. They take all kinds of risks in order to win someone they are chasing. When amorous and ardent, Leos may lose all sense of what is wrong and what is right.

Leos are sentimental and easily moved. Every love affair is serious to them. They may flirt from time to time, but when earnest in love they do what they can to make it permanent.

A Leo is very affectionate by nature and he displays this in private. He or she is not fond of being demonstrative in public places. Somehow Leo feels this is undignified. Love and affection should be kept between two people in private.

When in love, Leos are faithful. They do not believe in cheating. Constancy is important to the Lion and Lioness. But if a lover cheats, Leo cannot endure such unhappiness even long enough to resolve what might be only a testing situation. Leo quickly switches interest to another potential mate and wholeheartedly resumes the chase. The same is true of unrequited love. If the adored one is not responding, Leo doesn't hang around acting like a pest. He or she eagerly looks for another beloved on whom to lavish attention and affection.

Generally, Leo individuals are attractive and are never at a loss for company. The opposite sex falls under the charm of a Leo person quite easily.

When looking for a permanent mate, the wise and cultivated Leo chooses someone who is not jealous or possessive—someone who won't suspect him of infidelity if he finds someone else attractive and is quite frank about it.

Romance and the Leo Woman

The Leo woman is often charming and beautiful. She seldom has any trouble in finding a mate. Men are drawn to her almost automatically because of her grace and poise. Lady Lions are known for their attractive eyes and regal bearing. Their features are often fine and delicate. There is seldom anything gross about a woman born under the sign of Leo, even when they tend to be heavy-set or large. There is always something fine that is easy to recognize in their build and carriage.

The Leo woman is passionate by nature. She is very warm and giving when in love. Men find her a very desirable creature and are apt to lose their heads over her when in love. She has an undeniable charm for the opposite sex. Other women are not apt to care for her when men are in the vicinity, for she has no trouble in outshining them all. She is serious when it comes to love. She may have many love affairs before she settles down, but all of them will be serious. She almost never flirts. She doesn't like a jealous or possessive man. She wants the person she loves to trust her implicitly. She doesn't like her love to be doubted.

She likes to be active socially. She enjoys being catered to by the man who loves her. She is fond of parties and entertainment. The man who courts her may have to spend quite a bit of money in order to please her. Sometimes, she is dreamy and idealistic when in love, and so chooses the wrong man for a partner.

She is the kind of woman who stands behind her man in all that she does. She does what she can to help him ascend the ladder of success. She is an intelligent conversationalist and can often entertain her husband's business associates in such a way that her husband can make important gains. She is a charming hostess.

The Leo mother is affectionate and understanding. She will do all she can to see to it that her children are brought up properly.

Romance and the Leo Man

The Leo man is considered a real Casanova by many. He is passionate when in love and will stop at nothing to please the object of his affection. Women love his fiery, sure nature. They feel safe and secure when they are with him. He is a difficult person for many a woman to resist. When romancing someone, Leo does what he can to keep the affair exciting and happy. He lavishes gifts on the person he loves. Dining and dancing at the best places in town are something that Leo is fond of when dating.

If Leo loves someone, he is likely to be blind to her faults. He may be more in love with his idea of a person than with the person herself. So caught up is he in his passion that he is likely to forget all practical matters. Sometimes Leo marries unluckily because of this. He idolizes his love to such an extent that he feels she is incapable of human faults and weaknesses.

The Leo man is a passionate lover. He woos the woman of his choice until he wins her. It is important for him to love, and to have that love returned. Women are easily attracted to him because of his charming ways. He knows how to make a woman feel important and wanted.

He is serious about love. He doesn't believe in meaningless flings. He is very concerned with appearance and is easily attracted to a good-looking woman. He is apt to build a certain fantasy world around the woman he loves and set her on a high pedestal. He will do everything he can to make her happy. He is an attentive lover and is fond of presenting his loved one with presents. He does not like possessive or jealous women. He wants his sweetheart or wife to give him the freedom he feels he is entitled to. Although he may be attracted to other women after marriage, it is unlikely that he will ever be unfaithful.

As a parent and husband Leo is an excellent provider. He likes to be admired by his family. He may become quite irritable if he feels his family is not as loving and as affectionate as he is. He wants his family to be one he can be proud of.

Woman—Man

LEO WOMAN
ARIES MAN

The man born under the sign of Aries is often attracted to the Leo woman. After all, you are both fire signs. In you he can find that mixture of intellect and charm that is often difficult to find in a woman.

In some ways, the lamb and the lion are an idealized union. Your lively Ram lover may even lead the way. Aries has an insatiable thirst for knowledge. He is ambitious and is apt to have his finger in many pies. He can do with a woman like you—someone attractive, quick-witted, and smart.

He is not interested in a clinging vine for a wife. He wants someone who is there when he needs her; someone who listens and understands what he says; someone who can give advice if he should ever have to ask for it—which is not likely to be often. The Aries man wants a woman who is a good companion and a good sport.

He is looking for a woman who will look good on his arm without hanging on it too heavily. He is looking for a woman who has both feet on the ground and yet is mysterious and enticing—a kind of domestic Helen of Troy whose face or fine dinner can launch a thousand business deals if need be. That woman he is in search of sounds a little like you, doesn't it? If the shoe fits, wear it. It will make you feel like Cinderella.

The Aries man makes a good husband. He is faithful and attentive. He is an affectionate kind of man. He'll make you feel needed and loved. Love is a serious matter for the Aries man. He does not believe in flirting or playing the field—especially after he's found the woman of his dreams. He'll expect you to be as constant in your affection as he is in his. He'll expect you to be one hundred percent his; he won't put up with any nonsense while romancing you.

The Aries man may be pretty progressive and modern about many things. However, when it comes to wearing the pants he's downright conventional; it's strictly male attire. The best role you can take in the relationship is a supporting one. He's the boss and that's that. Once you have learned to accept that, you'll find the going easy.

The Aries man, with his endless energy and drive, likes to relax in the comfort of his home at the end of the day. The good home-maker can be sure of holding his love. He's keen on watching news programs and special reports from a comfortable armchair. If you see to it that everything in the house is where he expects to find it, you'll have no difficulty keeping the relationship on an even keel.

Life and love with an Aries man may be just the medicine you need. He'll be a good provider. He'll spoil you if he's financially able.

The Aries father is young at heart and can get along easily with children. His ability to jump from one activity to another will suit and delight a young child's attention span.

LEO WOMAN
TAURUS MAN

If you've got your heart set on a man born under the sign of Taurus, you'll have to learn the art of being patient. Taurus take their time about everything—even love.

The steady and deliberate Taurus man is a little slow on the draw. It may take him quite a while before he gets around to popping that question. For the Leo woman who doesn't mind twiddling her thumbs, the waiting and anticipating almost always pay off in the end. Taurus men want to make sure that every step they take is a good one, particularly if they feel that the path they're on could lead to the altar.

If you are in the mood for a whirlwind romance, you had better cast your net in shallower waters. Moreover, most Taurus prefer to do the angling themselves. They are not happy when a woman takes the lead. Once she does, he's likely to drop her like a dead fish. If you let yourself get caught on his terms, you'll find that he's fallen for you—hook, line, and sinker.

The Taurus man is fond of a comfortable home life. It is very important to him. If you keep those home fires burning, you will have no trouble keeping that flame in your Taurus lover's heart aglow. You have a talent for homemaking; use it. Your taste in furnishings is excellent. You know how to make a house come alive with inviting colors and decorations.

Taurus, the strong, steady, and protective Bull, could be the answer to your prayers. Perhaps he could be the anchor for your dreams and plans. He could help you acquire a more balanced outlook and approach to your life. If you're given to impulsiveness, he could help you to curb it. He's the man who is always there when you need him.

When you tie the knot with a man born under Taurus, you can put away fears about creditors pounding on the front door. Taurus are practical about everything including bill paying. When he carries you over that threshold, you can be certain that the entire house is paid for, not only the doorsill.

As a homemaker, you won't have to worry about putting aside your many interests for the sake of back-breaking house chores. Your Taurus husband will see to it that you have all the latest time-saving appliances and comforts.

You can forget about acquiring premature gray hairs due to unruly, ruckus-raising children under your feet. Papa Taurus is a master at keeping the youngsters in line. He's crazy about kids, but he also knows what's good for them.

LEO WOMAN
GEMINI MAN

The Gemini man is quite a catch. Many a woman has set her cap for him and failed to bag him. Generally, Gemini men are intelligent, witty, and outgoing. Many of them tend to be versatile and multi-faceted. The Gemini man could easily wind up being your better half.

One thing that causes a Twin's mind and affection to wander is a bore, and it is unlikely that an active Leo woman would ever allow herself to be accused of that. The Gemini man who has caught your heart will admire you for your ideas and intellect—perhaps even more than for your homemaking talents and good looks.

The Leo woman needn't feel that once she's made her marriage vows that she'll have to store her interests and ambition in the attic somewhere. The Gemini man will admire you for your zeal and liveliness. He's the kind of guy who won't scowl if you let him shift for himself in the kitchen once in a while. In fact, he'll enjoy the challenge of wrestling with pots and pans himself for a change. Chances are, too, that he might turn out to be a better cook than you—that is, if he isn't already.

The man born under the sign of the Twins is a very active person. There aren't many women who have enough pep to keep up with him. But pep is no problem for the spry Leo woman. You are both dreamers, planners, and idealists. The strong Leo woman can easily fill the role of rudder for her Gemini's ship-without-a-sail. If you are a cultivated, purposeful Leo, he won't mind it at all.

The intelligent Twin is often aware of his shortcomings and doesn't resent it if someone with better bearings gives him a shove in the right direction—when it's needed. The average Gemini does not have serious ego hang-ups and will even accept a well-deserved chewing out from his mate quite gracefully.

When you and your Gemini man team up, you'll probably always have a houseful of people to entertain—interesting people, too. Geminis find it hard to tolerate sluggish minds and impassive dispositions.

People born under Gemini generally have two sides to their natures, as different as night and day. It's very easy for them to be happy-go-lucky one minute, then down in the dumps the next. They hate to be bored and will generally do anything to make their lives interesting, vivid, and action-packed.

Gemini men are always attractive to the opposite sex. You'll perhaps have to allow him an occasional harmless flirt—it will seldom amount to more than that if you're his proper mate.

The Gemini father is a pushover for the kids. He loves them so much, he generally lets them do what they want. Gemini's sense of humor is infectious, so the children will naturally come to see the fun and funny sides of life.

LEO WOMAN
CANCER MAN

Chances are you won't hit it off too well with the man born under Cancer if love is your object, but then Cupid has been known to do some pretty unlikely things. The Cancer man is very sensitive. He is thin-skinned and occasionally moody. You've got to keep on your toes—and not step on his—if you're determined to make a go of the relationship.

The Cancer man may be lacking in many of the qualities you seek in a man, but when it comes to being faithful and being a good provider, he's hard to beat.

It is the perceptive Leo woman who will not mistake the Crab's quietness for sullenness or his thriftiness for penny-pinching. In some respects, he is like that wise old owl out on a limb; he may look like he's dozing but actually he hasn't missed a thing. Cancers often possess a well of knowledge about human behavior. They can come across with some pretty helpful advice to those in trouble. He can certainly guide you in making investments both in time and in money. He may not say much, but he's always got his wits about him.

The Crab may not be the match or the catch for many a Leo

woman. In fact, he is likely to seem downright dull to the on-the-move Leo girl. True to his sign, he can be fairly cranky and crabby when handled the wrong way. He is perhaps more sensitive than he should be.

Leo people are usually as smart as a whip. If you're clever, you will never in any way convey the idea that you consider your Cancer a little slow on the uptake. Browbeating is a surefire way of sending the Crab angrily scurrying back to his shell. And it's quite possible that all of that lost ground will never be recovered.

The Crab is most himself at home. Once settled down for the night or the weekend, wild horses couldn't drag him any farther than the gatepost—that is, unless those wild horses were dispatched by his mother. The Crab is sometimes a Momma's boy. If his mate doesn't put her foot down, he will see to it that his mother always comes first. No self-respecting Leo would ever allow herself to play second fiddle, even if it's to an elderly mother-in-law. If the Lioness is tactful, she'll discover that slipping into the number-one position is as easy as pie (that legendary pie his mother used to bake).

If you pamper your Cancer man, you'll find that "mother" turns up less and less both at the front door as well as in conversations.

Cancers make protective, proud, and patient fathers. But they can be a little too protective. Sheltering may interfere with a youngster's burgeoning independence. Still, the Cancer father doesn't want to see his youngster learning about life the hard way.

LEO WOMAN
LEO MAN

You probably won't have any trouble understanding the Leo man as you were born under the same sign. Still, some conflict is possible due to the fact that you both are very much alike. Be tactful and tolerant in a Leo-Leo relationship.

For many women, Leo is the sign of love. When the Lion puts his mind to romance, he doesn't stint. If he has it his way, he will be wining, dining, and dancing with his Lioness till the wee hours of the morning.

The Leo man is all heart and knows how to make his woman feel like a woman. More often than not, he is a man a woman can look up to. He's a man who manages to have full control of just about any situation he finds himself in. He's a winner.

The Leo man may not look like Tarzan, but he knows how to roar and beat his chest if he has to. He's the kind of man you can lean upon. He'll also give you support in your plans and projects. He's often capable of giving advice that pays off. Leo men are direct. They don't pussyfoot around.

Leo men often rise to the top of their profession, and through their examples prove to be great sources of inspiration to others.

Although he's a ladies' man, Leo is very particular about his ladies. His standards are high when it comes to love interests. He believes that romance should be played on a fair give-and-take basis. He won't put up with any monkey business in a love relationship. It's all or nothing.

You'll find him a frank, honest person. He generally says what is on his mind.

If you decide that a Leo man is the one for you, be prepared to stand behind him full force. He expects it—and usually deserves it. He's the head of the house and can handle that position without a hitch. He knows how to go about breadwinning and, if he has his way (and most Leos do have their own way), he'll see to it that you'll have all the luxuries you crave and the comforts you need.

It's unlikely that the romance in your marriage will ever die out. Lions need love like flowers need sunshine. They're ever amorous and generally expect equal attention and affection from their mate. Lions are fond of going out on the town. They love to give parties as well as go to them. You should encounter no difficulties in sharing his interests in this direction.

Leo fathers can be strict when they think that the rules of the royal kingdom are being broken. You'll have to do your best to smooth over the children's roughed-up feelings.

LEO WOMAN
VIRGO MAN

The Virgo man is all business—or he may seem so to you. He is usually very cool, calm, and collected. He's perhaps too much of a fussbudget to wake up deep romantic interests in a Leo woman. Torrid romancing to the Virgo man is just so much sentimental mush. He can do without it and can make that quite evident.

The Virgo man regards chastity as a virtue. If necessary, he can lead a sedentary, sexless life without caring too much about the fun others think he's missing. In short, you are apt to find him a first-class dud. He doesn't have much of an imagination; flights of fancy don't interest him. He is always correct and likes to be handled correctly. Almost everything about him is orderly. There's a place for everything and everything in its place is likely to be an adage he'll fall upon quite regularly.

He does have an honest-to-goodness heart, believe it or not. The Leo woman who finds herself strangely attracted to his cool, feet-flat-on-the-ground ways will discover that his is a constant heart, not one that goes in for flings or sordid affairs. Virgos take an awfully long time to warm up to someone. A practical man, even in matters of the heart, he wants to know just what kind of a person you are before he takes a chance on you.

The impulsive Leo girl had better not make the mistake of kissing her Virgo friend on the street—even if it's only a peck on the cheek. He's not at all demonstrative and hates public displays of affection. Love, according to him, should be kept within the confines of one's home—with the curtains drawn. Once he believes that you are on the level with him as far as your love is concerned, you'll see how fast he can lose his cool. Virgos are considerate, gentle lovers. He'll spend a long time, though, getting to know you. He'll like you before he loves you.

A Leo-Virgo romance can be a sometime—or, rather, a one-time thing. If the bottom ever falls out, don't bother reaching for the adhesive tape. Nine times out of ten he won't care about patching up. He's a once-burnt-twice-shy guy. When he crosses your telephone number out of his address book, he's crossing you out of his life for good.

Neat as a pin, he's thumbs-down on what he considers sloppy housekeeping. An ashtray with just one stubbed-out cigarette in it can annoy him even if it's just two seconds old. Glassware should always sparkle and shine.

If you marry a Virgo man, instill a sense of order in the kids, or at least have them behaving by the time he gets home. The Virgo father wants his children to be kind and courteous and always helpful to the neighbors.

LEO WOMAN
LIBRA MAN

If there's a Libra in your life, you are most likely a very happy woman. Men born under this sign have a way with women. You'll always feel at ease in a Libra's company. You can be yourself when you're with him.

Like you, he can be moody at times. His moodiness, though, is more puzzling. One moment he comes on hard and strong with declarations of his love, the next moment you find that he's left you like yesterday's mashed potatoes. He'll come back, though; don't worry. Libras are like that. Deep down inside he really knows what he wants even though he may not appear to.

You'll appreciate his admiration of beauty and harmony. If you're dressed to the teeth and never looked lovelier, you'll get a ready compliment—and one that's really deserved. Libras don't indulge in idle flattery. If they don't like something, they are tactful enough to remain silent.

Libras will go to great lengths to preserve peace and harmony—even tell a fat lie if necessary. They don't like showdowns or disagreeable confrontations. The frank Leo woman is all for getting whatever is bothering her off her chest and out into the open, even if it comes out all wrong. To the Libra, making a clean breast of everything seems like sheer folly sometimes.

You may lose your patience while waiting for your Libra friend to make up his mind. It takes him ages sometimes to make a decision. He weighs both sides carefully before committing himself to anything. You seldom dillydally—at least about small things—and so it's likely that you will find it difficult to see eye-to-eye with a hesitating Libra when it comes to decision-making methods.

All in all, though, he is kind, gentle, and fair. He is interested in the "real" truth. He'll try to balance everything out until he has all the correct answers. It is not difficult for him to see both sides of a story.

He's a peace-loving man. The mere prospect of an explosive scene will turn him off.

Libras are not show-offs. Generally, they are well-balanced people. Honest, wholesome, and affectionate, they are serious about every love encounter they have. If he should find that the woman he's dating is not really suited to him, he will end the relationship in such a tactful manner that no hard feelings will come about.

The Libra father is gentle and patient. He can be firm without exercising undue strictness. Although he can be a harsh judge at times, with youngsters growing up he will radiate sweetness and light.

LEO WOMAN
SCORPIO MAN

Many people have a hard time understanding a man born under the sign of Scorpio. Few, however, are able to resist his magnetic charm.

When angered, he can act like an overturned wasps' nest; his sting is capable of leaving an almost permanent mark. If you find yourself interested in a man born under this sign, you'd better learn how to keep on the good side of him. If he's in love with you, you'll know about it. Scorpio men let no one get in their way when they are out to win a certain heart. When it comes to romance, they never take no for an answer.

The Scorpio man can be quite blunt when he chooses. At times, he'll strike you as being a brute. His touchiness may get on your nerves after a while. If it does, you'd better tiptoe away from the scene rather than chance an explosive confrontation. He's capable of a firestorm of emotion that drives even fiery Leo away.

You're the kind of woman who can put up with almost anything once you put your mind and heart to it. A stormy Scorpio relationship may be worth its ups and downs. Scorpio men are all quite perceptive and intelligent. In some respects, they know how to use their brains more effectively than others. They believe in winning in whatever they do. And in business, they usually achieve the position they want through drive and intellect.

He doesn't give a hoot for home life, generally. He doesn't like being tied down. He would rather be out on the battlefield of life, belting away at what he feels is a just and worthy cause.

Many women are easily attracted to him. You are perhaps no exception. Know what you're getting into before you go making any promises to him. Women who allow themselves to be swept off their feet by a Scorpio man soon find that they're dealing with a pepper pot of seething excitement. He's passion with a capital P, make no mistake about that.

Scorpios are straight to the point. They can be as sharp as a razor blade and just as cutting. Don't give him cause to find fault with you, and you'll do just fine.

If you decide to marry him and take the bitter with the sweet, prepare yourself for a challenging relationship. Chances are you won't have as much time for your own interests as you'd like. Your Scorpio man may keep you at his beck and call.

In spite of the extremes in his personality, the Scorpio man is able to transform conflicting characteristics when he becomes a father. He is adept with difficult youngsters because he knows how to tap the best in a child.

LEO WOMAN
SAGITTARIUS MAN

If you've set your cap for a man born under the sign of Sagittarius, you may have to apply an awful lot of strategy before you can persuade him to get down on bended knee. Although some Sagittarius may be marriage-shy, they're not ones to skitter away from romance. You'll find a love relationship with a Sagittarius— whether it is a fling or the real thing—a very enjoyable experience.

As a rule, Sagittarius are bright, happy, and healthy people. They have a strong sense of fair play. Often they are a source of inspiration to others. They are full of drive and ideas.

You'll be taken by the Archer's infectious grin and his light-hearted friendly nature. If you do wind up being the woman in his life, you'll find that he's apt to treat you more like a buddy than the love of his life. It's just his way. Sagittarius are often more chummy than romantic.

You'll admire his broad-mindedness in most matters—including those of the heart. If, while dating you, he claims that he still wants to play the field, he'll expect you to enjoy the same liberty. Once he's promised to love, honor, and obey, however, he does just that. Marriage for him, once he's taken that big step, is very serious business.

The Sagittarius man is quick-witted. He has a genuine interest in equality. He hates prejudice and injustice. Generally, Sagittarius are good at sports. They love the great out-of-doors and respect wildlife in all its forms.

He's not much of a homebody. Quite often he's occupied with faraway places either in his daydreams or in reality. He enjoys being on the move. He's got ants in his pants and refuses to sit still for long stretches at a time. Humdrum routine—especially at home—bores him. At the drop of a hat, he may ask you to put on your party clothes and dine out for a change. He likes surprising people. He'll take great pride in showing you off to his friends. He'll always be a considerate mate. He will never embarrass or disappoint you intentionally.

His friendly, sunny nature is capable of attracting many people. Like you, he's very tolerant when it comes to friends. You will probably spend a great deal of time entertaining.

The Sagittarius father will dote on any son or daughter, but he may be bewildered by the newborn baby. As soon as the children are old enough to walk and talk, the Sagittarius dad encourages each and every visible sign of talent or skill.

LEO WOMAN
CAPRICORN MAN

A with-it Leo woman is likely to find the average Capricorn man a bit of a drag. The man born under the sign of the Goat is often a closed person and difficult to get to know. Even if you do get to know him, you may not find him very interesting.

In romance, Capricorn men are a little on the rusty side. You'll probably have to make all the passes.

You may find his plodding manner irritating, and his conservative, traditional ways downright maddening. He's not one to take chances on anything. He believes in the motto: If it was good enough for my father, it's good enough for me. He follows a way that is tried and true.

Whenever adventure rears its tantalizing head, the Goat may turn the other way. He's more interested in succeeding at what he's already doing.

He may be just as ambitious as you are—perhaps even more so—but his ways of accomplishing his aims are more subterranean or, at least, seem so. He operates from the background a good deal of the time. At a gathering you may never even notice him. But he's there, taking in everything and sizing up everyone—planning his next careful move.

Although Capricorns may be intellectual to a degree, it is generally not the kind of intelligence you appreciate. He may not be as quick or as bright as you; it may take ages for him to understand a simple joke.

If you decide to take up with a man born under this sign, you ought to be pretty good in the cheering-up department. The Capricorn man often acts as though he's constantly being followed by a cloud of gloom.

The Capricorn man is most himself when in the comfort and privacy of his own home. The security possible within four walls can make him a happy man. He'll spend as much time as he can at home. If he is loaded down with extra work, he'll bring it home instead of working overtime at the office.

You'll most likely find yourself frequently confronted by his relatives. Family is very important to the Capricorn—his family, that is. They had better take a pretty important place in your life, too, if you want to keep your home a happy one.

Although his caution in most matters may all but drive you up the wall, you'll find his concerned way with money justified most of the time. He'll plan everything right down to the last penny.

The Capricorn father's empire is rather like the Leo mother's royal realm.There are goals to be achieved, and there is the right way to achieve them. He can be quite a scold when it comes to disciplining the youngsters. You'll have to step in and bend the rules sometimes.

LEO WOMAN
AQUARIUS MAN

Aquarius individuals love everybody—even their worst enemies, sometimes. Through your relationship with an Aquarius man, you'll find yourself running into all sorts of people, ranging from near-genius to downright insane—and they're all friends of his.

As a rule, Aquarius are extremely friendly and open. Of all the signs of the Zodiac, they are perhaps the most tolerant. In the thinking department, they are often miles ahead of others.

You'll most likely find your relationship with this man a challenging one. Your high respect for intelligence and imagination may be reason enough for you to settle your heart on a Water Bearer. You'll find that you can learn a lot from him.

In the holding-hands phase of your romance, you may find that your Water Bearer friend has cold feet. Aquarius take quite a bit of warming up before they are ready to come across with that first goodnight kiss. More than likely, he'll just want to be your pal in the beginning. For him, that's an important first step in any relationship—love, included.

The poetry and flowers stage—if it ever comes—will be later. The Aquarius is all heart. Still, when it comes to tying himself down to one person and for keeps, he is apt to hesitate. He may even try to get out of it if you breathe down his neck too heavily.

The Aquarius man is no Valentino and wouldn't want to be. The kind of love life he's looking for is one that's made up mainly for companionship. Although he may not be very romantic, the memory of his first romance will always hold an important position in his heart. Sometimes Aquarius wind up marrying their childhood sweethearts.

You won't find it difficult to look up to a man born under the sign of the Water Bearer. But you may find the challenge of trying to keep up with him dizzying. He can pierce through the most complicated problem as if it were a simple math puzzle. You may find him a little too lofty and high-minded—but don't judge him too harshly if that's the case; he's way ahead of his time—your time, too, most likely.

If you marry this man, he'll stay true to you. Don't think that once the honeymoon is over, you'll be chained to the kitchen sink forever. Your Aquarius husband will encourage you to keep active in your own interests and affairs. You'll most likely have a minor tiff now and again but never anything serious.

The Aquarius father can be a shining example for the children because he sees them as individuals in their own right, not as extensions of himself. Kids love him and vice versa. He'll be as tolerant with them as he is with adults.

LEO WOMAN
PISCES MAN

The man born under Pisces is quite a dreamer. Sometimes he's so wrapped up in his dreams that he's difficult to reach. To the average ambitious woman, he may seem a little passive.

He's easygoing most of the time. He seems to take things in his stride. He'll entertain all kinds of views and opinions from just about anyone, nodding or smiling vaguely, giving the impression that he's with them one hundred percent while that may not be the case at all. His attitude may be why bother when he is confronted with someone wrong who thinks he's right. The Pisces man will seldom speak his mind if he thinks he'll be rigidly opposed.

The Pisces man is oversensitive at times. He's afraid of getting his feelings hurt. He'll sometimes imagine a personal injury when none's been made at all. Chances are you'll find this complex of his maddening; at times you may feel like giving him a swift kick where it hurts the most. It wouldn't do any good, though. It would just add fuel to the fire of his persecution complex.

One thing you will admire about Pisces is his concern for people who are sickly or troubled. He'll make his shoulder available to anyone in the mood for a good cry. He can listen to one hard-luck story after another without seeming to tire. When his advice is asked, he is capable of coming across with some pretty important words of wisdom. He often knows what is bothering someone before that person is aware of it himself. It's almost intuitive with Pisces, it seems.

Still, at the end of the day, the Pisces man looks forward to some peace and quiet. If you've got a problem on your mind when he comes home, don't unload it in his lap. If you do, you're likely to find him short-tempered. He's a good listener, but he can only take so much.

Pisces men are not aimless although they may seem so at times. The positive sort of Pisces man is quite often successful in his profession and is likely to wind up rich and influential. Material gain, however, is not a direct goal for a Pisces who devotes his life's work to helping people in need.

The weaker Pisces is usually content to stay put on the level where he finds himself. He won't complain too much if the roof leaks and the fence is in need of repair. He'll just shrug it off as a minor inconvenience.

Because of their seemingly laissez-faire manner, Pisces individuals are immensely popular with children. For tots the Pisces father plays the double role of confidant and playmate. It will never enter his mind to discipline a child, no matter how spoiled or incorrigible that child becomes.

Man—Woman

LEO MAN
ARIES WOMAN

The Aries woman is quite a charmer. When she tugs at the strings of your heart, you'll know it. She's a woman who's in search of a knight in shining armor. She is a very particular person with very high ideals. She won't accept anyone but the man of her dreams.

The Aries woman never plays around with passion; she means business when it comes to love.

Don't get the idea that she's a dewy-eyed damsel. She isn't. In fact, she can be pretty practical and to the point when she wants. She's a woman with plenty of drive and ambition. With an Aries woman behind you, you can go far in life. She knows how to help her man get ahead. She's full of wise advice; you only have to ask. In some cases, the Aries woman has a keen business sense; many of them become successful career women. There is nothing hesitant or retiring about her. She is equipped with a good brain and she knows how to use it.

Your union with her could be something strong, secure, and romantic. If both of you have your sights fixed in the same direction, there is almost nothing that you could not accomplish.

The Aries woman is proud and capable of being quite jealous. While you're with her, never cast your eye in another woman's direction. It could spell disaster for your relationship. The Aries woman won't put up with romantic nonsense when her heart is at stake.

If the Aries woman backs you up in your business affairs, you can be sure of succeeding. However, if she only is interested in advancing her own career and puts her interests before yours, she will surely be rocking the boat. It will put a strain on the relationship. The overambitious Aries woman can be a pain in the neck and make you forget that you were in love with her once.

The cultivated Aries woman makes a wonderful wife and mother. She has a natural talent for homemaking. With a pot of paint and some wallpaper, she can transform the dreariest domicile into an abode of beauty and snug comfort. The perfect hostess—even when friends just happen by—she knows how to make guests feel at home.

You'll also admire your Aries because she knows how to stand on her own two feet. Hers is an independent nature. She won't break down and cry when things go wrong, but pick herself up and try to patch things up.

The Aries woman is skilled at juggling both career and motherhood, so her kids will never feel that she is an absentee parent. In fact, as the youngsters grow older, they might want a little more of the liberation that is so important to her.

LEO MAN
TAURUS WOMAN
The woman born under the sign of Taurus may lack a little of the sparkle and bubble you often like to find in a woman. The Taurus woman is generally down to earth and never flighty. It's important to her that she keep both feet flat on the ground. She is not fond of bounding all over the place, especially if she's under the impression that there's no profit in it.

On the other hand, if you hit it off with a Taurus woman, you won't be disappointed at all in the romance area. The Taurus woman is all woman and proud of it, too. She can be very devoted and loving once she decides that her relationship with you is no fly-by-night romance. Basically, she's a passionate person. In sex, she's direct and to the point. If she really loves you, she'll let you know she's yours—and without reservations. Better not flirt with other women once you've committed yourself to her. She is capable of being jealous and possessive.

She'll stick by you through thick and thin. It's almost certain that if the going ever gets rough, she'll not go running home to her mother. She can adjust to hard times just as graciously as she can to the good times.

Taurus are, on the whole, pretty even-tempered. They like to be treated with kindness. Pretty things and soft things make them purr like kittens.

You may find her a little slow and deliberate. She likes to be safe and sure about everything. Let her plod along if she likes; don't coax her but just let her take her own sweet time. Everything she does is done thoroughly and, generally, without mistakes. Don't deride her for being a kind of slowpoke. It could lead to flying pots and pans and a fireworks display that would light up the sky. The Taurus woman doesn't anger readily but when prodded often enough, she's capable of letting loose with a cyclone of ill will. If you treat her with kindness and consideration, you'll have no cause for complaint.

The Taurus woman loves doing things for her man. She's a whiz in the kitchen and can whip up feasts fit for a king if she thinks they'll be royally appreciated. She may not fully understand you, but she'll adore you and be faithful to you if she feels you're worthy of it.

The woman born under Taurus will make a wonderful mother. She knows how to keep her children well-loved, cuddled, and warm. She may find them difficult to manage, however, when they reach the teenage stage.

LEO MAN
GEMINI WOMAN

You may find a romance with a woman born under the sign of the Twins a many-splendored thing. In her you can find the intellectual companionship you often look for in a friend or mate. A Gemini partner can appreciate your aims and desires because she travels pretty much the same road as you do intellectually— that is, at least part of the way. She may share your interest but she will lack your tenacity.

She suffers from itchy feet. She can be here, there, all over the place and at the same time, or so it would seem. Her eagerness to be on the move may make you dizzy. Still, you'll enjoy and appreciate her liveliness and mental agility.

Geminis often have sparkling personalities. You'll be attracted by her warmth and grace. While she's on your arm you'll probably notice that many male eyes are drawn to her. She may even return a gaze or two, but don't let that worry you. All women born under this sign have nothing against a harmless flirt once in a while. They enjoy this sort of attention. If she feels she is already spoken for, however, she will never let it get out of hand.

Although she may not be as handy as you'd like in the kitchen, you'll never go hungry for a filling and tasty meal. She's as much in a hurry as you are, and won't feel like she's cheating by breaking out the instant mashed potatoes or the frozen peas. She may not be much of a cook but she is clever. With a dash of this and a suggestion of that, she can make an uninteresting TV dinner taste like a gourmet meal. Then, again, maybe you've struck it rich and have a Gemini lover who finds complicated recipes a challenge to her intellect. If so, you'll find every meal a tantalizing and mouth-watering surprise.

When you're beating your brains out over the Sunday crossword puzzle and find yourself stuck, just ask your Gemini mate. She'll give you all the right answers without batting an eyelash.

Like you, she loves all kinds of people. You may even find that you're a bit more particular than she. Often all that a Gemini requires is that her friends be interesting—and stay interesting. One thing she's not able to abide is a dullard.

Leave the party organizing to your Gemini sweetheart or mate, and you'll never have a chance to know what a dull moment is. She'll bring the swinger out in you if you give her half a chance.

A Gemini mother enjoys her children, which can be the truest form of love. Like them, she's often restless, adventurous, and easily bored. She will never complain about their fleeting interests because she understands the changes they will go through as they mature.

LEO MAN
CANCER WOMAN

If you fall in love with a Cancer woman, be prepared for anything. Cancers are sometimes difficult to understand when it comes to love. In one hour, she can unravel a whole gamut of emotions that will leave you in a tizzy. She'll keep you guessing, that's for sure.

You may find her a little too uncertain and sensitive for your liking. You'll most likely spend a good deal of time encouraging her, helping her to erase her foolish fears. Tell her she's a living doll a dozen times a day, and you'll be well loved in return.

Be careful of the jokes you make when in her company. Don't let any of them revolve around her, her personal interests, or her family. If you do, you'll most likely reduce her to tears. She can't stand being made fun of. It will take bushels of roses and tons of chocolates—not to mention the apologies—to get her to come back out of her shell.

In matters of money managing, she may not easily come around to your way of thinking. Money will never burn a hole in her pocket. You may get the notion that your Cancer sweetheart or mate is a direct descendent of Scrooge. If she has her way, she'll hang onto that first dollar you earned. She's not only that way with money, but with everything right on up from bakery string to jelly jars. She's a saver; she never throws anything away, no matter how trivial.

Once she returns your love, you'll have an affectionate, self-sacrificing, and devoted woman for life. Her love for you will never alter unless you want it to. She'll put you high upon a pedestal and will do everything—even if it's against your will—to keep you up there.

Cancer women love home life. For them, marriage is an easy step. They're domestic with a capital D. She'll do her best to make your home comfortable and cozy. She is more at ease at home than anywhere else. She makes an excellent hostess. The best in her comes out when she is in her own environment.

Cancer women make the best mothers of all the signs of the Zodiac. She'll consider every complaint of her child a major catastrophe. With her, children always come first. If you're lucky, you'll run a close second. You'll perhaps see her as too devoted to the children. You may have a hard time convincing her that her apron strings are a little too long.

LEO MAN
LEO WOMAN

If you can manage a woman who likes to kick up her heels every now and again, then Leo was made for you. You'll have to learn to put away jealous fears—or at least forget about them—when you take up with a woman born under this sign. She's often the kind that makes heads turn and tongues wag. You don't necessarily have to believe any of what you hear—it's most likely just jealous gossip. Take up with a Leo woman and you'll be taking off on a romance full of fire and ice. Be prepared to take the good things with the bad—the bitter with the sweet.

The Leo woman has more than a fair share of grace and glamour. She is aware of her charms and knows how to put them to good use. Needless to say, other women in her vicinity turn green with envy and will try anything short of shoving her into the nearest lake, in order to put her out of commission.

If she's captured your heart and fancy, woo her full force if your intention is to eventually win her. Shower her with expensive gifts and promise her the moon—if you're in a position to go that far—then you'll find her resistance beginning to weaken. It's not that she's such a difficult cookie—she'll probably adore you once she's decided you're the man for her—but she does enjoy a lot of attention. What's more, she feels she's entitled to it. Her mild arrogance, though, is becoming. The Leo woman knows how to transform the crime of excessive pride into a very charming misdemeanor. It sweeps most men right off their feet. Those who do not succumb to her leonine charm are few and far between.

If you've got an important business deal to clinch and you have doubts as to whether or not it will go over, bring your Leo lover along to that business luncheon and it's a cinch that that contract will be yours. She won't have to do or say anything—just be there at your side. The grouchiest oil magnate can be transformed into a gushing, obedient schoolboy if there's a Leo woman in the room.

If you're rich and want to stay that way, don't give your Leo mate a free hand with the charge accounts and credit cards. If you're poor, the luxury-loving Leo will most likely never enter your life.

The Leo mother is strict yet easygoing with the children. She wants her youngsters to follow the rules, and she is a patient teacher. She loves to pal around with the kids, proudly showing them off on every occasion.

LEO MAN
VIRGO WOMAN

The Virgo woman may be a little too difficult for you to understand at first. Her waters run deep. Even when you think you know her, don't take any bets on it. She's capable of keeping things hidden in the deep recesses of her womanly soul—things she'll only release when she's sure that you're the man she's been looking for. It may take her some time to come around to this decision. Virgos are finicky about almost everything; everything has to be letter-perfect before they're satisfied. Many of them have the idea that the only people who can do things correctly are Virgos.

Nothing offends a Virgo woman more than slovenly dress, sloppy character, or a careless display of affection. Make sure your tie is not crooked and your shoes sport a bright shine before you go calling on this lady. Keep your off-color jokes for the locker room; she'll have none of that. Take her arm when crossing the street. Don't rush the romance. Trying to corner her in the back of a cab may be one way of striking out. Never criticize the way she looks. In fact, the best policy would be to agree with her as much as possible.

Still, there's just so much a man can take. All those dos and don'ts you'll have to observe if you want to get to first base with a Virgo may be just a little too much to ask of you. After a few dates, you may come to the conclusion that she just isn't worth all that trouble. However, the Virgo woman is mysterious enough, generally speaking, to keep her men running back for more. Chances are you'll be intrigued by her airs and graces.

If lovemaking means a lot to you, you'll be disappointed at first in the cool ways of your Virgo lover. However, under her glacial facade there lies a hot cauldron of seething excitement. If you're patient and artful in your romantic approach, you'll find that all that caution was well worth the trouble. When Virgos love, they don't stint. It's all or nothing as far as they're concerned. Once they're convinced that they love you, they go all the way, right off the bat—tossing all cares to the wind.

One thing a Virgo woman can't stand in love is hypocrisy. They don't give a hoot about what the neighbors say, if their hearts tell them to go ahead. They're very concerned with human truths—so much so that if their hearts stumble upon another fancy, they're likely to be true to that new heartthrob and leave you standing in the rain.

She's honest to her heart and will be as true to you as you are with her, generally. Do her wrong once, however, and it's farewell.

The Virgo mother has high expectations for her children, and she will strive to bring out the very best in them. She is more tender than strict, though, and will nag rather than discipline. But youngsters sense her unconditional love for them, and usually turn out just as she hoped they would.

LEO MAN
LIBRA WOMAN

You'll probably find that the woman born under the sign of Libra is worth more than her weight in gold. She's a woman after your own heart.

With her, you'll always come first—make no mistake about that. She'll always be behind you 100 percent, no matter what you do. When you ask her advice about almost anything, you'll most likely get a very balanced and realistic opinion. She is good at thinking things out and never lets her emotions run away with her when clear logic is called for.

As a homemaker she is hard to beat. She is very concerned

with harmony and balance. You can be sure she'll make your house a joy to live in; she'll see to it that the house is tastefully furnished and decorated. A Libra cannot stand filth or disarray. Anything that does not radiate harmony, in fact, runs against her orderly grain.

She is chock-full of charm and womanly ways. She can sweep just about any man off his feet with one winning smile. When it comes to using her brains, she can outthink almost anyone and, sometimes, with half the effort. She is diplomatic enough, though, never to let this become glaringly apparent. She may even turn the conversation around so that you think you were the one who did all the brainwork. She couldn't care less, really, just as long as you wind up doing what is right.

The Libra woman will put you up on a pretty high pedestal. You are her man and her idol. She'll leave all the decision making, large or small, up to you. She's not interested in running things and will only offer her assistance if she feels you really need it.

Some find her approach to reason masculine. However, in the areas of love and affection the Libra woman is all woman. She'll literally shower you with love and kisses during your romance with her. She doesn't believe in holding out. You shouldn't, either, if you want to hang onto her.

Libra is the kind of lover who likes to snuggle up to you in front of the fire on chilly autumn nights, the kind who will bring you breakfast in bed Sunday. She'll be very thoughtful about anything that concerns you. If anyone dares suggest you're not the grandest guy in the world, she'll give that person what-for. She'll defend you till her dying breath. The Libra woman will be everything you want her to be.

The Libra mother is sensitive and sensible, with an intuitive understanding of what a child needs. Her youngsters will never lack for anything that could make their lives easier and richer. Still, you will always come before the children.

LEO MAN
SCORPIO WOMAN

The Scorpio woman can be a whirlwind of passion—perhaps too much passion to really suit you. When her temper flies, you'd better lock up the family heirlooms and take cover. When she chooses to be sweet, you're apt to think that butter wouldn't melt in her mouth—but, of course, it would.

The Scorpio woman can be as hot as a tamale or as cool as a cucumber, but whatever mood she's in, she's in it for real. She does not believe in posing or putting on airs.

The Scorpio woman is often sultry and seductive. Her femme

fatale charm can pierce through the hardest of hearts like a laser beam. She may not look like Mata Hari (quite often Scorpios resemble the tomboy next door) but once she's fixed you with her tantalizing eyes, you're a goner.

Life with the Scorpio woman will not be all smiles and smooth sailing. When prompted, she can unleash a gale of venom. Generally, she'll have the good grace to keep family battles within the walls of your home. When company visits, she's apt to give the impression that married life with you is one great big joyride. It's just one of her ways of expressing her loyalty to you—at least in front of others. She may fight you tooth and nail in the confines of your living room, but at a ball or during an evening out, she'll hang onto your arm and have stars in her eyes.

Scorpio women are good at keeping secrets. She may even keep a few buried from you if she feels like it.

Never cross her up on even the smallest thing. When it comes to revenge, she's an eye-for-an-eye woman. She's not too keen on forgiveness—especially if she feels she's been wronged unfairly. You'd be well-advised not to give her any cause to be jealous, either. When the Scorpio woman sees green, your life will be made far from rosy. Once she's put you in the doghouse, you can be sure that you're going to stay there awhile.

You may find life with a Scorpio woman too draining. Although she may be full of the old paprika, it's quite likely that she's not the kind of woman you'd like to spend the rest of your natural life with. You'd prefer someone gentler and not so hot-tempered; someone who can take the highs with the lows and not bellyache; someone who is flexible and understanding. A woman born under Scorpio can be heavenly, but she can also be the very devil when she chooses.

The Scorpio mother is protective yet encouraging. The opposites within her nature mirror the very contradictions of life itself. Under her skillful guidance, the children learn how to cope with extremes and grow up to become many-faceted individuals.

LEO MAN
SAGITTARIUS WOMAN

You'll most likely never come across a more good-natured woman than the one born under the sign of Sagittarius. Generally, they're full of bounce and good cheer. Their sunny disposition seems almost permanent and can be relied upon even on the rainiest of days.

Women born under this sign are almost never malicious. If ever they seem to be it is only unintentional. Sagittarius are often a little short on tact and say literally anything that comes into their minds no matter what the occasion. Sometimes the words that tumble out of their mouths seem downright cutting and cruel. Still, no matter what she says, she means well. The Sagittarius woman is quite capable of losing some of her friends—and perhaps even some of yours—through a careless slip of the lip.

On the other hand, you will appreciate her honesty and good intentions. To you, qualities of this sort play an important part in life. With a little patience and practice, you can probably help cure your Sagittarius lover of her loose tongue. In most cases, she'll give in to your better judgment and try to follow your advice to the letter.

Chances are she'll be the outdoors type. Long hikes, fishing trips, and white-water canoeing will most likely appeal to her. She's a busy person; no one could ever call her a slouch. She sets great store in mobility. Her feet are itchy and she won't sit still for a minute if she doesn't have to.

She is great company most of the time and, generally, lots of fun. Even if your buddies drop by for poker and beer, she won't have any trouble fitting in.

On the whole, she is a very kind and sympathetic woman. If she feels she's made a mistake, she'll be the first to call your attention to it. She's not afraid to own up to her faults and shortcomings.

You might lose your patience with her once or twice. After she's seen how upset her shortsightedness or tendency to blab has made you, she'll do her best to straighten up.

The Sagittarius woman is not the kind who will pry into your business affairs. But she'll always be there, ready to offer advice if you need it. If you come home with red stains on your collar and you say it's paint and not lipstick, she'll believe you.

She'll seldom be suspicious. Your word will almost always be good enough for her.

The Sagittarius mother is a wonderful and loving friend to her children. She is not afraid if a youngster learns some street smarts along the way. She will broaden her children's knowledge and see that they get a well-rounded education.

LEO MAN
CAPRICORN WOMAN

If you are not a successful businessman, or at least on your way to success, it's quite possible that a Capricorn woman will have no interest in entering your life. Generally speaking, she is a very security-minded female; she'll see to it that she invests her time only in sure things. Men who whittle away their time with one unsuccessful scheme or another seldom attract a Capricorn. Men who are interested in getting somewhere in life and keep their noses close to the grindstone quite often have a Capricorn woman behind them, helping them to get ahead.

Although she is a kind of social climber she is not what you could call cruel or hard-hearted. Beneath that cool, seemingly calculating exterior there's a warm and desirable woman. She just happens to think that it is just as easy to fall in love with a rich or ambitious man as it is with a poor or lazy one. She's practical.

The Capricorn woman may be keenly interested in rising to the top, but she'll never be aggressive about it. She'll seldom step on someone's feet or nudge competitors away with her elbows. She's quiet about her desires. She sits, waits, and watches. When an opening or opportunity does appear, she'll latch onto it. For an on-the-move man, an ambitious Capricorn wife or lover can be quite an asset. She can probably give you some very good advice about business matters. When you invite the boss and his wife for dinner, she'll charm them both.

The Capricorn woman is thorough in whatever she does: cooking, cleaning, making a success out of life. Capricorns are excellent hostesses as well as guests. Generally, they are very well mannered and gracious, no matter what their backgrounds are. They seem to have a built-in sense of what is right. Crude behavior or a careless faux pas can offend them no end.

If you should marry a woman born under Capricorn, you need never worry about her going on a wild shopping spree. Capricorns are careful with every cent that comes into their hands. They understand the value of money better than most women and have no room in their lives for careless spending.

Capricorn women are usually very fond of family—their own, that is. With them, family ties run very deep. Don't make jokes about her relatives; she won't stand for it. You'd better check her family out before you get down on bended knee; after your marriage you'll undoubtedly be seeing lots of them.

The Capricorn mother is very ambitious for her children. She wants them to have every advantage and to benefit from things she perhaps lacked as a child. She will train her youngsters to be polite and kind and to honor traditional codes of conduct.

LEO MAN
AQUARIUS WOMAN

If you find that you've fallen head over heels for a woman born under the sign of the Water Bearer, you'd better fasten your safety belt. It may take you quite a while to actually discover what this woman is like. Even then, you may have nothing to go on but a string of vague hunches. Aquarius is like a rainbow, full of bright and shining hues; she's like no other women you've ever known. There is something elusive about her—something delightfully mysterious. You'll most likely never be able to put your finger on it. It's nothing calculated, either. Aquarius doesn't believe in phony charm.

There will never be a dull moment in your life with this Water Bearer woman; she seems to radiate adventure and magic. She'll most likely be the most open-minded and tolerant woman you've ever met. She has a strong dislike for injustice and prejudice. Narrow-mindedness runs against her grain.

She is very independent by nature and quite capable of shifting for herself if necessary. She may receive many proposals for marriage from all sorts of people without ever really taking them seriously. Marriage is a very big step for her; she wants to be sure she knows what she's getting into. If she thinks that it will seriously curb her independence and love of freedom, she's apt to shake her head and give the man his engagement ring back—if indeed she's let the romance get that far.

The line between friendship and romance is a pretty fuzzy one for an Aquarius. It's not difficult for her to remain buddy-buddy with an ex-lover. She's tolerant, remember? So if you should see her on the arm of an old love, don't jump to any hasty conclusions.

She's not a jealous person herself and doesn't expect you to be, either. You'll find her pretty much of a free spirit most of the time. Just when you think you know her inside out, you'll discover that you don't really know her at all.

She's a very sympathetic and warm person; she can be helpful to people in need of assistance and advice.

She'll seldom be suspicious even if she has every right to be. If the man she loves slips and allows himself a little fling, chances are she'll just ignore it—at least the first time. Her tolerance does have its limits, though, and her man should press never his luck fooling around.

The Aquarius mother is bighearted and seldom refuses her children anything. Her open-minded attitude is easily transmitted to her youngsters. They have every chance of growing up as respectful and tolerant individuals who feel at ease anywhere.

LEO MAN
PISCES WOMAN

Many a man dreams of an alluring Pisces woman. You're perhaps no exception. She's soft and cuddly and very domestic. She'll let you be the brains of the family; she's contented to play a behind-the-scenes role in order to help you achieve your goals. The illusion that you are the master of the household is the kind of magic that the Pisces woman is adept at creating.

She can be very ladylike and proper. Your business associates and friends will be dazzled by her warmth and femininity. Although she's a charmer, there is a lot more to her than just a pretty exterior. There is a brain ticking away behind that soft, womanly facade. You may never become aware of it—that is, until you're married to her. It's no cause for alarm, however; she'll most likely never use it against you, only to help you and possibly set you on a more successful path.

If she feels you're botching up your married life through careless behavior or if she feels you could be earning more money than you do, she'll tell you about it. But any wife would, really. She will never try to usurp your position as head and breadwinner of the family.

No one had better dare say one uncomplimentary word about you in her presence. It's likely to cause her to break into tears. Pisces women are usually very sensitive beings. Their reaction to adversity, frustration, or anger is just a plain, good, old-fashioned cry. They can weep buckets when inclined.

She can do wonders with a house. She is very fond of dramatic and beautiful things. There will always be plenty of fresh-cut flowers around the house. She will choose charming artwork and antiques, if they are affordable. She'll see to it that the house is decorated in a dazzling yet welcoming style.

She'll have an extra special dinner prepared for you when you come home from an important business meeting. Don't dwell on the boring details of the meeting, though. But if you need that grand vision, the big idea, to seal a contract or make a conquest, your Pisces woman is sure to confide a secret that will guarantee your success. She is canny and shrewd with money, and once you are on her wavelength you can manage the intricacies on your own.

Treat her with tenderness and generosity and your relationship will be an enjoyable one. She's most likely fond of chocolates. A bunch of beautiful flowers will never fail to make her eyes light up. See to it that you never forget her birthday or your anniversary. These things are very important to her. If you let them slip your mind, you'll send her into a crying fit that could last a considerable length of time. If you are patient and kind, you can keep a Pisces woman happy for a lifetime. She, however, is not without her faults. Her sensitivity may get on your nerves after a while. You may find her lacking in practicality and good old-fashioned stoicism. You may even feel that she uses her tears as a method of getting her own way.

The Pisces woman makes a strong, self-sacrificing mother. She will teach her children the value of service to the community while not letting them lose their individuality.

LEO
LUCKY NUMBERS 2002

Lucky numbers and astrology can be linked through the movements of the Moon. Each phase of the thirteen Moon cycles vibrates with a sequence of numbers for your Sign of the Zodiac over the course of the year. Using your lucky numbers is a fun system that connects you with tradition.

New Moon	First Quarter	Full Moon	Last Quarter
Dec. 14 ('01)	Dec. 22 ('01)	Dec. 30 ('01)	Jan. 5
3 7 6 2	8 1 8 2	5 3 3 1	1 8 6 8
Jan. 13	Jan. 21	Jan. 28	Feb. 4
1 9 1 8	8 8 3 9	6 7 1 8	8 6 5 4
Feb. 12	Feb. 19	Feb. 27	March 5
0 2 4 3	3 6 3 9	1 4 2 3	9 8 0 5
March 13	March 21	March 28	April 3
7 7 2 8	8 5 2 3	6 4 4 1	1 0 7 9
April 12	April 20	April 26	May 4
9 4 8 5	2 8 9 3	1 8 7 0	0 4 6 1
May 12	May 19	May 26	June 3
4 5 2 6	8 9 2 1	7 6 0 3	3 5 9 4
June 10	June 18	June 24	July 2
8 1 7 8	8 2 9 4	3 0 9 2	6 1 7 5
July 10	July 16	July 24	August 1
7 5 4 5	8 6 4 2	0 8 1 5	5 9 6 0
August 8	August 15	August 22	August 30
2 4 7 5	5 3 2 1	8 3 5 9	9 4 1 7
Sept. 6	Sept. 13	Sept. 21	Sept. 29
3 2 9 7	7 6 0 3	3 5 1 5	5 2 8 9
Oct. 6	Oct. 13	Oct. 21	Oct. 29
6 1 8 7	7 0 4 6	6 1 8 5	2 3 6 4
Nov. 4	Nov. 11	Nov. 19	Nov. 27
4 2 1 0	0 7 9 4	4 8 8 5	6 9 7 5
Dec. 4	Dec. 11	Dec. 19	Dec. 26
2 4 0 1	1 3 7 2	2 8 1 2	5 3 1 9

LEO
YEARLY FORECAST 2002

Forecast for 2002 Concerning Business
and Financial Affairs, Job Prospects,
Travel, Health, Romance and Marriage
for Persons Born with the Sun
in the Zodiacal Sign of Leo.
July 21–August 21

For those born under the influence of the Sun in the zodiacal sign of Leo, ruled by the vibrant and creative Sun, this promises to be an advantageous and effective year. You can make great strides forward toward achieving the success you want since you have a greater belief in your own skills and talents. Shifts in relationships will occur, so that you begin to understand more clearly the importance of friends and family members in your life. Creatively, this should be an exciting and productive time. The business world offers useful opportunities to go into partnership, although no decision should be arrived at hastily. You may prefer to branch out into your own enterprise rather than relying on partners or colleagues. Where your personal money is concerned, there is a strong temptation to take risks with spare funds. Investments should be made carefully. Spending on personal pleasure should be within reasonable limits. Whether you have a job or a career, this period can be useful for introducing a more individual element into your work. The more unique skills you can put into it, the happier you will be. Teamwork might prove rather frustrating by contrast. The outlook for travel suggests that holiday romance is not out of the question. Traveling for pleasure rather than business can be very educational. You will come across people whose outlook is very different from your own. Stress is the main aspect of your health to be concerned about. Guard against burning the candle at both ends. Alternative forms of exercise such as tai chi might appeal as a gentle way of getting fit while also calming your mind. As a Leo you like to reign supreme in someone's heart, and it seems you will have little difficulty finding a loving relationship that is close and emotionally intense. This is a year when issues of jealousy and trust may arise, offering valuable chances to learn more about yourself and how to deal with love and romance.

The prospects for business look quite good, although there may be some setbacks along the route to prosperity. You might be offered a partnership in a new enterprise that seems very promising. However, check out all aspects of the potential business before making a decision. Remember that you and a partner must not only get along well but also trust each other completely. This is not the best time to take any big chance financially. If you have been thinking of committing funds to a new product, do not get in over your head; leave a margin of safety in case success does not come immediately or even at all. It is very important to remember that your private life should not mingle too much with your business. Personal entanglements that would jeopardize your reputation should be avoided. Questions at important meetings may prove something of an embarrassment if you are asked about the way your enterprise is being run. Keep in mind to whom you are accountable, and play the game straight. During the first half of the year you may be taking a back seat in quite uncharacteristic fashion. However, you will probably find that there are many ways in which you can act behind the scenes to influence decisions, and that power does not always have to be in public view. By the end of August you should be ready to adopt a higher profile, perhaps even becoming a public spokesperson for your enterprise. Launching a new product or service can be quite tricky this year, but advertising campaigns ought to be effective between September and mid-October. Your personal creative flair should come into its own, so that by late November you are taking a much more active part in marketing and design. Just beware of imposing your own ideas without weighing them against those of your business partners. If you use your ability to enthuse both your associates and workforce, this should be a profitable year.

Your cash flow is unlikely to be much of a problem, unless you make it so. The tendency to spend on entertainment, hobbies, and sports can sometimes get out of hand. Keep tabs on your spending in these areas, so that you can pull back before you go into debt. It is wise to remember that investments are a gamble to a certain extent, so do not expect the financial market to always go your way. Risking funds on betting such as racing or lotteries is not recommended during most of 2002. You may have a few spectacular wins, but almost inevitably you will soon gamble away the money. Even if you do not think you can afford to do so, make regular contributions to charity. This is a positive use of your money, serving to remind you of how rich your own life is in many ways when compared to the less fortunate. Two periods during the year stand out as being potentially expensive: the month of January and the autumn months between mid-October and the beginning of December. It would be a good idea to regularly check your accounts at these times, just so that you know where you stand. Be careful, but do not forget that money is to be enjoyed.

As a Leo you have creative flair in one way or another. It is quite important that you have the chance to exercise it. This year you will probably find such an opportunity in the workplace. Even if you have quite a routine job, there are ways of making it your own. Ideally you need to be in a position that allows you freedom of decision and the chance to make an occasional theatrical flourish. You probably will not mind changing job this year, especially if you see one that looks more enjoyable than your current position. Some ups and downs with colleagues are to be expected, and that will not be a time when you relish teamwork. Joint effort may appear to cramp your style, but in fact there is much you can learn from cooperating and sharing decisions. Until the summer months you probably will not mind taking a back seat. As August progresses, however, it is vital that you take more initiative and be seen to be in control. Praise for good work will make all of your effort worthwhile.

Opportunities to travel may not be very numerous, but the trips you do take are certain to leave a deep impression on you. Going away for pleasure rather than business will be the focus of your attention, although that does not rule out the possibility of some enjoyable journeys made for work. You are likely to make new friends rather than useful business contacts. The people you meet in distant places are likely to stay in your memory more than local surroundings, no matter how beautiful these may be. You might also become embroiled in quite a passionate holiday romance. Even if it does not last, there are lessons to be learned from someone who is of a different culture. Vacationing with a group of friends might prove rather dull, restricting your opportunities to act spontaneously. You may even wish to travel alone so that you can fully enjoy experiences that come up unexpectedly. A spring holiday before the end of April is almost certain to leave you with very happy memories.

The main focus where health is concerned is having too much of a good thing. Burning the candle at both ends is fine if you do it from time to time, but you cannot live like that indefinitely without suffering the effects. Nor is it wise to compromise on your diet for the sake of saving time; fast foods can be very fattening as well as lacking in essential nutrients. This is a period when you may feel attracted to a discipline that has a beneficial effect on both your mind and body. Gentle exercise such as yoga or tai chi can be excellent if you live a busy, stressful life. During the later months of the year you may get a little flabby, especially if you have enjoyed an indulgent summer vacation. Walking can be good exercise, or swimming. Minor colds and viruses should not bother you too much if you build yourself up for the winter months. Leos with back problems should try to avoid trouble by moving and lifting in ways that create as little stress as possible. With good sense and moderation you can enjoy sound health all year.

Matters of the heart are unlikely to pass you by. Leo singles who are looking for a partner will find one who gives the emotional intensity you crave. Meanwhile, a settled partnership should bond closely as old feelings of romance are renewed. Issues that need to be worked on include a tendency to be demanding. Love should be a matter of give-and-take, and your partner's wishes should not always be subordinated to your own. You might also have to grapple with jealousy from time to time. Trust is not always easily won, but if you and your mate or partner face this issue openly and honestly, inevitably you will draw closer. A loving relationship can sometimes take up so much of your time and attention that you begin to neglect your friends. Try not to make this mistake, as the value of friendship is not to be underestimated. Someone a few years older than you might appear particularly attractive; a difference in ages can add a fascinating touch to romance. There may be elements of a parent-child relationship, which is fine as long as you are conscious of it. Otherwise it may complicate your emotions. Time spent alone this year can be very valuable for sorting out your feelings, whether you are between lovers or temporarily separated from your mate or partner. The deeper your understanding of yourself, the more you will have to offer in the way of love and affection.

LEO
DAILY FORECAST

January–December 2002

JANUARY

1. TUESDAY. Suspenseful. You could find yourself preoccupied with hidden motivations and deceit. You may sense that you can proceed smoothly and easily in all of your activities, only to find yourself blocked by people you thought were on your side. There is a cloak-and-dagger aspect at the moment. Not all hidden forces are against you, however. You currently have many allies and supporters. Although they may seem to be holding back at present, you can count on them when the time comes that you really need their assistance. In the meantime do not squander your resources on trivial matters. Use your power where it will have the most positive effect.

2. WEDNESDAY. Variable. Luck is taking a strange course at present. It could seem very much on your side one minute, then reverse course and leave you in the lurch. It is not a good idea to count too much on receiving help from your mate or partner at the moment. Too much is going on, making such support erratic at best. Instead on relying on anyone else, focus on your own personal power, which has considerable force right now. If you know where and how to apply your influence, you stand a good chance of creating some major shifts. These will not happen on their own, however. This is the time to utilize your own effort and initiative to help you get what you want and need.

3. THURSDAY. Unsettling. Efforts on the job can pay off handsomely. You are coming across as especially charming and charismatic, endowed with the gift of gab at present. If necessary, you can speak quite eloquently on your own behalf, although initially it is possible that your words will seem to have very little weight.

This impression is not entirely reliable since you can more than likely create a delayed effect. You can eventually get what you want, but you may have to wait for it to materialize. Your own secret life is apt to seem more intense and powerful than usual. You may find it beneficial to yourself to help someone by operating quietly behind the scenes.

4. FRIDAY. Frustrating. You will find it tough to make much progress in money matters. Investments could prove tricky. Although you may be thinking about them a lot, your judgment could be off. This can lead you to make hasty, unwise decisions. Avoid any temptation to speculate wildly. Nor should you bet anything that you cannot afford to lose, either money or possessions. It is possible that you will be able to make some headway soon, but caution is by far the better option at present. Romance may seem intense but difficult as well. Do not fall prey to any sort of aggressive or harmful behavior. Pay close attention to what a new relationship could mean in the long run.

5. SATURDAY. Fair. This is a good day for catching up with longtime friends and contacts. Make a phone call to someone you have not heard from in a while. You and your mate or partner are likely to feel an even stronger bond than usual, based on the sense of an intuitive or spiritual connection between you. However, you must put in some extra effort to make sure this connection surfaces sufficiently to be useful. There is a tendency for love and feelings of closeness to become buried, but do not force them to appear. It may be best simply to remember all the good feelings that you have toward your loved one and gradually reveal the depth of your emotions.

6. SUNDAY. Mixed. A brief outing today does not have to be anything elaborate. Even a visit to the park or some other favorite natural setting could work wonders for you. Or go to see some relatives you have been meaning to visit. You may also want to spend some relaxing time playing a team game. Today is much better for recreation than for anything relating to your career. If you were thinking of finishing up some project, you may want to delay your plans and instead enjoy what is left of the weekend. It is not always a good idea to force yourself to push ahead with work. Too much determination could end up taking more out of you and causing you to be less efficient in the long run.

7. MONDAY. Positive. Home life may seem a bit fragmented. Even if you actually want to spend some extra time with loved ones, circumstances could force you to go away. Your mate or partner is not likely to be as understanding as usual. If you need to talk things over, be as clear and straightforward as possible so that there is no chance of a misunderstanding. You will most likely consider this a positive day since there is a feeling of genuine goodwill in the air. Even if you cannot tell where it is coming from, you will benefit from its positive energy. It would be a good idea to help someone secretly, not expecting anything in return.

8. TUESDAY. Enjoyable. Today is likely to flow smoothly thanks to a strong sense of your firm home base. From there you can move outward to make your mark in the world. Work is likely to occupy much of your attention in a favorable way. You can expect it to proceed without any real difficulties. You can also make some significant headway on projects that have been delayed or which have proved frustrating for some other reason. There is a likelihood of arguments from a person who is not quite clear about where you stand. You need to hold your ground firmly but fairly. A strong, positive stance will serve you best. Although you do not need to argue, you do need to make your position crystal clear.

9. WEDNESDAY. Misleading. There is a strong focus on unusual forms of interaction. You could find yourself more in touch with your spiritual nature. If you are seeking information on religion, you can find some real help. The day strongly favors anything having to do with mysticism or the paranormal. It is not as favorable, however, for more customary pursuits. If you have to talk things over with a family member, be sure everything is clearly stated. There is a strong possibility of misunderstandings. If would be very unwise right now to make any agreement while in a highly emotional state. Even a minor upset is likely to blur your perceptions of people.

10. THURSDAY. Rewarding. Your personal dynamism will come to the fore, making you a powerful and charismatic figure to those around you. You could become immersed in some recreation that really shows your dynamic presence at its best. Luck is also on your side. If your usually good Leo intuition has seemed somewhat foggy in recent days, it is likely to be sharper now. You can trust your instincts more than you have been doing. Your feelings should also be easier to articulate. Your mate or partner may be more sympathetic to your points of view than in recent days. The time is right for that serious conversation you have been putting off.

11. FRIDAY. Changeable. You are apt to be more preoccupied with luck and good fortune than usual. This does not, however, guarantee that they are on your side; expect some dramatic swings. If you are at all tempted to gamble, be prepared to see wild variations in the course of the game. Overall it would be best to avoid betting any amount you cannot afford to lose. There is no guarantee that you will be able to stay in the game until your luck starts to turn. If you do not make a conscious effort to control your emotions, you could become angry at the course of events. You cannot logically blame anyone if your luck takes a downturn. Remain cautious in your speculations and you have nothing to fear.

12. SATURDAY. Disconcerting. Some hidden concerns about your own health, or someone else's, could surface. Realize that these are not just a sudden problem. Very likely there are some long-term medical issues that need to be resolved. If you have a tendency to be lazy or lethargic, try to be more active today. Avoid making any elaborate plans or dramatic gestures, which will not be effective in the long run. Instead, focus on some small, manageable steps. If you need to get more exercise, make sure it is in a form that you enjoy and can continue with in any type of weather. The same is true with diet. Avoid indulging in extreme measures or diet fads and think about how you can eat better in a way you can live with for the rest of your life.

13. SUNDAY. Buoyant. Today you should be in much better spirits. You will also feel more vigorous physically than you have in a long time. Use this extra energy to good advantage. Get more than your typical amount of exercise. Go for a long walk in your favorite locale, or spend an hour or two playing a favorite sport. If you do anything athletic you are likely to be more graceful and accomplished than usual. Overall it is possible to display just a little more style and artistry than usual. This is true not only with arts and crafts projects, but even in connection with the little details of life. Enjoy the chance to see how satisfying it can be to create beauty as well as be surrounded by it.

14. MONDAY. Useful. It should be possible to iron out difficulties both with your mate or partner and with your colleagues at work. In matters of love and romance, focus on the deep spiritual connection you feel. Even if you usually are not aware of your life together, you ought to realize that there is a reason the two of you are paired. Once you really reflect on this fact, you will feel more gratitude for the nature of your relationship. At work you can expect colleagues to be more helpful and easygoing than usual. If you have some problems with a co-worker that you have put off discussing, this is a good time for confronting the person. There will be more goodwill in the response than you can usually count on.

15. TUESDAY. Good. Your rapport with your mate or partner should be unusually strong. You can now express a great number of personal things that have been on your mind for a long time. Even if there has been some resistance to talking about these issues, you will probably find it surprisingly easy at this point. There is also a real possibility of taking responsibility for your own actions and inhibitions in the relationship. When you were first getting to know each other you may have felt that admitting these things could somehow hurt your position. Now you can do so without such worry. As a matter of fact, you will be stronger for it. It may take some courage to begin to speak, but circumstances will help once you open up emotionally.

16. WEDNESDAY. Disquieting. Partnerships of any kind will probably not be harmonious. You or the people you frequently deal with could show odd and rather contradictory qualities. You may start to act eccentrically without really knowing why. Or you could find yourself insisting that what you are doing is a matter of principle, making you very defensive about your position. The best remedy does not involve acting on your impulses; you probably will not succeed that way. However, if you realize that everything is a bit out of kilter at the moment, you will be more forgiving and accepting of whatever comes up. This is likely to help you ride over the rough spots without encountering a great amount of conflict.

17. THURSDAY. Frustrating. Your customarily outgoing Leo nature is not likely to be well accepted at the moment by other people. Either they will not understand you or you will not feel as outgoing as usual. This could lead you to withdraw, which basically is not a bad idea right now. If you demand too much, you are likely to be greeted with a cold shoulder. But approach people with a little more reserve and they are apt to be open and receptive to you. This is not the way you normally proceed in a social setting, but it is a good idea to stretch your personality. What works well one day might not work the next, so you need to be perpetually flexible. Do not rule out any possibilities.

18. FRIDAY. Quiet. On the surface everything may seem placid, but more is going on than you may think. Over the next three weeks you are likely to experience frequent glitches in communications and machinery. Today is not a favorable time for signing any agreement or contract. It is also not particularly helpful for activities having to do with computers; if you must work with them, be particularly careful to back up your work. Your personal energy is apt to be stronger than usual, displaying itself in stronger than average interest in romance and in a belief that you can win over anyone who appeals to you. You can enjoy your sense of power, but be sure to express it in appropriate ways and at appropriate times.

19. SATURDAY. Happy. You can look forward to an extremely romantic day. Going out on a special date could end up being a truly memorable time for both of you. You may even be drawn toward a more serious and lasting emotional commitment. Decide whether this relationship has a good chance in the long run or is just a passing fancy resulting from a few beautiful hours spent together. Most likely you will know the answer before even considering the question. If you are not sure what your lover's answer will be, this evening could be the right time to find out. Whatever happens, enjoy today's unique and wonderful memories. Take along a camera wherever you go, although today's sounds and sights will be in your heart for years.

20. SUNDAY. Favorable. Your thoughts could turn to matters of philosophy. Even if you do not normally think too deeply, it is likely that life's mysteries will cross your mind in some way. Do not stifle these impulses to understand the nature of the universe and your place in it. You may simply want to read a book or a magazine article that broadens your horizons. Or you could be drawn to plan a long trip of personal discovery in the future. Remembering that the world is larger than you would ever believe could give you a real sense of freedom and hope. You can use newly acquired knowledge to broaden and expand your day-to-day life.

21. MONDAY. Mixed. Partnerships are favored early in the day. With someone who is close to you either at work or in your personal life, ideals will draw you together and remind you of why you got together in the first place. There is something lasting and real in this belief, but it will probably be challenged later in the day. You may even experience some conflict between your home life and your place in the public. If you treat these as rivals for your attention, you can expect trouble. However, if you respect both of them and give both a fair measure of your time and attention, you will find that they enhance each other. You need both a public and a private face in order to have a satisfying life.

22. TUESDAY. Confusing. Your career life may seem topsy-turvy as you focus on your public presence. The more attention you pay to it, the more help you will seem to get from people behind the scenes who have your well-being at heart. If you need to do a little background research to consolidate your position, this is the time to start. Your customary supporters may not be quite so helpful, but do not blame them too harshly. There is a strong possibility that you have been giving mixed messages and confusing just the people you think are reliable. If you really feel conflicted, sort out your emotions and come up with a suitable response. If you have just been neglecting them, you need to remind them now of how important they are to you.

23. WEDNESDAY. Beneficial. Despite some minor inconveniences and aggravations, this should be an extremely powerful day. You will be made aware that the extra effort you put into making new connections is paying off more than you had hoped. If these efforts involve your highest ideals and aspirations, you will find that the effect has multiplied. This is an extremely beneficial day for enlisting support for a cause or project dear to your heart. It is also excellent for reinforcing the deeper and more sacred aspects of your love relationship. There is a point at which obligation meets the emotions in your heart, and you could very well touch that point this evening.

24. THURSDAY. Good. If you have been feeling isolated recently, this mood will probably pass today as you discover just how many friendships you have and how deep they are. You are in the midst of a powerful web of connections that spreads out in all directions. It includes all the people you actually know as well as the entire human race. Devote some extra attention to this web of connectedness. Even if it seems like a dream world, it can be much more factually true than you realize. You will make significant headway not by trying to use this knowledge for purely personal ends but by learning your proper role in the whole. Operating within your sphere leads to contentment.

25. FRIDAY. Satisfactory. The emphasis now is on the illusions of love. You could be easily swept into a powerful infatuation that seems to offer everything you have ever wanted. Someone you meet on the spur of the moment may at first seem like the person you are destined to be with for the rest of your life. As exciting as this can be in the short run, it is likely to have some painful lessons later on. It can be like a strong drug that leaves you feeling down after the effects wear off. It is hard not to want to sample the delights of love. However, as a Leo you are inclined toward sudden passion and infatuation, so try to keep in control today. The relationship can only gain from togetherness in a variety of situations and with a variety of companions.

26. SATURDAY. Stressful. There could be real pressure on you to enhance or end a relationship. You may be experiencing an attachment to someone that you cannot express openly. If you are currently frustrated by such a situation, you now have the chance to break through. You can make some real progress simply by speaking your mind; other people will listen attentively and fairly.

You could even find that something lasting develops from what you thought would be a temporary alliance. The chief danger at this point is allowing your bottled-up frustrations to make you so angry that you state your case in an explosive way that will not do anyone any good. Self-control is your best asset at this point.

27. SUNDAY. Rewarding. You have a fine opportunity to connect with your deepest self. This could cause you to withdraw somewhat from the world because you do not want to interact with people as much as usual. However, you will also find that the most direct way to personal understanding is through relationships with other people. In fact, you cannot really be yourself without people in your life. This has always been true, but you may not realize it until now. Today you can see that your individual path does not involve cutting off contact with people but rather uniting with them. Be especially open to a newcomer on the scene who is significantly older or younger than you.

28. MONDAY. Challenging. Your good Leo intuition is vital in your dealings with all of the people in your life. You should have a heightened sense of what is going on in other people's hearts, and it may at times seem as if you can read their minds as well. You can expect extra energy and restlessness, but do not jump to conclusions. Most likely this is nothing more than the mood of the moment. If you can set aside your personal emotions, which may be intense right now, you have a good chance of seeing more clearly than usual. You can use your insights to good advantage in dealing with your spouse or lover. Mix your basic understanding with a large dose of compassion. Guard against judging based on your own accomplishments or aspirations.

29. TUESDAY. Variable. You are likely to be more assertive and aggressive in all of your dealings. You may have the sense that you are the center of the world and that everybody is there to serve your purposes. This may be completely unconscious; you may not even begin to admit it to yourself, but it could be present. If this attitude is in play, you can expect it to receive a cold response from anyone and everyone you deal with. You will find a particularly severe reaction in matters of love. Eventually you will have a strong sense that other people are not simply around to suit your needs. The harshness of this lesson depends on how powerful your illusions are to begin with.

30. WEDNESDAY. Tricky. Concerns about property and money are likely. You may be aware of some reversals in financial matters, but these probably will not turn out to be as bad as they at first seem. There is a strong chance that some investments you have neglected or forgotten about could pay off for you. At present it is not necessary to sign any legally binding document. However, you could benefit from putting in some hard work that involves a detailed reading of legal papers or of the law. This may seem boring, but it is important. This studying is likely to dispel some old illusions, and you will be relieved to see them go. A rumor is probably based on fact; check into it further.

31. THURSDAY. Demanding. You cannot avoid putting in some hard work today. You may have good reason to be unusually concerned about money. It is even possible that someone is using finances to manipulate you. However, you do not have to give in to any inappropriate demands. It is likely that you will not get anything based on luck alone. Work is likely to demand some genuine sacrifice. One thing required of you is to devote much more attention than usual to small, apparently petty details. This is where you can expect your greatest financial rewards at the moment. It may not be glamorous to go over accounts and other financial papers, but when you are done you are likely to agree it was very worthwhile.

FEBRUARY

1. FRIDAY. Fortunate. If you need to get involved with a writing project, this is an excellent day to begin. You will be given a great deal of support from those around you, and they could also offer some much needed practical advice. It will be comparatively easy to maintain the disciplined attitude vital for carrying through the project. Your chief obstacle is procrastination or a fear of failure. It will be easiest to complete the project if you remember the high ideals that you begin with. This is not just a matter of pleasing yourself. You have an important task to accomplish right now, and remembering this should give you all the inspiration you need to do your best.

2. SATURDAY. Fair. This is a favorable day for short trips to run personal errands. You can probably get someone to go with you who will make the task easier as well as more pleasant. The outing could even turn out to include a touch of the romantic. You do not need to limit your journey to purely practical matters. Schedule some entertainment while you are out. A restaurant would be a pleasant setting for intimate conversation. There is a possibility that your trip could be slightly disturbed by some kind of conflict or argument. If you keep matters in perspective, however, there should be no cause for worry. Most likely tempers will quickly settle down and good feelings return.

3. SUNDAY. Variable. Early in the day is a good time to catch up with friends and relatives. Make a surprise call to someone you have not spoken to for some time. This person will be delighted to hear from you. Later on the day becomes somewhat quiet. You will then find the greatest satisfaction from staying home. You probably will not have much luck communicating with your mate or partner regarding important matters. Do not be surprised if your loved one wants some privacy. The two of you could end up pursuing totally separate interests. There is nothing wrong with doing so; you do not need a cult of togetherness. In fact, some time spent alone today could be extremely refreshing.

4. MONDAY. Challenging. Returning to the workaday world may be more of a challenge than usual. If you are tempted simply to stay home and take the day off, use your best judgment. It is possible that a quiet unscheduled vacation or sick day could be exactly what you need to restore your good mood. If there is nothing truly pressing, you could benefit from some time off for your mental health. If you do go to work, you may have to deal with some projects left undone quite a while ago or not done correctly. This is likely to be somewhat frustrating, but there is no alternative to buckling down to the task and making sure it is done right this time.

5. TUESDAY. Mixed. Neither frustrations nor accomplishments are foreseen today. There is the possibility that a domestic issue will demand more time than you thought. If you need to disagree with your mate or partner, be as gentle as you can to spare each other's feelings. Work should be satisfying as you catch up more easily than you anticipated with backlogged projects. Overall this is a better time to tie up loose ends rather than start any large new enterprise. You will have to clear up details eventually, so you might as well take care of them now and in the process take a big load off your mind. Skip evening socializing in favor of a quiet night at home.

6. WEDNESDAY. Satisfactory. Some clearing of the atmosphere is likely. Your mood is brighter and more positive, and you may also be more fun-loving. Spending time with children is an especially good idea. You might want to take them on an outing, or it may be necessary to help them with homework or teach some practical skill such as sewing or cooking. You will find a great deal of pleasure in the companionship of younger people. In all that you do, try to maintain a youthful outlook, aiming to make contact with your own inner child. If you devote too much attention to the serious side of life you are likely to become a bit gloomy. See the glass as half full and the grass as greener on your side.

7. THURSDAY. Lucky. Today should end up seeming like a fortunate day. You could meet a new romantic interest completely out of the blue. You probably will not have much success trying to force this to happen. However, if you just go through the day naturally and spontaneously, some delightful surprise is likely just when you least expect it. Married or engaged Leos may find that a loved one has done something unexpectedly nice, or you could take some time to create a pleasant surprise of your own. You might want to give a small gift for no particular occasion just as a gesture of thoughtfulness. You may be astonished to find out how much a certain person values your attention.

8. FRIDAY. Changeable. You may notice a shift in the efficiency of all kinds of communication. If messages and electronic transmissions have been more confused than usual during the past few weeks, now these problems will start to resolve themselves. Personal connections should seem to be opening up as well. There may have been some difficulties with friends and acquaintances recently as you sensed that you and they were not on the same wavelength. If you immediately made some real effort to overcome these limitations, it should start paying off now as your friendships move forward once again. Otherwise you need to have a heart-to-heart talk to resolve conflict. Be the first to apologize even if you were only partly to blame.

9. SATURDAY. Easygoing. Catch up on some much needed rest. If you have been feeling fatigued or under the weather, make a point of taking extra care of yourself now. Sleep late this morning or take a nap in the afternoon. Also go over your diet to determine if you are eating right. You do not need to indulge in food fads or make radical changes to the way you eat. Just make sure to have solid, healthy meals. Exercise is also a good idea providing it does not tire you too much. Start slow and work up to a more vigorous pace. Simple measures such as these are the best way to ward off illness. If you take care of yourself now, you can reduce the wear and tear on your body. Be sure to take only prescribed medications; avoid diagnosing your own condition if you are suffering any aches or pains.

10. SUNDAY. Useful. You should have more energy today than yesterday. Devote some time to catching up on old correspondence; paying bills is also necessary. Balance your bank account when you are finished. Anything that involves bringing more order into your life is very favored. If you have one or two drawers cluttered with items that you do not really need, go through them and sort out what you really want to keep. Put the rest in a bag to give to charity. This kind of tidying up will take a load off your mind as your life becomes less cluttered. As a result you will have more energy for the things you really need to do. Take on a part-time job if you will be paid well for it, but do not volunteer any help.

11. MONDAY. Good. The workweek starts out on a strong note. Your aspirations are nicely in line with reality right now. There is the chance that you could finally achieve a long-held dream. You have the energy and the resources to accomplish whatever you want. Concentrate on stabilizing your base. If you need to acquire financial support or other help, now is the time to round it up. Some of this help could come from people who live or work at a distance from you. Make sure to cast your net wide enough. Luck may seem to be on your side, but look closely. You will find that this luck is really the result of the careful preparations you have been making all along.

12. TUESDAY. Exciting. Today is likely to be somehow out of the ordinary. Romance is coming into focus. You could experience an especially intense bond with a romantic partner. Do not hesitate to go out on a date with someone you care about a great deal; it could lead to new heights of passion. Do not let preoccupation with what is conventional get in your way. You need to experiment somewhat. At this point you will feel happiest if you step outside the bounds you normally live within. You do not need to do anything bizarre or risky, but a few small variations in your daily routine could save you from becoming bored and dissatisfied with life.

13. WEDNESDAY. Disruptive. Events and announcements may seem to be coming from every direction. Just when you think you have everything figured out regarding a relationship, you may find that something new throws a totally new light on the affair. How upset you become by this discovery largely depends on how much you have been deceiving yourself in the past. This is a good time to take a realistic look at your current situation. You will probably have to do this now whether you want to or not. In the end it may not be as bad as you think. Many of the fears and anxieties you have been experiencing will prove completely groundless. Once you face up to them they will fade into distant memory.

14. THURSDAY. Disquieting. The world may seem sinister as you experience a strong sense of hidden motivations and drives. People will seem to mask their true feelings in order to gain leverage over you and others. In reality these dynamics are going on all the time, but they are just more obvious to you today. Try not to be shocked by the fact that things are not always what they appear. You can even make use of this knowledge for your own purposes, being careful to stay within the bounds of ethics and decency. People who try to manipulate others often end up being manipulated. Your true strength does not lie in controlling others but in managing your own life as best you can.

15. FRIDAY. Fair. You should be more mentally energetic than usual. Ideas will come rapidly, and you also can sort through them quickly. This applies not only to small details but also to the larger picture. If you look carefully, you can gain a wider view of the world and your place in it that can be tremendously uplifting. The day is not good for asking for favors. You may find that people are unreceptive to your requests or simply unavailable. If you schedule an appointment, it could be canceled soon thereafter. This is a temporary glitch rather than a long-term trend. It does not necessarily mean that you cannot get help, only that you might have to wait another day or two to receive it.

16. SATURDAY. Manageable. Powerful energy is working in your favor, especially if you are traveling or planning to travel. You can expect all of the details to fall into place for a work-related journey or a vacation. Ask yourself, though, what you expect to get out of the trip. You may want something romantic and adventurous. However, even if you settle for something tamer, this is a time when you can break out of the shell you usually live within. Look around and see how you fit into the scheme of the universe. An answer is waiting for you to discover. Your view of life could become broader and more tolerant as the result of travel or simply due to your more mellow and philosophic reflection on the ups and downs of everyday life.

17. SUNDAY. Happy. On the whole you will probably have the energy to lead a more unconventional life than usual. This is likely to follow some deep reflections you have been making about the nature of life. Even if you were not aware of what your mind has been doing, you will now benefit from brooding on some major questions and coming to some important decisions. These are apt to be somewhat at odds with the way things usually seem to proceed. You will also discover that you can be far more of an individual than you thought. The people whose opinion you are worrying about do not care nearly as much as you might imagine and will adapt readily to your new approach. Stick with what seems right to you.

18. MONDAY. Frustrating. Your concerns could turn to issues of money and an inheritance. You may wonder exactly how much you are likely to receive, but overall there is little you can do to influence these events right now. Do all that you can to make your professional reputation more secure. The more effort you put into your career at present, the more help you are likely to get. You could even discover that someone has been working on your behalf without your knowing it. Success depends less on ingratiating yourself with higher-ups and more on actually proving your worth. Take advantage of the chance to shine now by working hard even if you would rather be doing something else.

19. TUESDAY. Misleading. Today may see wild variations in career-related matters. You may try to enhance your future prospects by looking good, only to find that events and circumstances thwart your best efforts. There is no way you can be completely flawless, and no one really expects that of you. If you have been preoccupied with work lately, try to relax and be a bit kinder toward yourself. Today shows that since you cannot always be totally perfect you are going to have to cultivate some genuine self-acceptance and forgiveness. In the end you will find that this also makes you more tolerant of other people and better liked as a result.

20. WEDNESDAY. Mixed. Focus on your role in the community. Even if you do not usually pay much attention to community activities, you may find yourself thinking about them now. You could be torn in two directions. On one hand you want to put yourself forward in order to make new friends and win new status. However, you may also feel withdrawn or shy about making the initial effort. You will probably do best if you do not look on it as a matter of advancing your own public image. Instead, go out of your way to take an interest in other people. Ask about their life rather than talking so much about yourself. In this way you will find there is less pressure on you, and you will fit in more easily and get along better with everyone you meet.

21. THURSDAY. Discomforting. Expect to experience some conflict between your social circle and your romantic life. It may seem as if your friends do not really care for your partner or steady date, or that your mate is keeping you from people you like. You may feel weighed down by a number of different burdens. It could seem as if you are trying to please everyone but are succeeding in pleasing nobody. Do not let yourself become discouraged by such thoughts. Even if you have a gulf between your social and romantic interests, this is not a major tragedy. You can still function well in both capacities. Everyone is likely to be happier if they feel they are not being forced to accept one another. By the end of the year your partner and your friends may take more of a liking to each other.

22. FRIDAY. Favorable. You have a lot of energy for social pursuits at the moment. If you have been holding back about accepting an invitation to go out and have a good time, you might want to say yes this evening. You will probably come across as expansive and interesting, traits that will probably make you seem especially charismatic. You may also be drawn to these characteristics in somebody else. Allow yourself some extra freedom to explore. The only caution is not to insist on being center stage all the time. As a Leo you are naturally inclined to do this, but it is not always wise. You may alienate people without even knowing it. You can be outgoing and still allow others to be stars as well.

23. SATURDAY. Splendid. This could be a very important day. You need to have a serious talk with someone close to you. If you have been putting this off, consider doing it first thing today. You have the real opportunity now to go beyond any grudges that have been holding you back. You could also do quite well persuading someone to go along with an unusual request. Romance is favored, although you will probably find it most rewarding in a secluded or out-of-the-way setting. On the whole the day is extremely favorable for just about any pursuit. Do not hold yourself back in any way. The only problem is that you may be feeling so good at present that you will not take advantage of opportunity to its fullest.

24. SUNDAY. Tricky. This is not an ideal day for clear communication. You may become somehow confused, particularly if alcohol is involved. However, if you make a real effort to keep clear-headed, you could achieve some rare insights. The mystical and the supernatural are likely to seem very close. You could find it beneficial and inspiring to view a movie you have always wanted to see. Even if you go purely for entertainment, you are likely to discover a higher lesson in the story. You also have the opportunity to gain some important insight into the meaning of true kindness. This is very unlikely to be in public; in fact, you may be the only person who notices what is going on while it is occurring.

25. MONDAY. Variable. You may want to exert a great amount of effort in persuading other people to agree with you. As a Leo you are naturally somewhat charismatic, so this should not pose tremendous difficulties. You will do best if you invoke a sense of dignity and authority. It is not wise to be too chatty or superficial; this only turns people off. Also be cautious of seeming vague or obscure. You need to make your points clearly in order to be persuasive. The real question is what you are convincing people to do. Be very sure that you are not simply indulging in a power trip. If there is no real point in what you are doing, your intentions are likely to be overruled. Avoid saying one thing but doing another.

26. TUESDAY. Unsettling. Romance is not going to be smooth sailing today. You and your mate or partner may be headed in very different directions. Each of you will probably try to pull the other along. This situation could even start to seem obsessive as one of you begins to feel you have fallen prey to sinister motivations. In reality this is probably not the case. Most likely you and your loved one are simply pursuing what you naturally feel to be in your own best interests. However, if you cannot see things from the other person's point of view, you could cause some real unhappiness both in your own life and among family members.

27. WEDNESDAY. Sensitive. This is likely to be a more stressful day than usual. You may feel inspired and even somewhat restless, but a superior is apt to put a damper on your aspirations. This is not a good day to confront your boss about some complaint that you have been harboring toward management. If you do, you may find that your superior is far less understanding than you might have hoped. A confrontation now may just add fuel to the fire. You will succeed best by working quietly from a position behind the scenes. Some secret acts of charity could be extremely rewarding. Avoid gambling and all games of chance; luck is not on your side at present. Try not to do anything out of the ordinary.

28. THURSDAY. Up and Down. Your moods may be deep and quite erratic. You could be inspired to plunge into very practical work dealing with money or property matters. However, once you get into it, you will find yourself irked by countless petty details. You could become fed up with what you are doing and be drawn to the romantic and intuitive side of life. In any event you are likely to experience tension between day-to-day tasks and the dreamier side of your Leo nature. Do not expect to really succeed in mixing the two. Instead, give some of your time to each. Once you have taken care of business, turn your attention to emotional release. You may end up having a passionate evening with your mate or partner without having to spend a dime or make any promises.

MARCH

1. FRIDAY. Buoyant. For some time it seems your best intentions have been stagnating and hard to implement. Today you should start to see a change in that area. If you have been holding back from doing some good deed or offering help to someone, change course now. It will be best if you do this without making yourself known to the person you are trying to help. Secret aid is highly favored right now. Also try to avoid any thought of a reward for what you do. It is quite possible that you will never directly see how you manage to help someone, but you can be certain that the benefits are real. Even if you and your mate or partner have been together for years, do not neglect to show and express your love.

2. SATURDAY. Variable. You could experience some conflict between private and public life. You may want to stay home and enjoy the pleasures of being with family members. However, some kind of duty, real or imagined, is apt to pull you away. There is the chance that this conflict will create anger either in you or in another person. The best solution is to be very clear about what is happening. Decide how important these major issues really are. It is quite possible that you do not really need to attend to them today at all. You may be able to postpone them perfectly well till next week. Do not automatically assume that anything having to do with work or your career has to be attended to the moment it comes up.

3. SUNDAY. Fortunate. This is a day filled with fortunate influences. You will be able to harmonize best with them if you do not rush around too much. Even if you have a number of worries on your mind, try to put aside these concerns and make some time for peace and quiet. You could find satisfaction in puttering around the house. It will be best, however, if you are not too intent about any tasks you may begin. A gentle, leisurely approach will accomplish the most. As a Leo you tend to push too hard in general. Today provides you with a wonderful opportunity to try the opposite tactic and compare results; you will not be disappointed.

4. MONDAY. Disquieting. Your closest relationship is undergoing a major transformation. There is no absolute certainty about how it will turn out; that ultimately depends on you and your partner. If your relationship is based on fairly narrow or superficial interests, you can expect some kind of emotional upheaval.

You need to consider whether your partnership really has a deep aspect or whether it has been just a matter of mutual convenience. The answer may not be easy for either of you to face. It will require considerable honesty with yourself and with the other person. If more of a commitment is needed, now is the time to begin moving in that direction. Otherwise you risk losing all that you have gained in your time together.

5. TUESDAY. Mixed. Your relationships with children may be under some strain. They are apt to be unruly and even mischievous. You may have to play more of the disciplinarian than you like. This is the appropriate thing to do so long as you keep control of your temper and do not give in to a childish tantrum yourself. You could end up dealing with youngsters best by arranging some kind of entertainment that everyone will like, such as going to the movies or renting an action-packed video. Remember that you can take discipline too far. It is necessary to enforce limits, but if you are too inflexible you will only wind up defeating your own purpose.

6. WEDNESDAY. Positive. You have the chance of making some significant headway on creative enterprises. You could discover that you have a magic touch with a craft or hobby that you have pursued for a long time. Decide what you want to do with it now. There is always the chance that you could turn it into a profitable venture, but this is not automatically the best thing to do. You might only want to enjoy the pleasures of creativity for its own sake. This is an important source of satisfaction that is often overlooked. Do not assume that your efforts are being wasted just because you cannot justify them in terms of earnings or even public recognition. Pleasing yourself is most important.

7. THURSDAY. Challenging. You should have a high degree of energy and want to direct it into your career. This is a good idea, but be wary of coming on too strong with colleagues or a higher-up. There is the risk that you could prove to be too rigid and unyielding, especially in negotiations. Do not ride roughshod over others' feelings and objections. You may be tempted to ignore delicacy and tact, but by doing so you will find that even the best-laid plans will backfire. A more cautious approach is favored right now. Be sure to consult with colleagues and associates beforehand, giving as much attention as you can to their concerns. Only then can you proceed in full confidence that you are on the right track.

8. FRIDAY. Difficult. Some upheaval is likely regarding your innermost hopes and dreams. You may even find that you do not really know what you want, particularly when it comes to love and romance. These concerns could become almost obsessive if you allow them to monopolize all of your thoughts. Keep in mind that everyone has drives and urges that they are barely aware of and have difficulty integrating into everyday life. The key is maintaining a middle course. You do not need to deny whatever comes up, but neither are you obliged to give in to it. Keeping aware while being careful about the way you express your feelings could prove to be the best approach. Also remember that feelings of this kind come and go and do not stay the same forever.

9. SATURDAY. Sensitive. This is likely to be an unusual day but not necessarily an upsetting one. Your love life demands extra attention. You and your mate or partner may have been trying to force yourselves into the straitjacket of a conventional relationship even though your needs are very different. If you have such concerns, talk about them with your loved one. What you say may come as a suprise to you. And you may be very surprised how accepting and understanding your partner is. You could discover that there is a real underpinning of love and acceptance that you had never focused on before. Touching this level could put your relationship on a much more solid footing, enabling you to begin to make future plans together.

10. SUNDAY. Deceptive. This is one of those tricky days when you, or those near you, are likely to jump to all sorts of wild and unfounded conclusions. The danger of indulging in wild illusions is high. You could find yourself giving a great deal of attention to matters that are not very important at all. On the positive side, you should be much more aware right now of your deepest hopes and dreams. If you can separate them from mere wishful thinking, you have a good chance of accomplishing at least one of them. A realistic, hard-headed approach is best. Look at your aspirations seriously and you will be able to sort which ones are worth trying to achieve and which are just pipe dreams.

11. MONDAY. Variable. Your hopes and dreams involving a relationship that is very important to you demand some kind of dramatic action at this point. You may have the almost unstoppable urge to select a course of action and then immediately plow ahead at all costs. There is a very good chance that you will suddenly seem impatient with what you have taken for granted for a long time and will want to overturn it. Be careful that you do not do unnecessary damage or start saying things to your mate or partner that you will regret later. Remember that it is impossible to take back words once you have uttered them. If you are at all tempted to say something that is completely negative, hold back and wait till you can express it more lovingly.

12. TUESDAY. Unsettling. Love is not likely to be satisfying. You could experience a real clash between the urges of passion and true caring, with passion seeming to gain the upper hand. Your understanding and compassion, or your partner's, may seem submerged or nonexistent. No matter what happens, you will have a strong sense of the difference between your desires and what is truly good for someone else. Avoid lying. You will not be able to pull the wool over your own eyes or anyone else's. However, if you are open and honest about your concerns, you stand a good chance of resolving the tension. Just do not become impatient looking for fast results. Upsets that have been escalating for months or even years cannot be resolved in a day.

13. WEDNESDAY. Disconcerting. Expect to be preoccupied with long-term financial considerations, especially investments and inheritance matters. There is the strong danger of worrying too much. It is a good idea to plan for the future, but do not upset yourself. Try to think out a rational, long-term financial plan and stick to it. You do not need to chain yourself to any particular type of investment approach. Just control your worries by looking for some positive steps and then taking them. Once you have made a decision and put your money down, you can let it grow on its own and you can sleep easy at night. Be wary of a new job offer; you may not yet know all the requirements of the position.

14. THURSDAY. Calm. A placid, almost dreamy atmosphere prevails. You are apt to sense that a storm has passed by and left the air clean and fresh. Whether you will have a lot of odds and ends to finish up depends on how you have acted over the last week. Even if your life has been somewhat disrupted, there is no point becoming upset. At present you have the chance to start over with a clear conscience. You can do this quietly, almost casually. You do not need to indulge in any action that draws attention to yourself. Simply proceed naturally and easily toward your goals. If you are playing a sport today you can be confident of winning.

15. FRIDAY. Successful. This could be a day of major shifts. In your primary relationship you could see a major breakthrough that involves some integration between desire and commitment. If these two forces have been at odds lately, now you can find a balance between them. Your relationship will be all the stronger as a result. Talk to your mate or partner with as much clarity and sincerity as you can and a new, deeper love will arise. Be very careful, though, of being too assertive or aggressive about your views and feelings. You could end up bursting a beautiful bubble if you demand an answer to a very personal question. You do not need to know more than you have already been told.

16. SATURDAY. Happy. A lighthearted mood prevails today. If you are planning to give or attend a party or other entertainment, you can expect that guests will enjoy themselves. The event is likely to be more than just ordinary pleasure thanks to a special sense of participating in an unseen magical world. This may not be obvious to everyone or even to a majority of the people attending. They may just go home thinking they have had a fine time, but you will notice if you look for it. There is no real way of putting this sense of another world to practical use. However, if you are aware and participate in the aura as consciously as you can, you will find special rewards coming your way. An older family member is eagerly waiting to hear from you; write, call, or e-mail tonight.

17. SUNDAY. Cautious. Be careful. There is a higher risk of accident than usual, particularly with regard to the moving parts of machinery. If you are operating anything mechanical, be sure to follow all safety precautions to the letter. Also be as attentive as possible to what you are doing. Being aware is the best means of preventing an accident. Also be careful in choosing your words today. There is the possibility of a misunderstanding with friends. You may have the impression that they are holding you back. Even if there is some truth to this, you probably will not be seeing things in the same way in a couple of days. Do not take anyone or anything for granted, particularly friends and relatives.

18. MONDAY. Misleading. You should be constantly alert for any possibilities of conflict, particularly in the workplace. You may think you are not being taken seriously enough. Or a higher-up may not have followed protocol in wielding power and authority. Even if you are right in feeling slighted, choose your battle carefully. Also recognize the high probability of mixed messages and misread cues today that could lead to disputes. Someone could be offended by an offhand remark you make. If so, apologize promptly. On the other hand, if someone annoys you, do not take it to heart. You could be misreading what he or she is trying to say. If you have any questions, come right out and ask.

19. TUESDAY. Up and Down. The day is likely to be up one minute, down the next. There is chance of estrangement from one or two co-workers. You may conclude that a spirit of comradeship is lacking. Team spirit will be hard to arouse because there is likely to be a sense of every person for herself or himself. Influences are not entirely contrary, however. Although you may notice these problems, you should find it comparatively easy to overlook them or simply not to let them bother you. Upsets could be nothing more than the mood of the moment. If there is an underlying problem with your work relationships, it will surface more than once. If it has been around for a while, that is an important signal you need to attend to it without further delay.

20. WEDNESDAY. Confusing. Expect a powerful surge of impulses, not all of them harmonious with one another. If you have children your relations with them may require some major sorting out between now and early August. Something involving a friend or your circle of friends could trigger some new issues. Questions of control, power, and family dynamics could surface. If you have problems in these areas that you have not been able to resolve, now is an ideal time to start to sort through them. Doing so probably will not be easy as you reevaluate your own roles and the way you have acted in the past. Do not be too hard on yourself, but be willing to change.

21. THURSDAY. Complicated. There are new matters to resolve involving money and luck. You could discover that a speculative venture you entered into in the past is not going to be profitable. If some opportunity comes up to invest today, decline for now. If it is going to be favorable, it will present itself on another day. Your relationship with your mate or partner should strike a happier note. You could really warm your loved one's heart by preparing a pleasant surprise. Going out together for a social evening would be a nice idea. You may find yourself captivated by some pleasant community event you had not even planned on attending. If buying tickets for entertainment, get the best seats you can afford.

22. FRIDAY. Disconcerting. You are likely to feel a strong pull to be kind and generous at the moment, but there is a possibility that you will somehow be thwarted. You may be hindered by an inability to rise above petty emotional or practical difficulties. There is also the possibility that your own pride or someone else's will interfere with your best intentions. At the same time, however, you could discover that your Leo charm and graciousness will open doors that otherwise would stay tightly shut. In fact, the power of your personality is extremely high now. Put it to good use, but be careful. It is a double-edged sword and can easily be turned against you. If you are sincere, you have nothing to worry about.

23. SATURDAY. Fair. If you intend to pursue secret plans or goals in matters of your career, you can make some good headway at present. The energy and drive you have put into this lately is starting to pay off. All in all it is best to work as much as possible from a position behind the scenes. You can now set the stage for some significant progress later. Romance is not so well favored. If you have been planning a trip with that special person in your life, particularly a long one, consider putting it off for a while. Instead, enjoy the pleasures and comforts of home. You will find your domestic environment more comfortable than even the finest hotel. Stay home this evening. Have a quite dinner and then curl up with a good book.

24. SUNDAY. Unsettling. If you do not see a clear course ahead in dealing with your partner or spouse, do not press the issue. It is likely that you are not yet aware of the whole picture. You can help the situation most by strengthening your own sense of self-worth, even if your mate or partner is not interested in joining in. If this means solitary activity, do it. Physical exercise is an excellent idea; you may simply want to take a long walk in a natural setting, or go to a health club or exercise class. Even if you are concerned about your relationship at present, you can help it most by not pressing for a commitment at the moment. Just sit back and allow events to unfold at their own pace.

25. MONDAY. Tricky. The energy you are putting into your ambitions could be too much too soon. You may simply be trying too hard to impress those around you. Consider taking another approach today. You will probably find that your Leo talents will take you far. It will be easy to integrate these with your sense of dynamism and control, although on the surface it may seem like nothing much is going on. You will be able to get your way, if that is important to you, by utilizing your charm and ease of manner. Keep your goals very firmly in mind. Be soft on the surface but very clear and sharp mentally. Someone you think is on your side is only watching and waiting to make a move.

26. TUESDAY. Slow. Early in the day it may be hard to keep things in order. When you go to your job you may find that your workspace is messier than usual. Cleaning it up could seem tedious. However, accomplishing it will make performing your duties much easier. Later on your concerns will turn to material matters. You stand to make a profit if you can see the opportunity when it first is presented. It is unlikely to be a get-rich-quick scheme, however. Although the income potential is there, you will earn it through individual hard work. You could be tempted to enlist a friend in the enterprise, but in the end it will be easier as well as more profitable to do it yourself.

27. WEDNESDAY. Frustrating. Even though you could have all sorts of plans to be efficient, a certain dreaminess will make progress difficult. People could make vague promises, or they may agree to something only to take it back. Property negotiations are particularly likely to be frustrated in this way. It could be difficult to sell or rent a home today. Someone may seem interested but then leave on a long-distance trip. Any seeming misfortunes of this kind are only temporary. Later it may turn out that you were lucky to have these plans fall through, as the people you were dealing with turn out to be even more unreliable than you had feared. Or you may receive a much better offer a few days from now.

28. THURSDAY. Cautious. This is not an ideal day for shopping or for making any purchases. If you set out with an intention to buy, you could discover that you get the wrong size or color or style. Your judgment is apt to be slightly off in making a choice. You might become impatient with the whole process and simply buy the first thing that catches your attention, only to discover that you paid too much for it. You can succeed in shopping, but it will be a slow and time-consuming process. You have to do some research beforehand and consider options carefully. Make sure you have the patience before starting out, or postpone the trip until the weekend.

29. FRIDAY. Favorable. If you need to make a business proposal, it should go very smoothly. You will benefit from having props to enhance your presentation. Neatness counts, particularly today. Put in the time for careful advance preparation so that you do not need to fumble while putting on your show. You may be bitten by the travel bug but not actually end up going anywhere. It is likely, however, that you will at least find the idea of faraway people and places interesting. You might want to make a phone call or do some computer research to research a trip in the not-too-distant future. A package tour that includes transportation and lodging may be most economical.

30. SATURDAY. Exciting. You will probably notice electricity in the air. It is possible that you will hear from old friends or will run into someone you have not seen for a while who has just arrived in town. You may be restless in the midst of it all, wondering where to go or what to do next. There is a strong possibility of a new romance. If you are traveling today, you could meet someone interesting in an airport. You and an intriguing stranger could hit it off right away. There will be all the excitement of new love. Enjoy yourself, but do not become too attached or you will ruin your fun. You have plenty of time to discover whether there is something in the relationship that will endure for the long term.

31. SUNDAY. Rewarding. Try to reconnect with your spiritual roots. You may go to a religious service. Or if there is an older person whose advice you respect and trust, you might want to pay a visit. Talk over your current life and the meaning it has for you. Do not fret too much about the practical necessities of life. Allow your mind to range as far as it can, and try to see yourself as part of the whole universe. Some people might regard this kind of activity as a luxury or even as a waste of time, but it is vitally important to your mental health and to your sense of well-being. You can never understand too much about your role in life.

APRIL

1. MONDAY. Unsettling. You could be kept from performing customary tasks by some unexpected demands at home which could even make you late for work. Do not let this disrupt your focus. Deal with matters as they arise, one at a time. You can always catch up with routine chores later. As the day progresses, problems will iron themselves out. Soon you could find yourself experiencing some wanderlust. Because you are impatient with the demands of everyday life, you may yearn to break free. You can allow yourself a little time to explore, even if it is just taking a stroll down an unfamiliar street. You will not become lost if you do not follow your usual routine precisely. Try something that is daring for you.

2. TUESDAY. Buoyant. Your hard work in building connections and associations could really start to bear fruit. Although you may have been putting in a lot of legwork getting to know people, it may seem your efforts have had scanty results up to now. This could start to change today as you hear from someone you have been trying to contact for quite a while. If this person has not been interested in partnership previously, now could be the time to bring up the possibility again. Do not allow lingering hurt feelings from past neglect to stand in your way. Especially avoid any tendency to brood or sulk, which can interfere with some very positive forces that are about to come into play. Your marriage or other love relationship could also change for the better if you relax and let go.

3. WEDNESDAY. Exciting. Early in the day be ready for all sorts of stimulation. You may be impelled to go out into the world to somehow put your stamp on it. You could feel the urge to travel for fun and excitement. Allow yourself some such pleasure if you can. Later in the day the mood becomes more serious. This afternoon you may want to plunge headlong into a work project. If you follow through, you are likely to make a great deal of headway. Your love life has a certain special sweetness at this point. You will not find your mate or partner bold or dramatic. The dreamy, intuitive side of love comes into play now. Conditions are more favorable for a quiet evening at home than for a lively night on the town.

4. THURSDAY. Important. You may feel a tremendous pull to tell your story. It may be necessary to tell people what you really think about a situation without worrying about hurting their feelings. You will most likely discover that your hunches about certain people are surprisingly on target. The question is what to do with this knowledge. In the first place, you should rely more on your good Leo intuition. You have a tendency to push your feelings and reactions into the background or dismiss them as not really relevant. Today you will discover how valuable they really can be. However, this should not make you impetuous or flighty. In fact, it could give you a new sense of authority as you begin to feel more in control of all that is going on.

5. FRIDAY. Good. Try to end the workweek on a strong note. Circumstances are very much in your favor. If you give a final push to a project, you can probably complete it ahead of schedule. You have more than enough energy and resources to get the job done. If you encounter any obstacles, just say the word and the help you need will probably come your way. Concentrate on the practical, how-to side of things. You will not get quite as far if you allow yourself to theorize or brainstorm about the long term. It is best to apply yourself to the here and now. You can plow through a lot and leave yourself with a clean slate when you begin work next week.

6. SATURDAY. Deceptive. You or someone you know is likely to fall prey to the deceptions of love. This can be strangely appealing. You may even find that you want to play along with the illusion because it is so much fun. You can do this up to a point, but at the back of your mind hold on to the idea that everything today is not what it seems. It is also possible that you may be set up for a small romantic disappointment. This is almost certain to be minor, but it could start you thinking about what you really want in a relationship. There is probably some difference between what you want and what you only think you want. You have a wonderful chance now to sort out your feelings and focus on your needs as well.

7. SUNDAY. Excellent. Any lingering clouds of doubt should vanish, leaving you with a clear idea of how to proceed. Your relationship with your mate or partner should seem unusually easygoing. Take a long, hard look at your loved one and you will realize how lucky you are. Do not keep your feelings a secret. You have an opportunity to intensify your relationship by expressing your deepest love and admiration. Your partner is almost certain to respond in kind. You could share some new, unexplored depths of your relationship, but do not let this become serious. You are capable right now of real enjoyment and delight, so do not deprive yourself of getting all that you can out of the day.

8. MONDAY. Disconcerting. You can expect to encounter a few bumps in the road. If you decide to plot some grandiose plans for the future, your mate or partner is not likely to be sympathetic. Your ideas may come like a bolt out of the blue, and loved ones will respond with shock at first. There is the possibility that you will not see eye to eye for a long time. There is also the danger of a serious quarrel. You may become suddenly impatient with your partner's ways, feeling that love is a weight around your neck interfering with your plans to soar. This is probably quite a distorted picture. You need to look at your relationship in a larger context so that you do not jump to conclusions not based on fact.

9. TUESDAY. Misleading. Be careful about the illusions of romance. They could be far stronger than usual. There is something special in the air, but what it is seems uncertain. Pay close attention to all signals before making up your mind. It may be somewhat tricky to talk things over with your partner. Some of your hopes and dreams may be thwarted by harsh reality. Or you may insist on refusing to see the truth, causing you to cling to how you want to view the situation. In the long run if there is something between you it will withstand any and all disillusionments. If not, you are just as well off to discontinue the relationship. Even if this seems a bitter lesson right now, your heart will not suffer any real harm.

10. WEDNESDAY. Stressful. Do not expect smooth sailing, especially when you are in the public eye. You could make a tremendous effort to be flawless only to find that your presentation falls flat. It is not likely that you can control the situation entirely. Mishaps that arise are probably not going to be your fault, so do not take them to heart. The worst thing you can do is to launch accusations at everyone and anyone. This will not help in the slightest. If you find other people indulging in these actions, give them a wide berth. You can do a great deal to minimize conflict and tension right now even if you are not completely able to avoid the root causes. Just remain cool and in control of your own emotions, including your body language.

11. THURSDAY. Fair. This should be an agreeable but not particularly dramatic day. Many of the disruptions of the past few days are settling down, leaving you with the question of why they occurred in the first place. This is a good time to think about repeating patterns that you have noticed in your life. These include not only things that you habitually do, but also things that habitually happen to you. You probably think of these as being somehow accidental or out of control but they are not as accidental as you might like to believe. Your attitudes, behavior, and expectations have a tremendous role in shaping the events that happen to you, even when they seem to crop up automatically.

12. FRIDAY. Fortunate. Today is good for long-distance travel, particularly if you have to take a trip by air. A journey should go well and be a pleasant excursion. Even if you are making a routine trip for business purposes, try to see it as an adventure and a pleasure. Take advantage of a chance to meet someone new. If you are taking a vacation, you can count on a smooth beginning; most likely the remainder of the trip will be favorable and free of stress as well. If you are not going to be traveling, at least spend some time away from your customary habits. Opt to read a book on religion or spirituality, or find a magazine that uplifts and inspires you. You need to allow fresh ideas to penetrate your brain.

13. SATURDAY. Rewarding. You are likely to notice a significant shift of emphasis. Conditions favor putting a great deal of energy into building a better reputation for yourself. Call up people you know, especially if you have not been in touch with them for a while. Renew old acquaintances and see how far you can broaden your social circle. Even if you feel you have enough friends, one or two new connections could prove mutually beneficial. You have a lot more energy to devote to entertainment and socializing. Just make sure that you do not come on too strong; there is a slight risk of alienating a newcomer. Do not inhibit your extroverted Leo nature; just keep a close watch on how people are reacting.

14. SUNDAY. Mixed. You could experience some conflicts. Because of your tremendous appetite for work and your profession, you may want to plunge into these areas and really move ahead as far as you can go. Your mate or partner, however, may not understand this aspect of your nature and may even take it as a slight. While you do not mean any harm, this may not be entirely clear to your loved ones. If there is any possibility of alienating people who are close to you go out of your way to reassure them.

Even a small amount of tension could linger into the coming week. You do not have to put your work first all the time. You need to make sure it is integrated into a healthy and balanced lifestyle that includes fun and recreation.

15. MONDAY. Demanding. People may not give you a moment's peace. You are apt to feel like a celebrity being hounded for autographs. The effect will not be entirely pleasant because you could well be overwhelmed by what seems to be a sheer mass of humanity all around you, clamoring to have all of their demands met. This is especially likely at work. If you are not careful, you could lose your temper. If you sense the pressure starting to build, make your concerns known. If other people still do not seem to pay any attention, back off and insist on taking some time to yourself. Do whatever you need to restore your good spirits. You have a lot of energy and drive right now; do not squander it on an expression of negative emotions.

16. TUESDAY. Pressured. You are likely to feel the weight of upcoming as well as current social obligations. It may seem that all of your many friends and acquaintances all want something from you. You will probably not have much luck evading them. If you regard social commitments as a real burden, you are only going to make it tougher on yourself. The only way to cope with all of the demands is to take a long-range perspective. You are connected with these people and may need their help or companionship someday. Do your best to face whatever obligations you have with good cheer. You can make them not only bearable but pleasurable if you adopt the right attitude.

17. WEDNESDAY. Useful. Real luck could come your way in relation to property or finances. However, the best attitude is not to await it too eagerly or expectantly. If you find yourself eagerly rushing to the phone each time it rings, you will probably wind up disappointed. A light approach is much better, even if you have to force yourself to see the bright side. Let good news come to you. If you need to make a phone call or send a message, keeping a buoyant, upbeat attitude will be the most helpful way to assure success. Do not let friends bring you down emotionally. If anyone seems to be acting like a wet blanket, excuse yourself politely and go off somewhere else for a while.

18. THURSDAY. Satisfactory. Overall favorable influences predominate. If you have some legal matters to deal with, this is a good time to pay attention to them. You could be told of a reversal which will probably be in your favor. Distant friends will come to your assistance. You may have the best luck if you approach a problem from an unorthodox perspective. Try to break free of whatever preconceived notions are imprisoning you. There is the chance of some misunderstandings, particularly at work or with your partner, so be careful. Any impatience will be unhelpful. Even if your mind is racing, present an easygoing, pleasant personality to those with whom you must get along.

19. FRIDAY. Pleasant. Your domestic and professional duties should be in harmony. You could accomplish more by working at home today. Make a couple of phone calls and you will probably find that you can resolve problems that would have taken much longer to solve on another day. Even if you do go into the workplace, you should have an easy time dealing with people and projects. You can also catch up with the backlog of mail and phone messages. You may want to put in a little effort toward beautifying your surroundings. This can be something as simple as adding a picture or a plant, or taking away some item that does not please you anymore. You will benefit from sprucing up your environment and ensuring that people feel comfortable when they stop by to confer with you.

20. SATURDAY. Variable. Today may start out on an uneasy note as you find that your desire to stay home and enjoy a little extra privacy is not going to materialize. You may end up having to deal with someone from faraway, or even have to make an unexpected trip of your own. It is also possible that you will have to deal with a small but unpleasant police matter. Later in the day the mood shifts to a more pleasant phase as you become more outgoing. It would be useful to devote an hour or two to getting some exercise. You have more than your share of stamina right now. You will probably enjoy yourself more if you do not exercise alone; ask a friend or a neighbor to accompany you.

21. SUNDAY. Up and Down. Your desire to have things your own way, especially in your immediate surroundings, will not go unopposed. Quite possibly you will have to respond to someone else's unrealistic expectations. It will certainly be hard to get this person to see your point of view, much less to accept it. It is also unlikely that you can make your case by sheer explanation. You will have to wait the situation out, hoping that this person eventually comes around. If this does not occur in a reasonable time frame, bring in the heavy artillery and make your wishes known quite forcefully. A stronger rather than a more timid approach is favored at present. Your naturally powerful Leo presence can be a tremendous help in getting what you want.

22. MONDAY. Disquieting. Some hurt feelings are a real possibility, especially early in the day. You may be forced to listen to some harsh words or encounter inconsiderate behavior that you find personally upsetting. This is not likely to be a major trauma, but you will probably feel it more deeply than you normally would. You may also be taking upsets to heart far more than the situation deserves. Later in the day you could decide that it is simply not worth troubling yourself over the matter. Instead, turn your attention to more practical matters. Whether dealing with your finances or with some major task at work, your greatest salvation right now is to get your mind off whatever is troubling you. By doing so you will find it goes away quickly.

23. TUESDAY. Profitable. You can gain some real financial advantages but you will have to earn every penny. There is a strong possibility that you will have to go out and pound the pavement to deal with clients and customers. They are not necessarily going to be receptive, so you will have to put in more effort than usual to build some rapport with them. Do not let yourself become flustered by apparent adversities. People are unlikely to be sympathetic, so just put on the best face you can. You can get your way if you exercise patience. It could all turn out to be quite profitable. By the end of the day you will probably feel you have put in a full day and need to relax. Going out for dinner can help restore your optimism.

24. WEDNESDAY. Disconcerting. There is the chance of some startling news in the area of romance. A couple you know may announce that they are breaking up, or an unlikely pair may have fallen in love. No matter how disquieting the news seems to be, you will cope best by retaining a good sense of humor. Life can take some odd twists and turns. Probably there will be no harm in this situation as far as you are directly concerned. You may even see these changes as refreshing and stimulating. If you are somehow disturbed by them at some level, ask yourself whether it really is any of your business. Becoming too involved will not help your spirits nor improve the situation for those who are most directly involved.

25. THURSDAY. Positive. You are likely to have an unusual amount of mental energy, enabling you to think quickly and respond to any demands with sharp reflexes. If you are preoccupied with matters of love, you will probably learn over the next few weeks that a light, witty attitude is most impressive to the object of your affection. Avoid anything heavy or gloomy in romance. Adding a touch of sparkle to your conversation or appearance will be very helpful. You do not need to avoid discussing serious matters; in fact, it may be a good time to do so. Just keep in bright spirits and do not let anything seem to be too much of a grind or

a duty. A child may clue you in to how to proceed most effectively.

26. FRIDAY. Fair. This is not likely to be a day of major victories
or defeats. Instead, it will probably produce some small but pleasant surprise. You could come home to find a welcome letter from
an old friend. Or your mate or partner might buy you a small gift
for no special reason. This is not the sort of thing that makes or
breaks a relationship. However, it is wise to remember that just
as you can be worn down by small irritations, you can be strength-
ened by small gestures of kindness. Spend a moment or two in
silent gratitude for all you have been given in the past. If you do
not receive anything unexpected, at least you can make just such
a gesture. Doing so will be as beneficial for you as being on the
receiving end.

27. SATURDAY. Emotional. Brooding and melancholy are in
the air right now. You could find that your emotions turn inward.
There could even be a temptation to nurse a grudge or to take
perverse delight in your own grief. If this is the case, try not to
take yourself too seriously. That also means not being hasty to
judge or to try to force a reconciliation. Doing so is only likely to
prolong the condition. Instead, allow yourself to experience whatever is happening. It may be necessary even to open some old
wounds from the past in order to heal them once and for all. You
will of course benefit by letting them go, but sometimes taking a
detailed look is the best way to free yourself of them.

28. SUNDAY. Frustrating. The home situation could seem uneasy early in the day. There may be some harsh or cutting words
exchanged between you and a member of your family. If this happens often, you need to figure out how you are going to resolve
it. If you and the other people concerned allow this habit to continue, it could inject poison into the family situation. Take care
later in the day not to let unease spread to other areas of your
life. Be particularly sure to insulate children from any harshness.
If they take part in a game or creative project, they are not apt
to settle down as you would like them to do. Be prepared for this,
and try your best to control your temper.

29. MONDAY. Tricky. Anything involving fun or recreation is
likely to be somewhat upsetting. There may not be time for it in
any event, because you may have to handle some major problems
at work. Your professional standing is likely to suffer a bit from
some unforeseen circumstances. If it is your fault, own up to it so
that you can put it past you; if not your fault, do not trouble
yourself too much trying to prove your innocence. Just hold your
head up high and go your merry way. Your strong suit at the

moment is your creative drive and Leo spirit. You are likely to come across best if you remain something of a maverick or a loner. Following the herd is not recommended, particularly if you have any misgivings about where it might be headed.

30. TUESDAY. Enjoyable. You will probably start to be in regular touch with friends and acquaintances you have not seen in a while. If this does not happen on its own, take some definite steps to communicate. If you have recently been isolated or too immersed in your own routine, you could find that a broader social scene really opens your eyes. Take time to call or write friends; you might want to invite some for dinner in the near future. It is likely to be easy to host a get-together since your spirits should be brightening up at the moment. You may also want to reconnect with your basic ideals. Decide what you are doing with your life, and why. Do not make this a dreary question, but give it some thought when you have a few moments to spare.

MAY

1. WEDNESDAY. Variable. You are unlikely to have much patience with anything that is not based on solid facts and figures. If you encounter the unconventional in people or things, it could strike you as ridiculous or unpleasant. It is important to pay attention to these inclinations. Keep your interests and efforts as practical as possible. This is not a good time for brainstorming or making any long-term plans for the future. You probably will not follow through with them. Instead, adopt a matter-of-fact, almost plodding attitude. Take care of practical matters, particularly concerns in regard to work and health. Do not take it too personally if your home situation seems a bit strained. Problems take time to resolve in a permanent way.

2. THURSDAY. Quiet. Few dramatic incidents, either positive or negative, are apt to come your way. Instead you are likely to proceed with a solid, businesslike attitude. Take good advantage of this to squarely face all those practical matters that you have been putting off. If you feel more ambitious than usual, pour as much effort as you can into your work. You can do this in such a way that it is not exhausting if you keep focused on just one task at a time. Organize matters as you go along. Do this and you will have more stamina at the end of the day than when you started because you will not be putting energy into procrastination. Seeing results is sure to be inspiring.

3. FRIDAY. Useful. Conditions are favorable for negotiations or discussions, especially those that have to do with partnership matters. This will not necessarily involve your spouse. It could include anyone with whom you have or are considering a partnership. You are likely to find that you can connect closely with someone in your immediate circle of friends. Possibly what was only a casual acquaintanceship will lead to something permanent and meaningful, whether it is love, business, or even some hobby that you have in common. You should have little trouble cementing your relationship and making sure that you remain on the same wavelength. How far this develops will be decided by later events.

4. SATURDAY. Fair. Two major trends are emerging. You may find it unusually hard to get along with a good friend or acquaintance. It is even possible that an old resentment boiling under the surface will erupt today. Be careful about what you say. You will never be able to take back your words. In matters of love, however, influences are far more favorable. You may meet someone who seems like a potential mate, or you could realize that you and the person you are currently with are soul mates. There is even a honeymoon air at the moment, which will not last but can be enjoyed while it dominates. Just avoid making any long-term commitment concerning living arrangements.

5. SUNDAY. Disquieting. You are likely to make your romantic partner uneasy today, or you could find that your loved one is leaving a strange impression on you. If this goes beyond a certain point, it could even lead to a minor upheaval in your relationship. Possibly this is pointing to a major gulf that is looming between you. Far more likely, however, is a real chance that you are simply discovering the other person's uniqueness. This will not necessarily strike you as desirable, but it is part of the person's character that is not going to change. You would do far better to accept it as is rather than try for a change to suit your own whims. If you feel you are being pushed in a direction you do not want to go, you have to stand up for yourself rather than relying on lame excuses.

6. MONDAY. Slow. This is one of those days when you will not be very outgoing. You may have an urge to withdraw and hide yourself away from the noise of the world. Overall it would be best to follow this urge if at all possible. Relations with other people are likely to be frustrating. You may be at odds with authority figures, and you will probably see your colleagues more as rivals than as associates. Even your spouse or partner may be inaccessible for one reason or another. If you make up your mind to spend some quiet time at home, you will fare much better. You can take care of some household chores or just spend some time relaxing with a good book or video.

7. TUESDAY. Sensitive. Love and romance are likely to seem like something of a burden. You could become attracted to people who create difficulties for you. Or you might see your current relationship as one enormous chore. This undoubtedly is not the whole picture, but it may be impossible for you to avoid regarding it that way at the moment. If there is something that you need to talk over with your partner but you have been putting it off for a long time, you could find it just as difficult to bring up now. Regardless, try to break the ice and start to discuss the issue that has been troubling you. You can talk it out and at least agree to disagree until a solution is found.

8. WEDNESDAY. Disconcerting. It may seem that there is nowhere to go because your friends are not as available as usual. However, if you reach out to them some plans for fun can be worked out. You may end up making a long-distance phone call to catch up with an old friend. You could also discover that someone has not been as good a friend as you thought, which could cause some grief and worry. Beware of mentally going over and over old grudges and resentments. Doing so is of no use whatsoever. You need to calmly mull over the situation and see where you want the friendship to go. You do not have to continue it as is if it has caused you more grief than pleasure.

9. THURSDAY. Unsettling. The last day or two has highlighted some serious difficulties in your human relationships. There is a strong chance of heightened tensions both in friendships and in romance. If you are inclined to fall in love with someone at first sight, you may want to reconsider your approach today. You could become preoccupied with someone who just is not right for you. This person may not be interested in a relationship, or the mutual interest between you may not be to anyone's advantage. Be extremely careful about the way you proceed. It is wonderful to have someone in your life, but most of all you need someone who is going to be good for you.

10. FRIDAY. Happy. Love is apt to take on a more intense and more agreeable form. If you are in the mood for romance, you will find it easier than usual to connect with someone who appeals to you. Just do not come across as too serious or grim. The atmosphere at present favors fun. Use your good Leo sense of humor to your best advantage. You might even want to flirt by being a bit mischievous. This does not mean you cannot be intense or passionate, only that anything grim is likely to be a turnoff at present. You have a lot of natural charm and charisma; use it to your best advantage. If you are already in a stable relationship, think about refreshing the sense of novelty in your romance.

11. SATURDAY. Variable. You may need to put yourself forward in the public in some form. You could be drawn to attending some social event more as a means of making business contacts than for simple enjoyment. Ironically, if you do some public relations at present you could end up working against your own best interests. The reason is that it is possible you will leave a negative impression on someone important. The best way of advancing your career interests right now is to do nothing at all. Take a day off from work and worry. Stay at home and do something completely different. You do not always succeed with the direct approach. Sometimes holding back and letting things develop naturally is much more successful.

12. SUNDAY. Calm. This promises to be a peaceful day. If you like to garden, take advantage of the conditions by devoting some time to putting in spring plants. This is an excellent period for planting and sowing. You should gain an unusual amount of satisfaction from simple tasks that involve digging in the earth. The world of plants has tremendous calming powers; take some time to enjoy them. Do not become too preoccupied with how much you need to get done. It is not just a matter of accomplishment, but of being aware of the task itself. If you can be more in tune with nature and its glories, you will find that many of your worries and upsets vanish. Get to bed earlier than usual tonight.

13. MONDAY. Tranquil. It should not be surprising if your thoughts turn inward. Even if you find yourself in the midst of a crowd of people, which is quite possible, you will probably feel drawn to a more introspective view. The spiritual side of life is highlighted. If you have been ignoring this side of your nature in the busy course of life, try to take some time today to nourish your spirit. It is quite probable that you will discover something important that you have neglected. This may hold the key to successful relationships. However, the lesson is not just about making a partnership work; it has just as much to do with discovering something important about yourself. Keep plans simple and straightforward.

14. TUESDAY. Difficult. Some major issues are coming to the fore in regard to your friends and associates. Your relationships are not likely to be entirely smooth. In fact, you may encounter a certain amount of turmoil that will probably center around thorny issues dealing with passion and commitment. Some drama could ensue, with threats or tears. If you have been thinking of another person as a weight around your neck, it is time to do something to resolve the situation. You may even decide on some kind of face-to-face encounter. However, if you use your intuition as a way to understand the other person's point of view, you could find a discussion very rewarding. Just be willing to listen as much as you talk.

15. WEDNESDAY. Tricky. You could encounter some difficulties with communications and machinery. While things seem to be speeding up, they are not necessarily working any better. In fact, there may be a certain amount of counterproductive haste, especially with any club or association in which you are involved. Suddenly it may seem as if people do not know which way to go. Or they may be very determined but not be able to get their point of view across. Upsets could even take the form of simple crossed wires such as lost messages, missed phone calls, or bad timing that always makes it hard for people to understand each other. Try hard not to be overcome with resentment.

16. THURSDAY. Easygoing. You will not find the day packed with events and occurrences, but a certain calmness may be very welcome right now. You are likely to be in an open, generous mood. Take advantage of this to do something kind for someone, in secret if possible. Maybe you can arrange that the person you are helping will not even know about it. Once it is done, forget about it. You will find a real benefit from behind-the-scenes help that is subtle but important. The idea is not so much to get something in return as to open up the warm, generous side of your Leo nature. Whatever good deed you do for others will be returned to you in some measure when you need it most.

17. FRIDAY. Excellent. You can do something advantageous for your career by working quietly and unobtrusively on your own behalf. This goes against your basic nature, since you tend to like to be in the center of events. However, if you can overcome your inclination to steal the limelight, you could make some real progress in an area of vital professional interest to you. It is not always easy to accomplish things in full public view. Half of your energy is often expended putting on a show for onlookers. If you can set this temptation aside today and pretend you are operating backstage, you will be surprised how helpful and sympathetic other people will be. Follow the path of least resistance.

18. SATURDAY. Good. Your naturally outgoing nature is coming to the fore. You may be drawn to all sorts of social activities and ventures. There is likely to be a lot of conversation which no doubt you will want to take part in it. Be wary of gossip, however, or of spreading rumors. There is also the chance that some signals will be misread. You could give or receive the wrong idea about a romantic relationship. If you can avoid the consequences of miscommunication, this should be a good day overall. You have the opportunity to reassert yourself as an authority. If you felt less in control of a social situation recently, this may be the time to regain the upper hand by being positive and forceful.

19. SUNDAY. Changeable. The watchword for today is uniqueness. The degree to which you are your own person will to a great extent determine how and where the chips fall. It will not be easy to express your individuality because you may sense that you are butting up against stone walls when you try to do so. You could fear with some reason that other people will try to hold you down or will be offended. The good news is that your uniqueness could seem strangely attractive to a potential lover. If you are trying to catch the eye of a romantic partner, you are far more likely to succeed by being flamboyant rather than keeping strictly to the straight and narrow.

20. MONDAY. Mixed. You are entering a phase where you need to consolidate any romantic gains you have made since the start of this merry month. The current situation is more favorable to an established relationship than to making bold ventures. You may want to spend more time at home with your mate or partner, involved in cozy domestic activities. Or you could embark on some project around the house that appeals to both of you. Expect to encounter some obstacles in dealing with friends and associates. They will probably not understand you, or they may insist that you do not understand them. Do not waste a huge amount of energy explaining yourself. The best communication comes from the heart and is received intuitively.

21. TUESDAY. Frustrating. Your people skills could meet with some serious opposition. If you find yourself in a situation where you have to stand up for what you think is right, you could discover that you are on your own. Even people you have counted on in the past as loyal allies may not stay around to support you. Some discomfort as a result is unavoidable, but you will learn that some things you have to face independently. In fact, it could seem as if friends are not available precisely so that you can deal with these obstacles by yourself. Like most experiences that build character, it may not be pleasant. However, it will give you a much clearer sense of who you can count on and how much you can count on yourself.

22. WEDNESDAY. Sensitive. You can expect the pressure on you to lighten up a bit. Your love life may seem quite confining, making you want to break out of your shell and venture into the world even though your mate or partner is not in the mood. This should not be a major stumbling block. You may end up doing things separately if you cannot agree. You will benefit most by maintaining an attitude of real caring, even self-sacrifice. This is not a time for a me-first approach to life. You will find that the best way to fulfill yourself is by putting someone else first. Try to take this perspective if it is not the way you customarily proceed in life.

23. THURSDAY. Fortunate. The more generous side of your Leo nature could feel a bit wounded in the wake of some recent events. However, if you have managed to get through the past few days without falling apart, you could discover that it was all worth the effort. Supporters and allies you thought had deserted you will come back in full force. You may wonder where they were when you first needed them, but this is not a helpful way to look at the current situation. Stay in the present. If you think about it, you will probably find that you were expecting people to bail you out of a problem you needed to handle on your own. Quite possibly you were also blaming them for your own delays in acting. Put it all behind you now and look ahead with renewed confidence.

24. FRIDAY. Helpful. At present you are likely to thrive in a protected setting. If you get away from the world and all its noise, you will be able to accomplish what you need to do. Turn your attention to family members and loved ones. They could feel neglected because it seems you have been putting everyone else ahead of them. Spend some quality time around the house. This would be better than planning a lavish evening out on the town. You do not need to avoid the outside world, but there are times when you can most benefit from a home setting. After all, that is the place where you should feel most comfortable and able to be yourself.

25. SATURDAY. Favorable. This is an ideal day for any activity involving you with your family. If you have not had the chance to join loved ones in their favorite activities, try to do so now. Think about something you all love to do together, perhaps playing a game or piecing together a puzzle. However simple such things can be, they are important in cementing a bond among all family members. Your mate or partner probably feels the same way. If there are any lingering grudges or resentments from the past, do your best to set them aside. Make amends if that is possible at this late date. You will find that some basic recreation is more valuable than intense discussions. Avoid going out as part of a crowd tonight. A twosome will be much more fun.

26. SUNDAY. Challenging. This is likely to be an intense day. You may have been sensing or encountering some major obstacles in dealing with your social circle, including a strong element of manipulation and intrigue. These tensions reach their high point today; a crisis could ensue. If you choose, you can come through it all unscathed by letting go of your difficulties. Analyze the situation and you will realize that all will work out for the best. As hard as it may be to reach this state of mind, you are quite ready to do so now. A new sense of freedom could follow as you take back any control that you gave over to someone else, either consciously or without being fully aware.

27. MONDAY. Manageable. Your mind is likely to be running at full speed. You will prosper most if you create some distance between yourself and the images churning through your head a mile a minute. As hard as this may be to believe, they are not really helping you. In a state of calmness, you can sit back and view the most intense thoughts and emotions running by like images on a movie screen. It would be very helpful to try to detach like this. In fact, it is the only real alternative to mental restlessness and distraction. You will not be able to stop the train of thoughts, but you can free yourself of as much of it as you can. Focusing on a creative hobby may also slow down your thought process.

28. TUESDAY. Unpredictable. Watch for any signs of domestic difficulty or disturbance. They may not be easy to spot. The chief problem is unstated grudges and hostilities that could fester among those people who are closest to you. The best way of dealing with this is to be as clear and forthright with the person as possible. This does not mean challenging or confronting. Simply note that the person seems to be a little irritated by something, then offer to talk about it. You need to draw out the other person, but do not force the issue. As long as you are available to listen and to talk, the conversation will take place in good time. Fortunately you have the patience to wait if the right time does not come immediately.

29. WEDNESDAY. Uncertain. This is not a day for bold and decisive gestures, especially in the workplace. A simple, almost plodding approach is preferred. It may not seem particularly glamorous or charismatic, but glamour is likely to misfire at this time. Large, theatrical gestures will fall flat. As a Leo you feel more comfortable with boldness and flamboyance than with quiet routine. However, you have to learn that understatement has its place as well. If you are not sure of yourself, hold back and keep quiet.

And if you are sure of yourself, the same advice applies in order to avoid overconfidence. Spend the evening on your own.

30. THURSDAY. Rewarding. If you had to leave some lingering doubts in your relationships with friends in the past few weeks, now is a good time for resolving them. Anything that was left unstated or up in the air can be sorted out now. Definitely make an extra effort to talk about any problems that may have come up. You will probably find that the other person is remarkably willing and eager to listen. The same is true for your romantic partner. In fact, your mutual affection is likely to be stronger than usual. You may be almost compelled to express your feelings, which is a good thing to do right now. Being as lavish in your praise and encouragement as you sincerely can be will be much appreciated.

31. FRIDAY. Good. You are likely to be brimming with idealism, hoping to save the world. You may have a hundred ideas for doing so. Most of them are probably good, although it is unfortunate that you will not be able to accomplish all, or even many, of them. If your selflessness is really serious, you can show it by picking one or two of your best ideas and deciding to implement them in a practical way. Be realistic. If you want to help the underprivileged, you are probably not going to spend an afternoon each week doing so, even though this could be tempting right now. Instead, pick a more realistic goal and try to achieve it over a period of time. Even an hour or two a month is far better than doing nothing except talking about what you might like to do.

JUNE

1. SATURDAY. Enjoyable. Life is likely to seem strange and even funny. You will probably see the humor in most things. If your closest relationship has been too intense and serious lately, adopting a lighter attitude could really help. Step back and look at whatever situation is troubling you. You will probably find that it is nothing special and not all that important. Viewed from even a short distance, it is apt to strike you as a scene from a comedy. There is no need to make things out to be hard or serious. If you can laugh at all the amusing situations in your life, it will be a tremendous aid to your mental health because you will be able to put a lot of your supposedly heavy problems behind you.

2. SUNDAY. Active. You have a taste for life's stronger flavors today. Take this literally and venture out into the world of food. Try an entire meal from a cuisine you do not normally sample. If you can make it a romantic expedition, so much the better. Whisk your mate or partner off to some quiet, out-of-the-way place. Turn the occasion into something exotic and a bit wild. Do not bother trying to catch up with friends today. Leave the answering machine on and have some romantic time in total privacy. The whole point is to free yourself from the shackles of the routine and the everyday. If you can do this even for a short time, the world will seem larger and more exciting.

3. MONDAY. Promising. If you have been having any difficulties at home, they could go into reverse today. These will not necessarily involve the house as real estate or even your family. However, that which is most private and important to you is likely to experience a powerful surge of energy. You will experience the world most serenely if you view it from a quiet, safe setting. Think of this as the lion's lair, where you go when you are tired after the exertion of the hunt. Relationships may seem somewhat odd and strained. If you have left any ground uncovered, you need to deal with it now. Otherwise, in the weeks to come you will have to apologize and explain over and over again.

4. TUESDAY. Variable. You may discover some serious philosophical differences with friends. If you find yourself in a discussion about religion or politics, you may encounter some major disagreements which, if you are not careful, can escalate into a quarrel. Realize that these differences run deep and are also subjective. It is extremely important to keep in mind that the other person is just as likely to be as right as you given their twist of the issues. You will not sort anything out by arguing. There is also the risk that you are in the mood for a fight, and such a subject only serves as a pretense. It is wise to avoid this temptation if you can. Your mood will pass, but hurt feelings may not go away so easily.

5. WEDNESDAY. Easy. Overall the day should proceed smoothly. If you are involved with education in any way, you should find yourself particularly successful. The situation is favorable for some advancement. Leo teachers could come to realize how much students care. Leo students may discover some good fortune coming from a class situation. You may receive a higher than expected grade on a paper or a test. Do not become too preoccupied with turning your studies to some great career advantage at the moment. You are likely to benefit more in a quiet, unobtrusive way than through some major change in status. Opening your mind to new possibilities should be enough for your purposes.

6. THURSDAY. Good. You can advance your standing as an authority. This is especially likely in religion, philosophy, or politics. In fact, some totally unexpected circumstances may benefit you in a surprising way. Possibly some work that you have almost forgotten about will catch the eye of someone who can help you advance up the career ladder. This person may even want to enlist your help on a project. Watch out that you are not so taken by these events that you neglect matters of the heart. A mate or partner who is not a part of your work scene could feel left out. Do not let your love life sink totally into the background of all that is occupying your days and nights.

7. FRIDAY. Demanding. How well you succeed in your job will largely depend on two things. The first involves the amount of drive and initiative you put into it. Do not place too much emphasis on making sure the right people see what you do. Substance is more important than appearance. The second factor has to do with your ideals. If you violate these or think you can set them aside for the sake of personal interest, you will be seriously mistaken. Any belief of this kind could trip you up. Even if you feel under tremendous pressure to bend to the demands of necessity, be sure to maintain your integrity. Moral compromise is very hazardous at the moment. Accept some delays or setbacks if you must, but do not give in or give up.

8. SATURDAY. Satisfactory. Over the past few weeks you may have had a sense that things are not working out well. Machinery may have been a bit quirky. You may have tried to contact friends but succeeded in doing nothing more than exchanging messages on each other's answering machine. These problems have not been major, but they have been big enough to create some irritation. You can expect this situation to lighten now. Any contract negotiations or business deals that have been delayed will also begin to move forward again. Do not blame yourself for any of these problems; they were not your fault or anyone else's. Just put them behind you and move on.

9. SUNDAY. Frustrating. This is not the most opportune day for a social gathering. If you are planning to host one, expect preparations to take extra time. Some people you particularly want to see may not show up. Shopping and short trips could also take extra time, or you might simply find that you are not in the mood. A wait in the supermarket line may not be any longer than usual today, but it may seem longer. Accept these inconveniences as best you can and do not become overly impatient. Nor should you become too impatient with yourself because of your negative reactions. You are only human, so forgive yourself for any momentary bad mood.

10. MONDAY. Challenging. You may encounter some difficulty getting together for a professional meeting. Or you could become more involved in the politics of a group than you ever intended to be. If you let yourself get drawn into taking sides, you can expect some major frustrations. Avoid being made to feel guilty or in any way responsible for the actions of someone else, even a loved one. There is always the possibility of taking the high ground and trying to play the role of mediator. This could be a good idea in the long run, but today it is apt to backfire as you find yourself targeted as a common enemy by all the quarreling parties. Unless you want to unify everybody against you, this is not a good approach to take. A wait-and-see attitude will work out best.

11. TUESDAY. Pleasant. Any difficulties you have been having in dealing with your friends and acquaintances should lighten up today. If you have been worrying about how to deal with a particular person, some unexpected insight is apt to come to your rescue as you suddenly hit upon the perfect way of dealing with the issue. Or you could discover that your understanding of the situation was completely wrong and that the problem is something entirely different from what you thought. Once you see it clearly, it can easily be resolved. If you need to make a few phone calls to clear things up, do so early in the day. Communication will work in your favor, calming jangled nerves and hurt feelings.

12. WEDNESDAY. Stressful. Attention has to be given to someone else's health. A friend or family member may need professional medical attention, requiring that you spend time at a hospital emergency room or a doctor's office. Plan for some interruption of this kind, which could take a sizable part of the day. If you do not try to schedule this and instead try to accomplish everything as usual, you could end up very fatigued. Do not strive to do more than is humanly possible. Nor should you become frustrated or irritated because circumstances get in the way of making progress. This may not be pleasant, but it is an unavoidable part of life so try to accept it with as much grace as possible.

13. THURSDAY. Rosy. Wonderful opportunity is likely to arise out of the blue from a person or direction where you least expect it. It could come as a consequence of a duty that you performed earlier in the year and possibly even begrudged. If so, you will be very glad now that you performed this act of kindness. You may also find that someone all along has been helping you secretly, even though you only discovered it now. You are sure to feel a tremendous sense of relief from this good fortune. Do not worry too much about how to make the best use of it; that decision will come in its own time. You have a great deal to be happy about right now, so take some time to thank your lucky stars.

14. FRIDAY. Deceptive. A message that you receive early in the day may make it harder to understand your romantic partner. You may have thought you had this person all figured out, only to learn that some important information had been omitted. If you allow this new knowledge to make you suspicious, you will probably be defeating your own purposes. Instead, accept this knowledge as a part of basic reality and deal with it accordingly. You will probably have a sense that a blindfold has been lifted from your eyes, but do not jump to any conclusions. You still do not have as much of the picture as you really need. Adopt a hands-off attitude as you await further developments, which will soon become apparent.

15. SATURDAY. Favorable. You can move forward more easily in getting your way. You are coming across to friends and strangers alike as dynamic and forceful. People will respect you and take your word on important matters. There is a question of how useful this role is for your current purposes. If it causes you to put on a false front just to satisfy what someone else is expecting of you, step back and decide what you really want out of the situation. Do not confuse your true purposes with what you think other people want from you; you could get trapped in a hall of mirrors that way. If you can stick to your own purpose as much as possible regardless of the demands of the outside world, you should succeed handsomely.

16. SUNDAY. Confusing. It will probably be hard to get your bearings today. You, and everyone around you, are likely to feel that you are sliding down a slippery slope. Mutual misunderstanding is bound to occur. There could be a sudden shock from your spouse or partner early this morning that creates a lingering note of discomfort throughout the day. By the afternoon, communications with friends become important, although there is a danger that you will misread the other person. Even if you have high-minded ideals and motives, guard against being sidetracked by any form of intrigue. Even trickery is not out of the question. All of this is likely to make you want to give up in disgust and not bother with other people, but you will feel differently quite soon.

17. MONDAY. Fair. If you are concerned about getting ahead at work, be assured that you have friends in high places. You may not yet be aware of them, so at present it takes some faith on your part to know they are there. This is true even if you receive a reprimand from an associate that leads you to begin to doubt yourself. You need to recognize that this person does not have final authority and may even be working against you. Trust your own good instincts; your faith will not be misguided. Do not stoop to the same level of backbiting and arguing as those who are causing you some difficulty. You can rise above the situation and come through this difficult period with flying colors.

18. TUESDAY. Variable. Early in the day you may have to deal with some financial matters that you have been pushing aside. If they come up, face them; if not, do not go looking for them. This is not an ideal time for making financial moves or any major decisions. Later in the day the situation will seem to clear up a little. You may want to make a short jaunt to run necessary errands, which should be easy to do and even enjoyable. If you like to shop, this is a good time to stroll around and look at summer specials for the sheer pleasure of it. You do not have to buy anything. Just consider the outing a form of recreation. If you do make a purchase, be sure to save the receipt.

19. WEDNESDAY. Mixed. You could be reminded today how devoted you are to your mate or partner. You may want to express this by making some selfless gesture so that there is no doubt how you feel right now. You could also find it helpful to spend some time with youngsters. If you have children of your own, be an example they can look up to. Whatever the situation, realize that you have an almost magical power over them and need to exercise it wisely. Your relationship with younger family members may seem to have more to do with control than with joyful spontaneity. This is a necessary, unavoidable phase, but do not lose sight of the pleasure you take in their accomplishments.

20. THURSDAY. Lucky. Circumstances are on your side when it comes to money matters. You have a lot going for you at present. You should receive some good news concerning investments or property. Or you could look over some financial statements and realize that they have increased in value much more than you thought. If you are thinking about making a new investment, this is a good time to do so. Although your intuition is right on target, you still need to hedge your bets; you are investing, not betting at a racetrack. If you exercise ordinary care you should have reason to be very satisfied with the way your money grows. You could be starting to accumulate a nice little nest egg that will make the future even brighter for you.

21. FRIDAY. Buoyant. Your Leo dynamism is likely to surface. Throw yourself into a special project and it will bear fruit. Your challenge is to balance two somewhat different requirements. You have to put forth a lot of drive and initiative. However, you also have to emphasize the good-natured, genial aspect of your nature in order to enlist the support of other people. Do not overlook the aid you can receive from those at home. Those who are related to you see you as one of their tribe and feel that your best interests are tied to their own. For this reason they could be willing to do a lot for you. Just make sure your own feelings and actions are as helpful. Go out of your way to take part in an activity with a youngster or a group of children.

22. SATURDAY. Unsettling. There is a greater chance than usual of a domestic dispute that involves you and your spouse or partner. If there have been some tensions with parents or in-laws, they could come between you, making your home environment not as peaceful as you would wish. You may be tempted to run away from the whole situation. However, even if you do you could come back and find that nothing has changed. A high degree of patience may be needed on your part. You can trust the goodwill of friends, but take care not to take them for granted. Even among family members, goodwill and trust are not renewable resources if they are used up in a madcap fashion.

23. SUNDAY. Happy. Thanks to your fun-loving mood today you could want to take a trip to the beach or to a park. If you can gain the cooperation of your mate or partner, all should be well. However, there is a possibility of some hindrances. The chief one may involve spirituality or religion, perhaps something as simple as one of you wanting to go out and enjoy life while the other feels the urge to attend a religious service. Do not let this turn into some sort of emotional battle. Instead, compromise even if it means going your separate ways for the day. Do not try to force another person to have your sort of fun or to take part in your sort of worship. Live and let live is a good motto to keep in mind throughout the week ahead.

24. MONDAY. Manageable. You are likely to feel some connection with a higher dimension of reality. How well you cope will depend on your comfort with a world that you can only imagine. It is likely that some force is trying to convey a message to you, especially if you have never shown much interest in the mystical side of nature. This message probably will have some bearing on your relationships with other people. You may feel a particularly strong connection with your mate or partner at some point in the day. If you have never thought about why the two of you were brought together, you have a chance of unraveling that mystery today. Keep your schedule free and clear in anticipation of a special invitation tonight.

25. TUESDAY. Quiet. Take advantage of today's lull to rest and to recoup your strength. You do not need to play hooky or flee from your duties. Instead you can pursue them quietly and effectively, with a minimal amount of tension. If disruptive forces are usually in evidence at your workplace, they should be absent today. Use this time to focus on the way you work. If you tend to scatter your attention or are distracted as a rule, this is an excellent time to try to focus your efforts a little more. Do just one task at a time, giving it your full attention. If anything, you will be more productive than usual, and without the headache or cramps that occasionally plague you.

26. WEDNESDAY. Disconcerting. The workaday world may seem to be a nuisance because you just do not want to turn your attention to required tasks. There could be a strong pull toward daydreaming or idling. Do not try to force yourself too much. There is a reason that you are going through this downtime and it probably has to do with the fact that you often charge ahead without first thinking things through. As a result a small part of you may not want to go along with the program, and it is making its presence felt now. Do not blame yourself. Listen to your inner voice. It may be pointing your attention toward some important fact you have overlooked or have never stopped to consider. Turn down an evening invitation.

27. THURSDAY. Sensitive. An atmosphere of the mystical or spiritual is in the air. It will not be menacing or disruptive but instead should add a dreamy charm to the entire day. You may start to think about the world as it could be rather than as it is. You may envision your world as a delightful bubble that you do not want to burst by coming down to reality. There is nothing wrong with this mood, although of course you do not want to make enormous changes in your life while under its influence. Changes will have to be decided in the cold, hard light of day. At any rate, major disruptions may not be necessary. For now, allow yourself to dream of what could be in the best of all possible worlds.

28. FRIDAY. Intense. Romance could strike a strange but deep note. This is one of those days when you may see the proverbial stranger from across a crowded room, who will arouse emotions in you that are likely to be intense. You could suddenly feel the urge to throw away your life as it now exists and run off with your new love to live together happily ever after. Whether this is a good idea remains to be seen. No matter how intense the emotion, when it comes to expressing it you may find yourself slightly tongue-tied. Or the sheer attempt to express what you are feeling may suddenly cause it all to vanish. Be aware of the real difference in love between current intensity and lifelong duration. You can enjoy both stages but almost never simultaneously.

29. SATURDAY. Happy. Any difficulty or hesitancy you had in expressing romantic feelings yesterday is likely to vanish today. If you just met someone new and did not know what to say, a phone call or a message could put everything right. This is a good day to ask a new acquaintance for a date or to go on a group outing. Even if this person did not seem interested in you before, a sudden change of heart is likely. You will discover through your own interaction how far this relationship could go. If you are ever going to be able to talk on a heart-to-heart basis, it will probably happen now. Do not be so preoccupied with the possible outcome that you take no pleasure in the current period.

30. SUNDAY. Frustrating. You may have to keep explaining yourself over and over again to someone who is close to you. You could become confused and frustrated by various messages that seem to be coming through. Friends may try to help but only end up complicating matters further. Probably one of you is talking on an emotional level while the other is trying to be totally rational. This happens all the time in human contacts, and it explains much of the misunderstanding of daily life. Usually it is possible to muddle through without a clear understanding. Today, though, it may be harder than usual. Try to deal with whatever is going on by seeing where the other person is coming from and using that as a basis for reaching out.

JULY

1. MONDAY. Tricky. Passions are apt to come to the surface, but friends may seem to stand in the way of your desires. You are not likely to have much patience with anyone who opposes you. Very possibly their judgments are either unfair or misinformed. You have the ability to convince anyone of your point of view, at least for a little while. You may offer a mild bribe in order to get your way if that should be necessary. At any rate the best stratagem for attaining your ends is to alternate between a hard line and a more tolerant attitude. If you are convinced that you are right, you can make your case most persuasively. Avoid being too dreamy or muted in your response, and resist the temptation to play the role of martyr.

2. TUESDAY. Demanding. If you have been involved in any philanthropic or charitable pursuits, you could now face some obstacles. Taking part may have seemed like a chore for some time, and you may even be asking yourself why you bother. Such concerns come to a head today. If you have complaints or any difficulties with what is going on, now is the time to make them known. However, do not expect an entirely sympathetic response. In fact, a certain person or persons may view you as an enemy or rival, but that should not matter. Stand up for what you believe is right. Do not allow yourself to be outmaneuvered. You will probably receive some strong and extremely helpful support from your mate or partner.

3. WEDNESDAY. Challenging. Behind-the-scenes intrigue is coming to a head. You may have the impression that you are being judged behind your back, as if a secret trial is going on to decide your fate but you have not been informed about it. A great deal hangs in the balance. Do not attempt to interfere; you will not now be able to get to the bottom of things. Instead, sit back and allow the process to unfold at its natural pace. Trust that your own integrity will win out in the end. In romance, single Leos could be heading toward a commitment. Obstacles in the path of greater intimacy will fade, even working in your favor. Be bold and forthright in discussing your hopes and dreams. You do not need to hold back.

4. THURSDAY. Good. If offered a sudden trip to some faraway place, by all means take it. Or you could win a travel vacation. Either will give you a means of expanding your horizons. If you just find yourself suddenly bitten by the travel bug, this is a good time for planning a vacation trip or for taking one. Allow yourself to experience a little more of the world. If you sense that you have been hiding out in a little corner of the universe, it is now time to emerge. Your mate or partner is likely to be a willing and eager companion. At the very least take a drive to a favorite spot. You should not experience too much traffic or any trouble with your transportation.

5. FRIDAY. Fair. Your romantic partner may not quite understand or accept your desire to be in the limelight. Your need for public attention may confound people who are close to you. If you have been somehow dishonest about your intentions, that could be all too clear now. Your motives and drives may not be so clear, however. You have the opportunity to set things right, but only if you decide once and for all to be completely honest. You may also need to consider whether a certain ongoing relationship is right for you. It may be doubtful right now; you have the opportunity to decide, as does the other person. Do not automatically assume that you are in complete control where romance is concerned or that what you think is conveyed without saying it out loud.

6. SATURDAY. Satisfactory. You could receive some good news that has to do with romance or another relationship. If you had some serious doubts about the feelings between you, a message from your mate, partner, or friend could bring some welcome relief. You may not have been communicating well recently, maybe not even speaking. If so, this is the right time to pick up the phone and break the ice. Forget about who is right and wrong. Such questions only confuse the issue, which you will probably never get sorted out to everyone's complete satisfaction. Once you cut through the red tape of complicated feelings, something new and beautiful can begin to blossom.

7. SUNDAY. Placid. Today's peaceful, somewhat spiritual atmosphere may find you concerned with discovering more about life and love. This is a good day to devote at least a little attention to spirituality. A religious service could prove very uplifting. If you are interested in mysticism or the occult, you might want to look into these areas. Do not be too concerned about being taken in by mystical nonsense. Just be sure to keep your feet on the ground and not to lose touch with your good Leo common sense. Remember that the die-hard skeptic is also somewhat of a true believer. Investigate your interests without being bound by your own preconceptions or anyone else's.

8. MONDAY. Changeable. This will be a quirky day when it comes to your dealings with other people. There is likely to be some obstruction from an acquaintance or a colleague. This could lead you into an intense power play that may even arouse basic philosophical differences. Open conflict is not a good idea at this point because it will be too costly and disruptive for both of you. Instead, try using your Leo charm and charisma. A touch of originality will also help. Your sense of humor could prove to be your salvation. Even if you cannot reach a real agreement, you can at least get to the point of laughing about your mutual differences. Accept that no one is quite like you.

9. TUESDAY. Disconcerting. Your love life may be highly charged. You could attempt to plunge forward with a relationship, only to find to your surprise that your advances are not completely welcome. This is part of a long-term struggle between you and the object of your desire and affection. On the surface it could look like a power struggle, but this is only the most superficial view of the situation. In fact, the two of you are probably both seeking the same thing but just not sure if the other person can supply it in a way that feels safe. Much depends on how you handle the situation today. If it becomes too explosive, as it has been for some time, you may simply have to let the whole relationship fade into the background for a while.

10. WEDNESDAY. Lucky. The situation brightens considerably today. You now have the opportunity to give yourself some real comfort and assurance. There might be some question about whether another person figures in the equation. In the end you are the only one you can forever count on. Love and reassurance are necessary; so are relationships with people. However, if other people are not around, or if they are not giving you what you need, it is your responsibility to provide it for yourself. Now is a good time to remind yourself of your special strengths and abilities. You could find that the best thing for yourself right now is to enjoy being alone but definitely not lonely.

11. THURSDAY. Successful. The pace of life is likely to speed up. You may find yourself in the position of a stagehand at a theater, hurrying madly behind the scenes to make sure the show goes on. This can be fun if you allow it to be. However, if you try to occupy center stage yourself, you are likely to be booed lustily. Stand aside and allow other people to have their moment in the limelight and the situation could proceed very smoothly. You may even want to watch the whole panorama from a distance. You may also have to deal in some way with household matters, especially structural problems. You may need to call a plumber or a general contractor if you are not experienced in handling the problem.

12. FRIDAY. Rewarding. You will probably want to put yourself in the public eye. This is a good time for taking a leadership role. Enlist support to get the help you need for achieving your goals in life. You have the chance to establish yourself as an authority among your circle of friends. There is a likelihood that close friends may not quite grasp what you are trying to do. If you want to branch out in a new area of business, be straight with them about your needs and goals. Otherwise friends and family members could fail to understand your motives and you could be the recipient of some hostility. You have the drive at this point to get your message across. Do not handicap yourself by sending out unclear or conflicting messages.

13. SATURDAY. Easygoing. You will be at your best if you set aside your usual Saturday routine and do something novel. You may choose to engage in some new form of exercise, preferably something fairly easy and nonstrenuous. There is a slight possibility of an accident, so observe all safety precautions if you are taking part in a sport that entails physical risks. If you want to shine in the romantic sphere, find some activity that takes you out into the public arena. The best place to meet someone would be at a professional conference or gathering. Even if this does not seem like the ideal way to spend your weekend, you can make it seem recreational by setting aside business matters and just socializing. Be alert for the obvious or it may escape your attention.

14. SUNDAY. Mixed. Take some time to go over financial and property matters. You will function best by staying at home. Spend some time doing repairs around the house. You will enjoy the opportunity to work by yourself, especially if your social life has seemed like a merry-go-round lately. You are not likely to enjoy anything having to do with parties, socializing, or games. Also stay away from games of chance. Even refuse an invitation that you know is quite special. It will help tremendously to root yourself in simple, solid tasks that you have been putting off for some time. Tackling them can give you a new lease on life as you get to use skills that rarely come into play in your day-to-day affairs.

15. MONDAY. Productive. You are likely to have a burst of energy. Look through your investment portfolio and you may discover some new ways of enhancing your retirement funds. This may not involve radical new ventures; in fact, it probably will not. However, if you think of a way to restructure your resources, you have the opportunity to make quite a lot of money. It may be something as simple as cutting your losses on a poor investment and putting the money into a financial sector that has been paying off much better. Do some research. Also consider the possibility of an investment in real estate if it fits in with your overall financial goals. You could find some real opportunities buying, fixing up, and reselling rundown properties.

16. TUESDAY. Active. The accent is on mental activity. You will find that your thinking processes are exceptionally sharp. As a result you may discover the answers to some problems that have been hard to solve. The difficulty may have been that you were trying to think things through in too much detail. At this point solutions may come as much from your good Leo intuition as from calculation. Sudden insight is likely, which may even leave you somewhat stunned, wondering where it came from. The answer is quite simple: it came from depths of your mind that you have not even begun to explore. Your discoveries today suggest that what has come about accidentally could be developed by sustained, conscious work.

17. WEDNESDAY. Exciting. You are likely to be running around from one place to another. You could get halfway through a task when another job demands your immediate attention. Actually you have the resources to get it all done right now. If you feel your energy start to fade, slow down and focus on one thing at a time. There will probably be some pressure to speed up, but you will accomplish the most if you work slowly and steadily. Make sure to do things your own way. It is not a good idea to work according to someone else's idea of how it should be handled. As a matter of fact, you may need to discard some of your own work habits and invent new ones if you are to function most effectively.

18. THURSDAY. Deceptive. You will probably derive the most satisfaction from being in your home. There are likely to be some intense emotions among family members. You may plunge passionately and completely into your family, almost as if you were diving into a pool. Even if your interest does not reach this high a pitch, make the effort to spend extra time with your loved ones. You might enjoy a game together or some kind of common art project. Make sure that your spouse does not feel left out. If your mate misunderstands your motives and tries to interfere, the two of you could become adversaries. However, you both want your family to be unified and content, so keep the lines of communication wide open.

19. FRIDAY. Buoyant. This is one of those days where you feel that everything, or almost everything, is working in your favor. And this will probably be an accurate perception. Strong emotional intensity is in the air. Feelings will seem to run deeper than usual and have more of a life of their own. Although there is the risk of some disruption as a result, the overall mood will be positive. At one point you will probably be brimming with love and gratitude for all the blessings you receive in your life. When this happens, pay attention and act accordingly. This impression is apt to be even more profound than you could ever imagine. Share your feelings with that special person in your life.

20. SATURDAY. Rosy. A tremendous amount is going on just beneath the surface right now. Under most circumstances you are an outgoing Leo. Whatever you feel or believe, other people are going to hear about it. That is why the present situation could leave you feeling at a loss. You have some very positive forces working in your favor but they may be hard to identify. You may observe them only out of the corner of your eye, and when you turn in that direction they disappear. Try not to be concerned; you do not have to personally witness everything that happens.

There are some things that work better sight unseen, so let go of trying to make everything happen based on your willing it to occur.

21. SUNDAY. Useful. You are likely to receive some clarification of a mystery that you have been experiencing for some time. Some communication has been going on behind your back, that much you know. If this inclines you to be suspicious or paranoid, you are mistaken. Soon you will learn that these background activities have been working in your favor. Even if helping you was not the primary intention, you will find that you have been given a tremendous lift. If your friends are working in your best interests they will succeed. If you have adversaries who are working against you, their efforts will misfire to your long-term advantage.

22. MONDAY. Calm. On this placid, uneventful day you can focus on the nitty-gritty details of your job. Although this may make you somewhat impatient, you will function best if you do not paint on a large canvas today. Instead, take some time to fill in important holes that have been neglected until now. Once these are handled to your satisfaction, devote some attention to your health. You should be feeling as well as possible. You do not need to become compulsive about diet and exercise, but you might want to devote a little more attention to these areas. If a doctor has suggested that you give up a particular food or has told you to get more exercise, today is as good a day as any to start following the advice.

23. TUESDAY. Enjoyable. If you have been somewhat reclusive lately, today you may want to turn back into your usual outgoing self. It is a good occasion for social activity. Consider doing some work on your image and appearance. You could take pleasure in enhancing your looks by having your hair cut, restyled, or colored. It is also the right day to add a few new stylish items to your wardrobe. Your taste is likely to be at its best, do not hesitate about your choices. Even if your preferences tend toward the flamboyant, you are likely to hit just the right note at present. There is no need to follow fashion trends; just be yourself.

24. WEDNESDAY. Difficult. This is a difficult day for romance and for all of your relationships. It would be best not to get together with someone you want to impress. If you just met an interesting person and are wondering whether to call, you may find it best to wait until early next week. If you have a mate or partner, be aware of the push and pull of personal dynamics right now. This could come to play in matters of fun and recreation. Either you may completely disagree about what to do, or the activity may turn into a very heated competition between you. If you take part in a sport or game, you could find that the urge to win is compelling. However, do nothing that might make spectators question your basic integrity.

25. THURSDAY. Tricky. You may be overconcerned with your image. Although you want to come across at your best for personal or professional reasons, expect to face some obstacles. The chief one involves being too loud and coming on too strong. It could be as simple a matter as having too loud a voice or standing too close to someone when talking. You may be comfortable with this kind of intensity, but the other person may pull back. Especially today, you may contact someone who gets upset by this kind of gesture, so tone down the impression you are trying to make. It may be hard to be low-key, but if you can be more restrained than usual you will do your overall image a world of good.

26. FRIDAY. Demanding. You may not like the idea of compromise or of putting someone else first, but today you are probably going to have no choice. Your mate, partner, or associate may make a demand that you cannot agree to. The two of you may find it extremely hard even to understand each other. Some of this is genuine confusion, but at least part comes from a stubborn unwillingness to listen with an open mind. Once you realize this, you will grasp the situation all too well. Then you will be faced with the question of whether you want to agree. Unless the matter involves some real compromise to your integrity, you probably should give in without much of a fight.

27. SATURDAY. Unsettling. Expect a quiet but distinct unease today. You may find children, in particular, harder to deal with than usual. You could be left with the suspicion that they are not as innocent as they seem and that they are cunningly trying to exploit you. There is probably some truth to this idea. You already know that children have many strategies for getting their way, so there is no real reason to get upset about it. They may try to make you feel that you are not a good person unless you give them what they want, which is nonsense. Do not let yourself be manipulated. Do your best to decide what is really best for them, then stick to your decision despite pleas or threats.

28. SUNDAY. Disconcerting. Your biggest job at present is to keep your sense of humor at all costs. There will be some challenges to overcome today. For example, you may have an overwhelming passion to break free of the constraints of your home life. The place you live in may not feel like a pleasant setting. You could sense that love is there but is somehow inaccessible or not the kind of love you want. You might even feel that you have never received the affection you wanted at home, which may be true in part. However, you are probably painting too dark a picture. Be aware that much of the gloom you are experiencing at present is exaggerated and will soon pass.

29. MONDAY. Rewarding. You will have at least one conversation today that is deeper than usual. It may come totally out of the blue, perhaps while you are walking in a building and encounter someone you met a long time ago. You may have a talk with this person that includes an idea that moves you profoundly. It may be only casual remarks, and the other person may not be aware of what you are experiencing. Still the message will strike home and should be both heartening and encouraging. You are likely to discover that you are on the right track in a major area of your life, and this could be confirmed by an important stroke of luck.

30. TUESDAY. Inspiring. This is a time for expansion, for building on the foundations you have been laying. The best way to do this is by continuing to pursue your education. You do not need to sign up for a course or think about going for a degree, although you could do so. Anything that uplifts and informs you will be both inspiring and productive. If you have been wondering about what to do in your profession, for example, broadening your outlook could supply the answer. This is not merely a matter of technical training. In fact, you are most likely to receive the kind of boost you need by looking into a field you currently know very little about. A book on a subject different from the ones you usually follow will supply you with vital knowledge.

31. WEDNESDAY. Positive. Bright trends continue, although not as strongly as yesterday. You may find that your thirst for learning is not quite as acute as it was. You could still want to expand your horizons but start to worry that doing so will be too hard or that you are too set in your ways. Ultimately it is a matter of time and energy. Sometimes a very small push in the direction you want to move could provide all the impetus you need. Be wary of the danger of getting into ruts and habits. While they are useful, they can also be deadly. You will only stay healthy and vibrant if you retain your flexibility and versatility. If you make an attempt to break loose, it will be handsomely rewarded.

AUGUST

1. THURSDAY. Misleading. Your natural outgoing Leo personality is being boosted. Over the course of the next year you will advance greatly in your ability to master the world around you. You will also be putting yourself forward as a more dynamic, creative individual. This is a long-term trend. While you will start to see its effects right away, do not take them as a cue to barrel ahead with all of your plans. You may experience some frustration in achieving your career goals in the short term. Carefully choose where to put your energy. Do not come on too strong and attempt to ride roughshod over your colleagues. Your basically good intentions may not be recognized. Quarrels are a distinct possibility if you insist on having your way all the time.

2. FRIDAY. Bumpy. Romance could take a rocky course. There is a strong focus on sheer practicalities. You and your mate or partner may not be able to agree on a time or place to meet. However, if you can rise above petty difficulties, they should pass quickly. It is also possible that minor upsets are symptoms of underlying disagreement between you. Together you should think carefully about how these differences have surfaced in the past. Also consider how basically compatible you really are. If you get along quite well and are generally content, there will be no problem. On the other hand, if your differences outweigh the similarities, you will have to face the facts and consider changing the relationship.

3. SATURDAY. Helpful. The problems and difficulties of the past few days should vanish. You can expect a brighter, sunnier atmosphere. Your willingness to work at communicating with another person is likely to bear fruit. You could discover that someone you thought was your enemy is actually sympathetic to you, which is likely to take a tremendous load off your mind. You could even be in a mood for celebration. It would be good to give yourself a small treat or present, even something as simple as an ice-cream cone. Consider it a reward for work that was well done despite opposition or your own qualms.

4. SUNDAY. Demanding. Computers and other electronics could behave oddly. If there is any defect in a home appliance or machine, it may make its presence known. Do not blame your spouse or partner for such problems. It is likely that it would have happened no matter what anyone did or did not do. Avoid trying to solve your problems all at once; you will not be able to do so. For starters, take some steps to simplify your life. If you have to deal with routine matters, take them one step at a time. You could obtain some relief by spending time outdoors with friends. Going for a hike or a trip to the beach with people you like to be around can put current worries in proper perspective.

5. MONDAY. Variable. Standing up for your own integrity is the key to improving your self-esteem. It is also the best way to win the regard of people around you. It does not matter if this makes you seem like an eccentric or a loner. If you want to prime yourself for leadership, you have to take this risk. Do not be surprised if other people follow you on what may look at first like a lonely course. You may want to strike out in a completely new direction in regard to your workplace. You could discover that your best allies are people you have not paid much attention to in the recent past. Networking is a good idea at this point. Circulate and you will make some new contacts who may eventually prove valuable.

6. TUESDAY. Intense. You are be going through some inner turmoil that is not necessarily reflected in your appearance or attitude. In fact, you could seem somewhat withdrawn and quiet while inside a battle rages. This should eventually work out in your favor. You may be experiencing some tension between your desire to have fun and the call of solid, practical duties. Now you have the chance to bring the two together. If you are not enjoying what you are doing, change course now. However, do this only if you are going to move toward what you truly love. While some upheaval may result, in the end it will work to your advantage. Ironically, you will find that moving toward more creativity and play is the most solid and practical thing you can do.

7. WEDNESDAY. Starred. This is the right time to talk about your romantic feelings. You can speak effectively and even eloquently about what you are experiencing. There could be some ambivalence about an ongoing partnership. On the whole, however, today could be a turning point in your life that is likely to be for the better. Your true Leo nature is making itself clear. You have some special inner power working to your advantage right now. If there is ever to be a time when you can make your wants and desires known in the world around you, it is now. Do not waste one minute of this opportunity. If there is something that you have always wanted, now is the time to go for it.

8. THURSDAY. Promising. You are likely to get a very favorable response from a person you are interested in romantically. What you make of it will, of course, be up to you, but the moment is right for a relationship to develop and grow. If you are already involved in a relationship, you have the power now to take it to new heights. The only current danger is that you will feel overly cheerful and comfortable and thus fail to take advantage of a major new opportunity. If there is someone you want to get to know better, take steps to do so now. The situation could hardly be more favorable. Although this is not a guarantee of success, it means that if you are going to succeed at any time it will probably be right now.

9. FRIDAY. Fair. This is a day of minor successes and upsets. You have the chance to expand your authority and prestige in any group you are already connected with. Relationships, however, will be tricky. If you quarrel with your mate or partner, the two of you are likely to consider it a matter of principle. This is a tempting but ultimately defeating strategy. There are no principles at stake. One or both of you should realize that it is only a question of two well-meaning people who are trying their best to get along in the intricate world of human feelings. If you really understand this, you will be able to overlook many little problems and upsets as you focus on the overall picture.

10. SATURDAY. Stormy. This is likely to be a day of upsets due to stormy tempers. If you feel you must have your way no matter what, you are almost certain to find yourself in a battle of wills. You could interpret even the slightest resistance to you as a major affront. On the other hand, you may encounter someone who feels that way. This is not a time for fighting it out because the situation could become far more tense than anybody ever expected. Conflict can always be avoided, even if you simply have to leave until your temper cools down. Do whatever you must to avoid the danger of coming to blows. You know yourself well enough to understand what you have to do, and you have the self-control to do it.

11. SUNDAY. Manageable. Early in the day you could find that taking care of some practical matter around your property is harder than you expected. You may have figured on spending five minutes on a small repair only to find it takes an hour or two. Or you could be going through a bank statement or your checkbook and encounter a discrepancy that you need to puzzle through. Later in the day the situation should improve. You will probably want to get out of the house this evening, even if it is just for a short walk or drive. You might enjoy doing some shopping or just taking some time to chat with neighbors. Getting some physical exercise would be ideal. It could even be quite strenuous if your health and current condition permit it.

12. MONDAY. Good. Find time to catch up on phone messages and correspondence. If you are in the mood to write a love letter, this is the perfect day to pour out your feelings. Put a little extra into making a letter as appealing as you can, either in the writing style or by including graphics. You do not need any elaborate designs; just pay a little extra attention to beauty in whatever you do. Touches like these might seem an unnecessary frill, but they are not. As a Leo you have a need for beauty, just as you need food, water, and air. If you have been somewhat starved for such things, make sure to get your fill of them now. Do not stay up very late tonight.

13. TUESDAY. Enjoyable. Do whatever you can to enhance your physical appearance. It is a good day for a haircut or a beauty treatment. You may also treat yourself to some new clothes, especially at an end-of-summer sale. It might also be helpful to give yourself some solid exercise or to get a massage. These can be the best and healthiest ways of making yourself look better. Consider joining a gym or health club. You could also spend some time socializing with friends or enjoying the company of your mate or partner. A get-together could be either low-key or quite lively, depending on your tastes. Going out dancing might be fun. You will probably have the best time if there are a lot of people around, plus lights and music to stimulate all of your senses.

14. WEDNESDAY. Disconcerting. Family relations are apt to be somewhat difficult. Probably you can all agree on fairly practical matters like money and property. Differences may arise, however, about how you treat one another as opposed to your relations with friends. Someone could complain that you behave better with people outside the family than you do with those who are closest to you. This could be a thoughtless accusation, at least look to see if there is any truth to it. If you are ignoring your loved ones, it could be that you have felt somehow slighted or hurt by them in the past. Do not try to ignore such feelings if they exist. You have to acknowledge them and then see the best way to get back on good terms.

15. THURSDAY. Mixed. If you are not totally satisfied with the house you are living in, problems could come to a head now. You may be exasperated by some small inconveniences that can be easily dealt with. Or you could discover that the place really does not suit you. Examine the situation carefully to see if it is just a temporary annoyance or a real dissatisfaction that might make you move. You do not have to feel stuck with a place just because you are living there right now. It is always possible to move. Of course, if you own you will have to consider the pros and cons of selling. Leo renters should find it easier to relocate. Either way, though, it is a major step. Trust your good intuition.

16. FRIDAY. Excellent. You could find yourself in a party mood. If you are planning to entertain or to go out to a social event, you can count on having a good time. You will probably come across as the life of the party. The pleasures of socializing and romance should fit together very nicely. Love is apt to have an intense and highly spiritual note. You could find that you have a deep connection to your love interest, whether this person is your mate or partner of many years or someone you just met recently. Love is likely to seem alluring and more than a touch intoxicating. Allow yourself to enjoy the delight and mystery, but keep your feet planted firmly on the ground. This is not the time to make a commitment.

17. SATURDAY. Chancy. The emphasis today is on recreation. You may enjoy playing a game or even gambling. Just make sure that whatever you choose to do does not become too intense or cutthroat. Even if there is no money involved, you could become so involved in the proceedings that you lose your perspective. Be sure to keep your sense of humor. Remember that the activity is only a game. If someone else is playing too intensely, do your best to calm down the situation. Assert yourself if you must. Make sure that your own good sense is not overcome by the competitive spirit. In the end you should be able to walk away with a light heart and a clear conscience, pleased to have had a good time even if you were not the big winner.

18. SUNDAY. Calm. Step back from the world and all its noise and commotion. You might want to take part in some light amusement, even just watch television or go to a movie. If you have been thinking about your health, you will probably come to the conclusion that the best thing you can do is to occasionally have a day away from all the stress and strain. This should be entirely feasible now. Do your best to take a rest from even thinking about day-to-day concerns, perhaps by going for a drive or a hike. If you have pressing family duties, try to get away for an hour or two. Do not make a chore of your need for privacy. If you can find some time for rest and relaxation, it will do you a world of good.

19. MONDAY. Satisfactory. If you have had some ongoing concerns about your future at work, today these should be put to rest. If you felt somehow stuck in your job or profession with no way out, you are likely to discover that you really have a lot of good options. At this point you can call upon some of the contacts you have made over the years and receive some valuable assistance from them. You can find another job if that is what you decide you want. Or you may discover that your concerns about your present situation are unfounded. In either case, pressure concerning your professional future will be removed to a greater degree, allowing you to apply yourself to present tasks without fear or distraction.

20. TUESDAY. Unsettling. The focus at present is on who comes first in your life. You may naturally think that you always put other people first. However, you could get a sharp comeuppance when someone close to you tells you that you have been very selfish. Or you may need to confront your mate or partner with such a statement. Either way, the situation could become quite uneasy. It will probably seem harder than usual to forgive and forget, but that is certainly what is called for. The best way to view these upheavals is as momentary disturbances that you will barely recall in a few weeks or months. You will find some real peace and harmony once you are able to let go of anger and jealousy.

21. WEDNESDAY. Positive. Some major restructuring is taking place as far as you and other people are concerned. All of your relationships, from the closest to the most distant, are now highlighted. This should be a positive experience overall. Some old friendships are fading into the background and new ones are developing to take their place. This does not mean that you will totally overhaul your circle of acquaintances. It is just that as your interests change your friends will shift as well. You also have the chance to rebuild some relationships on a far higher and more elevated basis. In addition, you could discover some special connections with people you had barely noticed until now, probably neighbors or even someone you commute to work with regularly.

22. THURSDAY. Sensitive. You will probably discover that romance is more intense than usual. You are deeply in touch with your passionate Leo nature. To some extent this will show, particularly because you will be strongly moved to express your feelings somehow. If this is new for you, it could seem unusual and perhaps even frightening. However, you will soon learn there is nothing to fear from being open and aboveboard. You have a much wider range of possibilities in expressing yourself than you tend to imagine. At this point you are becoming more aware of them. It is wise not to constrain yourself too much. You can be open and expressive without damaging your self-respect or any of your relationships.

23. FRIDAY. Easy. The day is apt to be uneventful and routine with few disruptions to the smooth functioning of life. You are likely to be more aware of your emotions and intuition. You could even have a desire to look more closely at them in order to understand what makes you tick. If you look at this as something to be solved or settled with a definitive answer, you will probably be disappointed. What comprises your basic Leo nature is much richer and deeper than you may ever have thought. You have the chance to plumb some of these riches today. A vivid dream or some inspiring piece of art may be the trigger that gets you thinking about the whys of life and love.

24. SATURDAY. Tense. Strong and potent conflicts are brewing. A chief question is whether you can assert yourself without being hostile or provocative. There is some risk of a major upset now. You may discover that a close partner is not all that you thought. There could be a blowup, particularly if some financial irregularities are involved. Your initial reaction may be to explode in anger and lash out at the offender. This may even prove necessary, but it does not help you determine what to do next. More important than initial reactions is who will pick up the pieces and how that will be accomplished. Do not slam any doors; keep your options open.

25. SUNDAY. Buoyant. You are likely to experience a burst of vigor. Your body should be feeling superb and you will be functioning at your very best. It is also quite possible that you realize this has not come about by accident. Benefits of the effort you have been making to discipline yourself recently in matters of diet and exercise are beginning to be noticeable. If you have not yet made such a move, this is an excellent time to start. One key is to find supportive friends who can encourage you. You may want to join an athletic club or start taking an exercise class. Anything that will prompt you to start a program and then stay with it in the long run is highly favored.

26. MONDAY. Fulfilling. You will probably notice two major trends. If you have been reconsidering your relationships with one or more children, your own or someone else's, you should sense real progress now. You may have had to backtrack to catch up with some areas that had been neglected. For example, you may have decided that you were not paying enough attention to your children and circumstances were forcing you to do something different. You should now start to notice some relief in this area. Your mental agility is heightened. If you need to sit down and write some letters or make phone calls, this is an excellent time to do so. Keep your words short, polite, and to the point.

27. TUESDAY. Positive. Try to look at things from a philosophical point of view. It is a tremendous advantage to open up your mind in whatever way you can. If you enjoy reading, make some extra time for this. You do not have to sit down and work through some huge tome. Even light reading can serve as a wonderful stimulus to your imagination. If you decide to read inspirational writing, so much the better. What will be most beneficial at the moment is to reawaken your Leo idealism and benevolence. This requires standing back from your customary gripes and preoccupations in order to look at the great universal principles of ethics and religion. See how you can fit them into your life on an everyday basis.

28. WEDNESDAY. Tricky. This is a good day for looking over your financial records and getting a clearer idea of where you are and where you should be heading. Do this only as a matter of research and clarification. If you make some investments right now they could be misguided. Most likely your attention will be drawn to matters at work. Some rivalries could surface. You may only be an observer of these, or they may directly involve you. If you are involved, it will most likely be a question of who deserves the credit or the blame in regard to some important project. Do not be too stubborn. Back down rather than fight unless it is a matter of basic principles; if so, you must hold out.

29. THURSDAY. Quiet. This should be a fairly uneventful day. Blowups in the workplace should simmer down. Concentrate on consolidating your current position. Your energy may turn toward ways of improving your financial situation. You can accomplish some significant advances because your drive and initiative are real assets. You also have a sharp eye for detail. A tendency toward perfectionism could surface, which will be very helpful if you customarily tend to be somewhat sloppy in keeping your financial books and records. Look over bank statements and make sure your checkbook is in good order. Keep evening plans open until the last minute so that you can accept a phoned invitation.

30. FRIDAY. Stressful. You will probably have a full plate today. There is the chance that every time you think you have come to the end of your work, someone will drop some more on your desk. This could cause some premature fatigue. You may also simply not be in the mood to be a team player. You could be tempted to rebel, to fling up your hands and storm out. However, you would be smart to talk it over with a superior or someone else in a position of authority. They will be more sympathetic than you may guess. If you do not have this opportunity, be ruthless about how much you are going to take on. Finish it and leave the rest until next week even if this means missing a deadline.

31. SATURDAY. Fair. You may not have much patience for money matters, so it would be best to simply set them aside for now. Your judgment in connection with financial matters is probably somewhat clouded. You are likely to be in the mood for company, however. Call some friends to see if they are ready to join you in a good time. You may even want to just lie around the house as a means of relaxing from the strains of the week. Games may not be a good choice because of the danger that tempers could get heated. The best thing for the moment is good humor and joviality, in whatever forms are most suited to you.

SEPTEMBER

1. SUNDAY. Lively. This is a good day for any social activities. Your natural Leo idealism will be a great help to you in building and sustaining friendships. If there is any need for charm or tact in dealing with other people, you should have very little difficulty with that. You may encounter one person who seems unpleasant or awkward, throwing a wet blanket on your hopes and wishes. Even here, however, you should be able to exercise enough natural charm to offset the hostility and defensiveness. It may even turn into an exciting challenge as you take on someone who is making difficulties and turning him or her around. You will both feel better in the end.

2. MONDAY. Happy. You should find life sunny and happy. You have a great deal working in your favor and are likely to hear some news that cheers you even more. You will probably get the go-ahead on a project that is of real importance to you. There is a good chance to go forward with plans and goals you have been thinking about for a while. This will probably seem effortless, but it is building on the groundwork you have laid in the past. It is a good idea at present to focus your attention on what really makes you thrive; this is the direction in which you need to move. Do not be handicapped by outworn ideas of what you think you should or should not be doing.

3. TUESDAY. Exciting. Expect some real advances in a romantic relationship. The best way to help it along is to release your natural spontaneity. Take that special person in your life on a short surprise trip. You may have some special place that is not too far away where you both like to go. Take your time getting there, even if this means a minor disruption to your plans. You can deal with routine matters another time. If you can make today a special occasion and add a touch all your own to the proceedings, so much the better. You may, for example, want to go to a nice out-of-the-way restaurant that offers fine service and accommodations. Your mate or steady date will especially appreciate any romantic gestures.

4. WEDNESDAY. Manageable. You now have a stronger sense than usual of mystical nature. Not all dreams are meaningful or important, but some are. It is quite possible that you may have just had one of those meaningful dreams. You may even want to keep a notebook beside your bed to write down your dreams as soon as you wake up. In that way you will remember more. You could completely forget that you dreamed anything until random images start coming up during the day. You do not need to sit down and figure out these images in some kind of therapeutic fashion. However, at least try to sense the general flavor of the dream since it may contain some important knowledge or insight that your unconscious mind is trying to convey to you.

5. THURSDAY. Satisfactory. Get an early start. Your attempts to build a solid network of friends and associates is paying off. you may soon be involved in an effort to get a group or organization going, or you may have already done so. Expect some ups and downs. Today, however, there could be a major breakthrough. What seemed vague and unformed in the past is now becoming something you can count on. If you have already put in the work you may have forgotten how much you did. However, you will be reminded in the results that you are starting to see. Keep your goals in the forefront of your mind to give you the encouragement you need to persist in your cause.

6. FRIDAY. Fair. Early in the day focus on social concerns and how you relate to other people. As a Leo you seem like a natural leader. Do not be afraid to go for what you want. You have both the authority and the charisma to make your presence felt. Later in the day the mood shifts somewhat. Money concerns could come to the fore. You may encounter a small amount of financial pressure, but this is not going to be as important as it may seem. Try to keep it in proper perspective. You may be more upset by what it symbolizes than by any real challenge it poses to your long-term economic security.

7. SATURDAY. Demanding. Some concerns about money may linger or even be heightened. You could be tempted to micromanage as details, facts, and figures start to obsess you. Beware of becoming pennywise and pound-foolish. Step back and try to get a better perspective about your financial affairs. If you cannot do this on your own, you may want to consult an accountant or financial adviser. These concerns may end up taking more of your time and attention than you want. In fact, they could even go so far as to interfere with recreation you planned. There is not much that you can do about this except keep your good humor. The situation is likely to correct itself very soon if you avoid meddling.

8. SUNDAY. Productive. The mood brightens as your financial concerns seem to lift. A friend or acquaintance could bail you out of a current money crunch. Later you may want to get out and take a short trip. Bring along your mate or partner. Your relationship is about to shift slightly to become less outgoing and more intense and introverted for a while. The fun of going out and seeing friends may be somewhat muted as romance shifts to a more domestic context. If either your own mother or your partner's has had some difficulty in accepting your relationship, she could come around now. There is a good chance that you can set aside differences and actually begin to get along quite well.

9. MONDAY. Challenging. The lure of getting out and seeing a little of the world could be strong. You need not make a long journey; even a short excursion could prove extremely enjoyable. It could also somehow revolutionize your way of seeing things. You may want to visit a museum or go to an art exhibit. Doing so can free your mind while not changing your beliefs. Be open to the unusual. It is really more a matter of opening up your perceptions of the world and all it holds. If you can do this, you will feel better able to cope. You will be less preoccupied with small, petty matters that take away your peace of mind. Do not stay out past your usual bedtime.

10. TUESDAY. Good. Early in the day you can firm up an agreement that has only been tentative until now. You can also contact people you have been missing on the phone or in person. Later on you will become preoccupied with domestic matters. This is a good day for taking care of repairs and maintenance around the house. You will find it worthwhile economically to do these without delay, and you have the energy right now. Your interests in spirituality may seem blocked. If you pray or meditate, you could find doing so more difficult than usual, but persist. The effort itself is an important part of the process. Input from a friend can get you back on the right track.

11. WEDNESDAY. Misleading. You are likely to see a sharp difference between your dreams and reality. You may have a strong desire to expand personal control over your life. Perhaps you would like more responsibility in your place of work, for example. Or you may yearn to enter politics or become more powerful in a volunteer organization. You can go ahead with these plans, although at first you are likely to take on too much. You may have a serious misunderstanding about what you are willing to do. You could even be completely thwarted. Let the situation teach you not to come on too strong right away. Try to be aware of the signs that you are receiving from a variety of reliable sources.

12. THURSDAY. Fortunate. You should be feeling exceptionally lucky, and in many ways you are. Do not take this too literally, however. You would not be smart to gamble at cards or the race-track and expect to come away with more than you start out with. Making a killing probably will not happen. Instead, focus on human concerns. You may want to devote a little extra time to those who are closest to you. It will be most helpful if you bring them a spirit of cheer. If your mate or partner is feeling a little depressed, it is your job to introduce a spot of humor into the day to improve the atmosphere.

13. FRIDAY. Difficult. There is some possibility of difficulties with children. If you have experienced a power struggle in your relationships with them on other occasions, these could come to a head now. Try to be realistic about the current situation. It is true that relationships with children should be based on spontaneous love and affection. However, there is also a strong element of control and even manipulation. It would be a great mistake to pretend that these factors do not exist. Instead, be as aware of them as you can so that you can rise above them. Do not assume that power and control are matters only for grown-ups. Children often understand far more than you may believe or even would want to believe.

14. SATURDAY. Satisfying. Enjoy some fun and entertainment early today even though it may bring on a slight sense of guilt. You have responsibilities that you should not neglect, so the best thing to do is to enjoy yourself early in the day. Later on you can turn your attention to more serious and practical matters. You should feel some genuine satisfaction doing work around the house. Small details such as cleaning spots on the carpet, washing windows, or touching up chipped paint could give you real satisfaction and joy. You may end the day deciding that you had a better time doing your jobs than you did when you were trying to entertain yourself.

15. SUNDAY. Manageable. You will be kept busy today restoring a sense of structure to your life. This could involve some financial or property considerations. You may have to sit down and write checks to pay a stack of bills. Once you have done so, you should feel a great sense of relief. If you have to send out payments, allow a little extra time for them to arrive. Delivery of letters and other communications could be stalled or could even go astray. It would also be wise to pay special attention to maintenance of automobiles and other types of machinery. There is some chance that one of these could start to malfunction over the next few weeks, so some preventive maintenance now could more than repay its cost.

16. MONDAY. Favorable. It will be easier and more enjoyable to return to work than it usually is. You might even look forward to going back to your actual job and plunging into its challenges and compensation. Your capacities for hard work and your ambition are both heightened, and they will harmonize well. You have a clear sense of the rewards and incentives that lead you to your present occupation. Whether you realize it consciously or not, you have a natural affinity for the work you have chosen to do. In addition, you are quite capable even when you do not necessarily like what you have been assigned. Today you are likely to derive some real enjoyment from your labor.

17. TUESDAY. Mixed. You are seeing your partnerships in an extremely idealistic light, which has both pluses and minuses. You probably are aware of the tremendous potential of these relationships, but you could also experience a sense of disappointment when you see how often they fail to live up to the ideal. These realizations could heighten any tendency you have to be a loner. You may be somewhat disillusioned as you witness the comparatively selfish motivations in other people. However, you will be mistaken if you let these thoughts lead you to feel bitter. You need to guard against being blind to your own selfishness. Being aware of it could help you become more forgiving.

18. WEDNESDAY. Sensitive. There is some danger of becoming dissatisfied with your mate or lover. Passion may not seem to be what it once was. A sense of remoteness may prevail, although this will not necessarily lead to hostility. Instead, you could be tempted to withdraw, behaving in a completely acceptable manner on the outside while on the inside you have gone cold. Or you could become aware that the other person has become distant. Either scenario is probably just a passing mood. Everyone has rhythms that alternate between emotional closeness and distance. Today's feelings will probably change in a couple of days. If you become upset about a certain relationship, getting some professional counseling could be reassuring.

19. THURSDAY. Deceptive. You probably are seeing life as a cloak-and-dagger enterprise. Life has its own strange rhythms whereby things are alternately revealed and hidden. You will be very aware of these cycles now. There is also a possibility that you will become aware of the span of life. This does not mean that you will experience a loss, but you will recognize that life is not infinite. This will possibly be brought to your attention in a small way. You may, for example, see an injured bird or squirrel on the street. You will be especially sensitive to these matters today. Do not become upset, but let the awareness help you to reflect on life in general and on your own goals.

20. FRIDAY. Demanding. It could be somewhat difficult to concentrate on your assigned tasks. The situation may require that you be all business. There will be facts and figures to deal with, plus a thousand little details that demand your attention. It will not be possible to escape these, but you will not be naturally drawn to them. Instead, you are likely to be in a dreamy, reclusive mood. The needs of everyday life could seem to intrude upon your peace of mind. One possible side effect of this situation could be a temptation to brood or obsess. The same thoughts may run round and round in your mind and not allow you to either relax or engage fully in your tasks. Even pleasure could seem like a chore.

21. SATURDAY. Challenging. You are likely to be aware of an array of negative and positive forces. On the less positive side, your desire to consolidate your financial position may not go over well with your circle of friends. Someone you know may ask for a short-term loan or want you to make an investment. If this happens, refuse as politely as possible. The brighter part of the picture is that you are now able to communicate your needs clearly and persuasively. This does not have to be a matter of asking for favors. Instead, it is about making your presence felt. If you need to give orders, you should be able to do so without hurting anyone's feelings. Just act as though you know exactly what you are doing.

22. SUNDAY. Chancy. You could be inclined to speculate by making a real estate purchase or you may get into something as daring as day trading. There is the chance that you will feel completely sure of yourself and will have an unusually clear sense of what you are doing and where you are going. Someone could give you a tip and guarantee it to be a sure thing. If it sounds too good to be true, it almost certainly is, so beware. Take as few outright risks and gambles as you can since they are not well favored at the present. There is a chance of a physical accident as well, although it is considerably less likely. Even so, you need to take as many safety precautions as you can while still going about the day.

23. MONDAY. Successful. Your interests are apt to turn toward higher education. Consider whether you really have the education and training that you need, suited to the profession that you most want to get into. If there are some gaps in your knowledge and skills, now is the right time to start filling them. It would be best to consider returning to the classroom apart from purely professional interests. Decide what sort of knowledge you want to acquire for your own personal satisfaction. Looking through a catalog for a local college or adult school can set you thinking. Some continuing study could be beneficial in expanding your horizons and could also help you meet some new people.

24. TUESDAY. Stressful. There is apt to be some tension over confidentiality in love and romance. You may have some feelings that are very difficult to communicate to that special person in your life. It may not be a good idea to talk these over with your partner. An intimate matter calls for extra vulnerability, and you may feel the need to protect yourself. However, you will almost certainly find it valuable to at least talk with yourself about these matters. They may just be passing issues that have no substance, but if they have been nagging at you for some time it could be helpful to consult a professional. If you decide to get some counseling, shop around for someone you can trust.

25. WEDNESDAY. Disquieting. Attention is focusing on your relationship with men in your family. If you normally get along quite well, some disturbance could shake up this picture. If your relations with your father or an uncle have not been good for some time, consider why this is so. If you have lingering grudges, try to do away with them as much as you can. You may be waiting for this person to change so you can then forgive him. If so, you are likely to wait a long time. You need to try to accept him as he is. This may not make genuine intimacy or warmth possible since that is a matter of time and circumstance, but it is a necessary first step toward a reconciliations.

26. THURSDAY. Unsettling. Your public reputation may suffer a noticeable though temporary reversal, probably due to some minor slipup. Avoid the inclination to berate yourself about it. You know that mistakes are an integral part of life. However, there is another side to the issue that may not be quite as obvious. Frequently there is a reason for mistakes. They often mean that you were not ready to take a step in the direction you wanted to head. Almost as often they mean that the step was not really the right one for you at the time. This can be hard to accept, especially if you like to think of yourself as a person in control of your own destiny. You are not able to control every aspect, and this is not entirely a bad thing.

27. FRIDAY. Exciting. Today finds a number of strands coming together at last. For some time you may have been trying to contact certain people but they have proved elusive. This could be the day when you finally manage to get together. It is almost certain to be a good experience for everyone. You and your new acquaintances have a high chance of getting along very well. If these people are business contacts, you could hit upon an opportunity that promises to benefit all of you equally. If it is purely a social matter, you may well make a new and lasting friend. Do not close your eyes to any possibility. Someone considerably, older or younger than you could spark your life.

28. SATURDAY. Disconcerting. Some social discomfort is likely today. You may be looking forward to a party or a dinner only to find that it has to be canceled. Or you could go and discover that the other guests are argumentative or just not as exciting as you had hoped. It may get to the point where you wish you had stayed home with a good book. You and your mate or partner may exchange glances at this event, silently telling each other to leave the gathering, and quickly. If you excuse yourselves and go off together, you will end up having a much better time. You can probably manage to escape without being thought of as rude. In fact, you may not even be missed and your departure may go unnoticed.

29. SUNDAY. Mixed. This is not a good day for parties or other social gatherings. If you go to one, it could turn out to be more like a chore than a pleasure, even for naturally outgoing Leos. Any trips and errands should be done as early as you can. Later in the day you are apt to be in a stay-at-home mood. If at that point you have to go out to shop or take care of some small errand, you will probably view it as an irritation. Allow yourself to be somewhat introspective. This is not an ideal day for accomplishing a great deal in terms of physical work or for dealing with other people. However, you do have a real opportunity to reconnect with yourself. You will feel far better and more refreshed if you review your goals and accomplishments, then make plans for the last quarter of the year.

30. MONDAY. Pleasant. Today has a slight flavor of domesticity. This does not necessarily mean that you will stay at home. Even if you go out to work or to run some errands, you are likely to be drawn to places that seem warm and hospitable. You may opt to go to a restaurant where you always feel comfortable and welcome. Romance could flourish in such a setting. At work you may want to hide away in your private space and just work quietly at assigned tasks rather than immerse yourself in meetings or in dealing with the outside world. If you must interact with other people you will probably do quite well. A low-key, folksy approach should work best.

OCTOBER

1. TUESDAY. Positive. You are likely to be more outgoing than you have been in the past few days. Your mini retreat has probably done you a lot of good, making you ready to meet the world again on your own terms. In the midst of all this activity you may notice that something else is going on. This is likely to involve a deeper, more spiritual quality to all of your activities. It may seem as if your core is in close touch with the essence of the universe. This can be extremely subtle and can easily go unnoticed. However, if you set aside even a few minutes to seek it out, you will benefit greatly. Meditation will be helpful; otherwise some time in a natural setting could give you the same sense of peace and tranquillity.

2. WEDNESDAY. Confusing. Disruption and disharmony could be in evidence. If you have not been completely careful in your financial affairs, some little detail could come back to haunt you. This is not likely to be a major problem, but there is the possibility that you will have to deal with an uncashed check or a charge on your credit card that requires immediate attention on your part. You can handle this without great difficulty. Be careful that you do not let overindulgence come between you and your mate or partner. If you are tempted to eat or drink too much, be aware that it could not only leave a bad impression but could make you feel physically sick. Moderation is the key.

3. THURSDAY. Frustrating. You will have continuing money and financial upsets. It may not be a matter of personal finances. On the other hand, the books of a group or organization in which you are closely involved may not be quite as clear as you hoped. This is not necessarily your fault, but it will require some work on your part to clear up the matter. You may end up feeling somewhat disgruntled about the whole procedure. You might even find yourself asking why you need other people at all. Of course, you realize that you do. Looked at objectively, you have probably caused grievances of much the same kind. No one is immune either from causing problems or from having to solve some that were created by other people.

4. FRIDAY. Fair. Beware of a tendency to obsess about your problems, particularly concerning money and bill payments. Worry will not help. In any case, your difficulties are probably not nearly as bad as they may appear. In fact, there is a good chance of some reassurance regarding current financial matters. By taking on some extra work you may be able to earn enough to cover extra expenses of the season. Work in general is likely to have a satisfying aspect. You will probably have the urge to roll up your sleeves and plunge into the heart of a project. Act on this inclination without delay. Pay attention to small details, which is where perfection and excellence lie.

5. SATURDAY. Stressful. The emphasis is on feelings and emotions. Recently you have been somewhat overburdened with the tasks and responsibilities of life. You may have a sense of yourself struggling alone and unappreciated, waging the battle for basic survival. Tension and even anger could surface. You may have a strong urge to express these feelings; in fact, it may be hard to avoid doing so. Whatever emotions come up are real enough and should be acknowledged, but they also should not be taken too seriously. At this point you are likely to exaggerate the difficulties you are facing. Try to get a more realistic picture of the overall situation before making any long-lasting judgments.

6. SUNDAY. Bright. Today the situation is likely to brighten. Follow any urge to be more outgoing. You may want to reconnect with friends either in person or by telephone or e-mail. Any form of communication is highly favored and could even lead to some new financial or job opportunity. Probably you will be made aware that you are not alone and that help surrounds you; all you need do is ask. This is a good time for future planning and for putting some projects into motion that are geared to pay off down the line. As usual, you will probably have to scatter many more seeds than will actually grow into something real and rewarding.

7. MONDAY. Favorable. You may have noticed over the past few weeks that communications have been more challenging than usual. Lost messages, missed phone calls, and even computer malfunctions may have been adding to the stresses of day-to-day life. Now, however, you should start to notice some improvement in the situation. You will not have to do as much backtracking or apologizing for small errors or omissions. Machinery should also start to behave better. Mass communications can work well for you. If you are planning some work involving radio, television, or the Internet, you should meet with considerable success. Advertising campaigns or publicity promotions will very likely thrive as well.

8. TUESDAY. Intense. Action now centers on your house and home. Your attachment to where you live is intense, so you are likely to react to any perceived threat with a special fervor. You probably think of your place as a love nest and may be somewhat puzzled when your mate or partner does not quite see things in the same way. It would be best to focus any extra energy on practical matters such as cleaning or repairing. Another area that requires some extra attention involves your brother or sister. Take some time to reconnect if you have not been in touch lately. If you have been worried about a loved one for any reason, you now have the chance to find out what has been happening and lay your fears to rest.

9. WEDNESDAY. Disquieting. You could have to deal with someone who is unscrupulous. This tendency may not be easy to spot immediately. This person might pose as a friend, or might actually be a friend who does not have your best interest at heart. It would be foolish to confront this person right away, however tempting that may be. Instead, watch carefully before deciding when to speak up. It does not necessarily serve your interests to have dishonesty revealed publicly. You could derive some benefit from knowing the game without giving yourself away. At any rate you no doubt have to deal with some complicated human relations that come as a total surprise to you.

10. THURSDAY. Good. Turn your attention to the creative aspects of life. Art offers deep access to levels of your mind that you barely know exist. It is not just a matter of self-discovery, however. Once you connect to art in some form, you will probably feel better and have a better outlook on life. You do not have to make a great project of this. Simply sit down and write a few lines in a personal journal, pick up a sketch pad and do some doodling, or play a tune on a musical instrument. Activities of this kind could lead you into a pensive, dreamy state, which is the true source of your creativity. Turn down an invitation to go out tonight. You will be happier on your own.

11. FRIDAY. Demanding. If you have been hurrying and hustling to keep your finances healthy, today you will probably begin to see some rewards for all your activities. If you need to contact the media for any reason, this is an auspicious time. You may want to place or answer an ad or do some publicity work. Relationships with friends are somewhat unsettled. This is a phase of life when your dealings with other people are undergoing a major change. While this will cause some current difficulties, soon you will land on much more solid footing, knowing who you can count on and who is untrustworthy. Today requires rethinking these matters without being emotional about it.

12. SATURDAY. Happy. Your love life should be a major interest today as you find some special satisfaction working on a small project with your mate or partner. For example, you may want to go through old photographs and put them in an album. A sense of nostalgia and fondness for the past could surface. You are also inclined to look back on your own past relationships and see where they have led you. An old flame could reappear on the scene causing some excitement as well as some doubt about your current relationship. This could be exciting, even thrilling, but be careful. There is a strong inclination to cast a warm glow on a past that actually was not that ideal as you experienced it.

13. SUNDAY. Changeable. Pay at least some attention to matters having to do with your health. If you were cooped up at work all week, take time to get out for a walk and some fresh air. It would also be a good idea to eat solid, healthy food, especially if you do not normally have a nutritious diet. Try to cut down on junk food if you usually eat a lot of it. You could find that contacts with siblings and other family members are slightly strained. Some old rivalries having to do with power and dominance could crop up once again. Most likely this will not turn into an argument. Even so, be especially sensitive about saying anything that could cause hurt feelings. Give loved ones the benefit of every doubt.

14. MONDAY. Frustrating. Some irritations are likely in regard to your mental or intellectual activities. Your mind wants to rush ahead to all kinds of innovative solutions, only to find that these ideas really are not so clever after all. What is basically a good idea can be ruined or defeated by small details that are being overlooked. You may have to go back to the drawing board more than once. Patience is necessary, so do not be in too much of a rush to complete any project. You will do best if you take the time to get it right at the outset. Clashes with associates about ideas is also a possibility, so try to avoid arguing about sensitive subjects like politics or religion or finances.

15. TUESDAY. Mixed. Your relationship with your mate or lover is going through some difficult times, but these can be sorted out if you have patience. One or both of you may be somewhat lazy about the relationship, indifferent toward responsibilities that once were accepted without question. You could be taking each other too much for granted. Your love interests could also be out of kilter. The remedy involves going back to basics. Bring to mind the reason that the two of you got together in the first place. It has to do with a real connection at the deepest level. Each of you has something important to learn from the other and to give in return. Just do not insist that everything be equally shared or divided.

16. WEDNESDAY. Sensitive. Friendships are likely to be more intense than usual, verging on the eccentric. You may be attracted to someone who seems offbeat. What usually repels you may suddenly hold a strangely powerful allure. Romantic attraction may involve someone who is considerably older or younger than you. If you are already involved in a love relationship, the connection with your current partner could be thrown into turmoil. This probably does not mean that you will break up. Rather your attraction to someone different could remind you of an important element that has been missing in your current relationship. Think about how you can find this missing part of the puzzle that is love and life.

17. THURSDAY. Disconcerting. Love is likely to be a tricky proposition. There will be a strong and conflicting pull toward being both outgoing and secretive. You or your mate will probably want to socialize and spend time with new people, while the other partner does not find this particularly appealing and wants to spend time alone at home. Each of you could feel held back, kept from acting naturally. You may not be able to reconcile these contradictory urges in any way that is totally satisfying to both of you. As a compromise, one person may go out while the other stays home. This is not ideal for togetherness, but it may be the best thing for the relationship as a whole. Being apart for a short while can actually be what pulls you back together.

18. FRIDAY. Quiet. Today there is an unusual focus on the mystical and the paranormal. You could have a sense of unseen worlds, possibly through a dream or an experience that seems to come from another dimension. Consider the possibility that these forces are always present. Today it just so happens that the veil between them and your reality is slightly thinner. Do not make the mistake of becoming spooked or superstitious. As a matter of fact, solid day-to-day reality is the best angle from which to approach the supernatural. Both have their own truth and their own reality. Your task is to become aware of all aspects so that you can pick and choose what is best for you.

19. SATURDAY. Variable. You may come into contact with someone from another nation or culture. This is not likely to be an entirely pleasant encounter. You will probably find this person different from anyone you have ever known and therefore somehow threatening or disruptive. In current times many people and nations are brought together in ways that were once unimaginable, providing intense stimulation from this contact. There are also times when enforced togetherness leads to fear and a defensive posture. However, you do not need to give in to this temptation. Try hard to accept the different faces of humanity without anxiety or bigotry. This is an important step to achieving inner freedom. Once you can treat every person as a valued individual you will be on your way to accepting yourself.

20. SUNDAY. Positive. Your mood is likely to be generous and expansive. Try to do something that elevates your consciousness, perhaps reading a book that deals with spirituality or the philosophy of happiness. This is a good time for making contact with a source of wisdom, no matter what form it takes. You will notice a shift in your attitude toward all things spiritual after today. If you have been slightly blocked or distant, you are likely to become free now. How revolutionary these changes seem will have a great deal to do with your attitude toward unseen realms. You are probably going to have to acknowledge a presence with the power to influence your actions and reactions.

21. MONDAY. Lively. Energy is riding high at the moment. If you do not have adequate ways of expressing it, you can expect to experience some irritation or anxiety. The present season tends to have a slightly unreal aspect, which you may notice in the air. You probably will not find it particularly disturbing or threatening because it will probably take the aspect of a child's costume rather than anything truly ghoulish or frightening. Ask yourself, however, why this has such an allure. It could have to do with the fact that people want to remember the existence of supernatural realms no matter how down to earth their daily life may be.

22. TUESDAY. Rewarding. There is a great probability that you will make some significant contact with another person. This is not likely to be of the romantic variety, but it will go beyond the limitations of ordinary social exchange. You and this person are apt to hit it off immediately; it may seem as if there is some very deep and important reason that you have been brought together. It could be that you have an important task to undertake in common. Or you may simply need to talk over important issues that no one else can really help you iron out. Whatever it is, this encounter is likely to strike you as something far more than a mere coincidence that will soon be forgotten.

23. WEDNESDAY. Successful. Something startling and favorable is likely to happen, probably as the result of a message or letter. You may discover that your own interests in communicating are the key to success. If you need to do some serious writing or revising in whatever form, this is an excellent time for it. Catch up on your business or personal correspondence. If you enjoy creative writing, jot down a few lines of poetry or an entry in your journal. Even something as routine as paying bills could prove satisfying. At any rate, the emphasis is on reaching outside yourself. Whatever you can do to extend your interactions with other people is likely to proceed extremely well.

24. THURSDAY. Favorable. Your thoughts are apt to be moving as swiftly and effortlessly as the wind. This is an extremely good day for brainstorming, particularly if you need to come up with some new ideas for a group or organization you are connected with as an officer. It will be comparatively effortless to apply all your energy to mental tasks. You will also find that your Leo intuition is unusually sharp, harmonizing nicely with your rational powers so that you can intuit answers to questions and also figure them out rationally. Let your mind go directly to important matters without a lot of emotional fog to obscure your way ahead. Put aside personalities and deal with facts.

25. FRIDAY. Buoyant. Today is a good day for charity and good works in all its forms. You might want to think about giving some money to a favorite cause. If you do not have a lot of extra cash, there is always the possibility of contributing some time to volunteer work. You will learn the truth of the statement that charity benefits the giver as well as the receiver. At a very deep level you may find that you can only give to yourself; no one else can truly fulfill all of your needs. This is not a roundabout way of saying charity begins at home. You will find that giving to someone else opens you up so that you can graciously receive what you need. If you do not do so, you can be closed off from people, and that can be a very hard situation to overcome.

26. SATURDAY. Fair. On the social front some sudden upheaval may give you new authority among your circle of friends and acquaintances. Whether you find this a blessing or a burden remains to be seen. Your own preferences may turn toward pleasures of a more domestic nature. You could want to busy yourself in your home, keeping your mate or partner with you so that you can snuggle cozily together. Any tension that you experience will probably come from this conflict between being social and being alone with the person you love. You will probably find it most advantageous to devote a little time to each. This is not the time to consider relocating, even if your job involves a long commute.

27. SUNDAY. Important. You are likely to learn some hard lessons about the true meaning of power. To some people, power is sheer, naked force, leading them to believe that if you dominate others, you have power over them. You are about to discover that this is not really true. Of course, there is a need to govern and regulate. However, doing so in a high-handed way is not the best approach. You have a real chance to learn now that control comes through a mild, generous spirit. In choosing between a carrot or a stick as your philosophy, keep in mind that no one can be forced beyond a certain point. If you have children or spend time around children, you will discover the truth of this through them, particularly if you are dealing with teenagers.

28. MONDAY. Challenging. You have a special opportunity to resolve some issues involving your home and family. Devote more time and effort than usual to talking things over. It will be astonishing to see how much can be accomplished through simply stating needs and wants. Also find a way to put more effort and energy into your everyday domestic life. A small amount of work on your part is apt to reap many benefits. It could even seem that you are being assisted by some unseen hand. The beneficent forces in the universe are more than willing to help you, with just a small push on your part to make it happen. Emphasize all that is good and rewarding in your relationships, and make allowances for occasional disagreements.

29. TUESDAY. Mixed. Some difficulties could arise from too much rigidity in your life. You may want to stick to your guns on some issue on the home front, but other members of your family could see things from quite a different angle. It will not be easy to get anyone to budge even an inch. Stubbornness could be the chief obstacle to harmony. You will have to become somewhat assertive in order to settle matters. At the same time, you should guard against showing too much aggression or domination. Fortunately you are not likely to argue today. Just state your needs and perspectives clearly and definitively. Chances are other people will do the same, and the solution will gradually develop from there. Patience is the key to finding a permanent solution to ongoing problems.

30. WEDNESDAY. Deceptive. There is the possibility that you are being misled, or believe you are being misled, in romantic matters. For example, it may seem that someone you are interested in does not feel the same way. It could also work in the opposite direction. You may be exaggerating the possibilities of love with someone you barely know, so be extremely careful. The danger of jumping to the wrong conclusions is extremely high at present. Avoid excessive jealousy. If someone is jealous of you, you may find it somewhat difficult to justify your recent actions. Do not concern yourself with proving too much in the short run. If you are innocent, it will be made quite obvious very soon.

31. THURSDAY. Opportune. The emphasis is on money and property matters. You can expect some good fortune. A real estate investment may turn out to be unexpectedly profitable right away. It might also be a good idea to expand your personal contacts. An older person could give you some very helpful advice based on personal experience. This person may be particularly helpful in setting you straight in some area where you have been experiencing real confusion and uncertainty. Your home could be a special source of comfort at present. However, be alert for hidden deception among and between family members. Suspicion could linger on you and your partner. You can overcome this if you want, but you may opt to sweep any differences under the rug and just adopt a sunny attitude.

NOVEMBER

1. FRIDAY. Pressured. Put some emphasis on the practical side of life. You could find that you have to overcome some serious obstacles in your financial arrangements. Something you buy may wind up costing a lot more than you budgeted. Reconsider whether the purchase was really worth it. You are not stuck with it. It is entirely possible that you can find the same item for a cheaper price elsewhere and return the more costly purchase. Watch out while shopping. Sales pressure could be intense, and you are more susceptible to it than usual. Never buy something just because you like the salesperson or think you might hurt his or her feelings if you say no. That is exactly how they want you to feel, but it makes for a poor buying decision.

2. SATURDAY. Variable. You are much more persuasive than usual. If you have to convince someone to take a particular view, you could surprise yourself with your own gift of gab. There is one major caution, however. You could easily slip into half-truths or even deliberate deception in order to make your point. This might happen so naturally that you are only barely aware of it while it is happening. All the same, it is bad policy. You cannot justify your action by saying it is really in the other person's best interest. You truly have no way of knowing that. Be very careful to stick to the truth in your words and actions and you will have a clear conscience as a result.

3. SUNDAY. Good. You have the chance to draw together a number of different ideas and get them working harmoniously. This is one of those days when you mix with assorted people in your social circle. If you introduce some of your friends who do not know each other on a first-name basis, some unexpected benefits may develop. This could lead to new business or social contacts that take some surprising but positive twists. Alternatively, someone to whom you are introduced, or a whole new social circle, could be extremely advantageous. Try to focus as much on the pleasure of socializing as on any ulterior advantage.

4. MONDAY. Favorable. Today has an intense but generally harmonious aspect. Your sense of perception and your reflexes are unusually balanced, which could be quite helpful if you are involved in anything athletic. In addition, because of this special harmony, your thoughts and words will be in unusual accord. There is often some strain in human interactions as you feel the contrast between how you really are and how you appear to other people. Today this discrepancy is likely to be small, allowing you to be more natural and comfortable in dealing with people from all different walks of life. Even communicating well with a total stranger should not be difficult.

5. TUESDAY. Misleading. Be careful if you are taking any drugs or medication that could affect your balance or physical coordination. There is a chance of some problem involving a ladder or balcony. Your perceptions are not as accurate as they may seem. Alcohol could affect you more powerfully than usual. The danger is that you may think you are perfectly capable of functioning and that it is having no effect at all. However, you could be misleading yourself. Even if you have not been drinking, be extremely watchful of any tendency to be careless while driving. There is danger of a mishap due to lack of attention. Talking on the phone while driving or operating any machinery should be avoided.

6. WEDNESDAY. Exciting. You can expect a burst of creative inspiration. Your intuition should be sharper, or at least more vivid. You will also be led to some creative effort by a new friend or co-worker. It can be a bit tricky to sort out the initial inspiration from all of the various ideas and images swirling around in your mind. How you express it will largely depend on the talents and abilities you have been developing throughout the year. Write or draw whatever comes to mind. If your creativity is even more deliberate than this, you could profit from letting inspirations jell until you are sure of the best way of expressing them. Just be wary of revealing your ideas to people who might claim them as their own.

7. THURSDAY. Good. If you have been debating with yourself or with your mate about how to discipline your children, today is a good time to bring those issues into focus. Discipline requires a careful balance between severity and indulgence, and it is not always clear which is the best tack to take at any given time. Today you are likely to reach a genuine understanding of this delicate balance. Overall, the subtler you can be in your dealings with children, the more positive the effect will be. Do not give a harsh punishment when a word or two may be all that is needed. A response that shows you are in control will pay off best.

8. FRIDAY. Variables. Early on in the day your urge to be up and out may not sit well with family members or co-workers. Your desire for freedom and spontaneity could come up against a stone wall of resistance. Very likely this will take the form of a friend or colleague who does not see things quite the same way you do. Later in the day it will be somewhat easier to get down to serious business. You can then make some real headway dealing with small details and could even derive some real pleasure from doing so. You may also finally discover how caring for the small things in life can further your long-term ambitions. Direct some effort toward improving and beautifying your home or office.

9. SATURDAY. Disconcerting. There is an underlying current of disruption or irritation. One form it could take is you being outgoing and social while someone in your family insists on being more introverted and withdrawn. There is a tendency to become stuck in your own perspective, so try to maintain a flexible attitude. A solution to this dilemma is not readily apparent. You may have to cope by focusing on the practical details of everyday life, which should proceed more smoothly. You could spend some time working on small projects around the house. Try to catch up on repairs or minor maintenance that you have been meaning to do for quite a while.

10. SUNDAY. Rewarding. You are likely to notice a powerful focus on control. Your drive for self-promotion and self-advertisement are now beginning to pay off. There could be some question, however, about the ultimate meaning of such activities. Consider whether you are really ready for the kind of success that you seem to be preparing for. There is likely to be some discrepancy between what you think you want and what would actually make you happy, and this will not be easy to sort out. In fact, your judgment could be somewhat clouded in this regard. The best approach to take is simply be aware that to some extent you are stabbing in the dark. Make allowances for possible errors and poor decisions that have to be reversed almost immediately.

11. MONDAY. Sensitive. The major question facing you today is deciding what really makes you thrive. As a Leo you are not the type of person who does well playing second fiddle to someone else. You prefer to occupy center stage, to feel like a ruler surrounded by a court of admirers and subordinates. The good news is that you have the vitality and dynamism to achieve this goal, if that is really what you want. The bad news is that you do not necessarily have the clear vision to see how your action or inaction may affect other people. Your family is apt to be the focal point of any tension in this regard. Be very slow to dismiss their input or deny that they have a real understanding of the available options.

12. TUESDAY. Active. This will turn out to be a worthwhile day. You are likely to be more idealistic than usual and an active humanitarian, although you may express this in slightly unorthodox ways. The curious paradox is that any ideas you have in this regard may actually turn out to be quite practical. It is not always possible to make a dream come true, but today it may be feasible. What will also help is that your intuition is a touch clearer and sharper than is customary. You will certainly have no trouble saying the right things to the right people. You can use your Leo charm to very good advantage at present to get what you want.

13. WEDNESDAY. Pleasant. On this uneventful, serene day you are likely to be more moody and introspective than usual. You could wander off into the realm of daydreams. This is not necessarily bad. Your dreams could penetrate to a deep level of your psyche, revealing and expressing layers of insight that you do not normally bring into play. Pay serious attention to what drifts across your mental screen. Insights will not necessarily give you any advantage in the world of work or of love. However, you could gain a measure of self-knowledge that is far more important. Try to avoid arguing with your mate or partner about what has been done and cannot be reversed.

14. THURSDAY. Useful. Your mind is sharper and penetrating. You have the chance of some real insight into the thoughts of other people, particularly family members. You may tend to jump to conclusions in judging them, but these judgments are likely to be right on target. It may even seem as if everyone is an open book which you can read easily and plainly. The danger is not that your insights may be inaccurate. It is more a matter of what you choose to do with your knowledge. If you reveal certain things to other people when they are not prepared, they could be hurt and you could find yourself facing an enemy. The outcome of a legal matter may depend on how well you can recall events of long ago.

15. FRIDAY. Mixed. In the early part of the day you may be more sarcastic than anyone has ever heard you be before. Your wit could touch a vital nerve that rubs friends and associates the wrong way. You are likely to hear about this now and for a long time to come. Later on the mood lightens as you become more open, outgoing, and optimistic. You may have a desire for some fresh air. A jaunt out in nature could be very refreshing, especially some spot where you can enjoy a beautiful sunset. You might also find it beneficial to look into spiritual or religious interests that seem like a figurative breath of fresh air. What you were taught as a child is not necessarily the only answer to questions of life and death.

16. SATURDAY. Disruptive. At present your mental processes are going through an upheaval. If you have been troubled by a minor inconsistency or an annoying habit you perceive in someone else, the issue could come to a head now. You and your mate or partner may have a misunderstanding about such issues. It could be something as simple as the other person's habit of humming constantly or sniffling that has always irritated you. You may have not said anything until now, managing to ignore it in the interest of harmony. Now it forces itself on your attention. You could suddenly find yourself intolerant and irritable about what may be quite insignificant. This feeling may be covering up some deeper grievances which need to be examined.

17. SUNDAY. Confusing. Today's focus is on some problem that you have always had in a religious context. Even if you do not consider yourself particularly spiritual or religious in a traditional way, you probably have some questions about the why and how of the universe. These questions are now coming to your attention more forcefully. You will probably come to the conclusion that your usual views of these matters are limited and even a bit absurd. However, you may not have anything real or meaningful to replace them with. This leaves you with the eternal problem of how to confront the mystery of life in a way that is neither foolish nor simplistic.

18. MONDAY. Deceptive. You will probably want one thing in regard to your work while your business partner or a colleague wants something quite different. There is a possibility that some deceit is going on. You may start to suspect that someone you work with is not being entirely honest about future plans or current finances. There is some truth in this suspicion, but only a small measure. You would be well advised to investigate any concerns you have before confronting the other person about them. This is not only good politics but will keep you from looking like a fool if you happen to be wrong. This is not an ideal day for sorting out truth from illusion, facts from fiction.

19. TUESDAY. Unsettling. The workplace is likely to be somewhat disrupted as conflicts start to surface concerning business relationships. Your natural Leo inclination is to take charge and move front and center. However, you may find that this inclination does not go over well with the people you have to work with. There is a very real possibility of shooting yourself in the foot because what you thought was helping your cause could in fact be holding you back. The best solution is to take careful stock of how your colleagues see things. Be as generous as you can in sharing any credit or recognition you receive. Turn down a social invitation for this evening.

20. WEDNESDAY. Intense. The intensity of your moods and emotions could heighten. You are likely to see a strong difference between your public and private attitude. Watch that professional necessities do not keep you away from your home too much. Your family could have some sharp words for you if they feel you are neglecting them. Later in the day you are likely to be preoccupied with social contacts. There is a possibility that you may miss a phone call or two that proves slightly inconvenient. On the other hand, you will probably have a strong sense of goodwill toward people. You should find this enjoyable and heartwarming, although it could be difficult to put into practice in the real world.

21. THURSDAY. Tricky. One of the most noticeable things today is that matters of love will shift subtly. Recently either you or your romantic partner may have been penetrating deeply into the relationship. This has probably not been entirely pleasant or comfortable, even though the discoveries may be quite accurate. There could also be some ongoing jealousy, but this probably has no basis in current reality. If you or your partner has been irrationally jealous of some former lover, you will probably feel foolish now as you realize such anxieties were unfounded. Show your love and affection openly; do not hesitate to say those three little words that add joy to a relationship.

22. FRIDAY. Good. The general atmosphere shifts now toward greater optimism. Your relations with friends and associates should proceed smoothly. Any dealings with an older person are likely to be very beneficial for both of you. You have a chance to learn something of lasting value from a person with more seniority and experience than you. It is possible that you will have to actively seek out a mentor, which will be worth the effort. Try to keep from automatically dismissing a person who does not seem to offer anything you want. Your most important lessons are likely to come from someone who is a bit odd or eccentric. Just beware of being manipulated by a smooth talker.

23. SATURDAY. Buoyant. You are likely to be bursting with energy and enterprise. Your intellectual life will be active and might even become hyperactive. This is a superb day for finding new and unexpected solutions to familiar problems. These solutions may not come from you. You may idly mention a problem you are thinking about to someone you know and then find that, almost magically, this person furnishes an answer. The moral is to turn your attention far and wide. The kind of input and inspiration you are looking for will probably come from many unexpected directions. Do not shut your eyes to any possibility.

24. SUNDAY. Tranquil. This is a good occasion to reflect on religious and spiritual issues. You may go to a religious service if you are so inclined. Some information or knowledge in regard to an unseen realm is likely to come to you. Pay special attention to it; it has some important implications in resolving an issue that has been plaguing you for some time. You will not necessarily find help through a spiritual organization or a sacred text. Knowledge is actually all around you. For example, you may make a sudden decision to go to a movie for pure entertainment, only to find that a line or two in the film speaks to you in an unusual and profound way. A TV personality might also inspire you.

25. MONDAY. Fair. Your personal willpower is likely to be a major preoccupation at this point. What you want could occupy your whole day. You may be unusually single-minded in deciding how and when to get it. Your determination is highly energized and you have the mental power to think of good solutions. You will have some concerns, however, regarding the effect you are having on other people. Your actions could set up certain crosscurrents that you could not have predicted. For this reason you should be extremely careful in pursuing your goals. Tact and diplomacy are an absolute necessity. Also make sure you are clear in expressing yourself to other people and that you understand them clearly.

26. TUESDAY. Sensitive. Today emphasis continues on personal will. The danger of alienating other people is smaller than it has been. Your mate or partner may not be entirely sympathetic to your wishes, however, and may in fact be something of a wild card in your plans. You can overcome any such obstacles by maintaining a spirit of kindness and goodwill. It may be necessary to consciously hold this attitude even when other people do not seem to share it. There is no need to react to their negative behavior. Do your best to maintain a positive attitude no matter what kind of response you get in return. The more you do so, the more you will find it pays off in the long run if not immediately.

27. WEDNESDAY. Successful. This promises to be a memorable day. You have a rare opportunity to see how your energy and initiative have been working for you, even if you may not have understood all that was going on. People often feel that their efforts are wasted or only pay off marginally. You should see some real rewards for your hard work now. If not, it is a starred time to begin some projects. Anything involving a group or society is particularly favored. Keep a close eye not only on short-term goals but on the ultimate purpose of your organization. You can advance it significantly if you are willing to take the lead or at least share a leadership position.

28. THURSDAY. Demanding. At present you may be immersed in considerations of money and property. Wealth may seem elusive, or it may be there but you are not aware of it because your records and statements are not in good order. Avoid any temptation toward wild or reckless speculation. Investments that are touted as a sure thing may be the exact opposite. You will probably benefit most from a slow, almost plodding attitude toward money matters. Play the investment game conservatively. Luck is even more elusive now than it usually is. There is also the possibility that an adviser is not giving you the whole picture. Keep your money where you know it is safest.

29. FRIDAY. Challenging. Early in the day a friend or associate may deliver some unpleasant news regarding money matters. This is not likely to be a major problem, so do your best to take it in stride. Later on focus on the world of communication. Try to make your voice heard far and wide. It could be beneficial to contact people in other parts of the country or even in other nations. You may also find that your competitive spirit receives a boost. If you have been at a loss lately in terms of your work, you have the chance now to reverse the picture. By conveying an image of strength, competence, and vision you can land a rewarding new contract or assignment.

30. SATURDAY. Manageable. Some deep issue or question may be gnawing at you. This could have to do with children or with a love affair. You might find yourself compelled to confide in someone so that you can get these matters off your chest. This would be an excellent relief, but choose your confidant wisely. One option is to speak to a counselor who guarantees confidentiality. There is also the chance that you need to talk to the people who are directly concerned in the matter. Frankness is favored because it could cause a real transformation in your life in the end, however it seems in the short run. Do not hesitate to apologize if you were wrong.

DECEMBER

1. SUNDAY. Favorable. There are so many favorable influences at work right now that you can get involved in nearly anything and expect to succeed. There are days when everything seems not only to be in good order but to function joyfully and harmoniously. This is one of those rare days. If you need some luck in an area such as gambling, you could find that it is there for you. One caution, however: nothing is absolutely sure. Remember this when you act. On the whole, you are likely to have a breezy, carefree attitude even toward fairly humdrum duties. This is one of those times when it seems as if you can sail through life. Enjoy it while it lasts, but be prepared for some changes in the days ahead.

2. MONDAY. Difficult. Some adversities, mostly minor, will come your way in dealing with family members. There is a general belief that a family should be a source of constant comfort and support, but it does not always work that way. You may be feeling hemmed in with the restrictions your loved ones are inflicting on you. How intense this is depends on how deeply rooted these patterns have become. If it is something new or not part of the ordinary, the feeling is likely to pass quickly. However, if it is the sort of difficulty that you have always experienced in dealing with your family, new irritation may just be more salt rubbed into some very old wounds that have yet to heal.

3. TUESDAY. Unsettling. Domestic discord could continue. Yesterday's misunderstandings could turn into today's upsets. Your mate or partner may feel that this is the last straw. You need to be ruthlessly honest with yourself in determining if current problems are really your fault. You will naturally want to free yourself of any blame, but resist this urge as much as possible. Try to see the situation from the point of view of a neutral third party. You are likely to learn that the difficulties are at least partly your own doing. You have a hard choice to make right now. The best thing to do is to repair any damage you caused even if your partner does not follow suit. Doing so requires real maturity and wisdom.

4. WEDNESDAY. Productive. You should be seeing things somewhat more brightly at this point. Your concerns could turn to personal creativity as your natural artistic touch surfaces. This does not necessarily mean that you need to take up a pen or a paintbrush. Rather, you should apply your natural Leo creativity to whatever you have been asked to do, whether it is a matter of baking a cake, fixing a broken piece of furniture, or writing a business letter. The point is not to focus on the work but to experience the joy of the task itself. Let creativity be for pleasure, not for profit. You will find that your artistic urgings are being fed by your natural desire to contribute the best you have to offer.

5. THURSDAY. Excellent. If you can express yourself in unconventional ways you could derive real benefits. You are likely to be more agile and clever than usual. A certain cleverness could emerge either in you or in people who are closely associated with you. This is not likely to be dishonesty. It is more like a game of hide-and-seek as you encounter someone who is daring you to act or react. What you decide to do may contain some unusual twists and turns. The chief way that problems will arise is if you take the whole thing too seriously. Guard against turning every activity into a chore or a job. Just be very clear about the situation, take it lightly, and do your best with what you are able to give at the moment.

6. FRIDAY. Dissatisfying. Some disruptions are likely in your ideas and your way of thinking. You may have to face a mental challenge that seems beyond your current abilities. This may be some kind of mathematical problem, a legal matter, or simply making sense out of a long written report. You may be strongly tempted to drop the whole matter into someone else's lap, but you will probably not be allowed to do so. Most likely the other person will either refuse or be unable to give you any real help, forcing you back on your own resources. The problem is not impossible to solve; it just requires some long, intense thought that will be good mental exercise for you.

7. SATURDAY. Quiet. Although there should be few disruptions in anything you want to undertake, it may be best to spend most of your time on fairly routine tasks. For example, you may want to go through a closet or cabinet and clean it out. You will be surprised by how much it lightens your mood to do this. Even if you have not given much conscious attention to neglected corners of your life, they probably have been nagging away at you. Once you really reduce clutter, you are likely to experience real relief. Put away work this evening and do something enjoyable with your mate or partner, even something as simple as a nice dinner and a movie close to home or even at home.

8. SUNDAY. Tricky. You and your mate or partner should be very much on the same wavelength. Even though you normally understand each other quite well, you are now unusually sensitive to each other's moods and reactions. However, this may not necessarily lead to peace and harmony between you. In fact, you could end up becoming so sensitive to perceived moods and whims that you become somewhat annoyed with each other. Watch out for a tendency to react to what you imagine the other person is saying or implying. There is no guarantee that such intuitions are accurate. Even if they are accurate, there is a significant difference between thinking something and coming right out and saying it directly to the person.

9. MONDAY. Sensitive. The person who you feel yourself to be is likely to be revaled through games and recreation. The reaction to this is apt to vary wildly. One possibility if you take part in some sport or game is that you will be drawn to winning at all costs. You may discover that your true self comes out naturally and fully on the playing field. There is some danger, though, of taking such a competition far more seriously than it deserves. If you can let go of your sense of having to control everything, you should fare quite well. Your emotions are a major source of strength at this stage, and your feelings can be trusted to guide you in the right direction. Once you make up your mind do not back down.

10. TUESDAY. Lucky. Today offers some extremely bright prospects. Your luck is better than usual, so you could find yourself in the right place at the right time. Capitalize on any fortunate coincidence that will put you in the limelight. Your natural Leo charisma is extremely strong. Your intuition is penetrating and will be a more reliable guide to investments than more rational and conventional methods. You can find a way of getting a little ahead financially to provide for your retirement. You may even be lucky enough to make a gamble worthwhile, always bearing in mind that no bet is a sure winner. A game of chance involving cards could be very lucky for you.

11. WEDNESDAY. Disquieting. Do not expect anything to be simple. There is the possibility that your thoughts will be drawn toward the deeper meaning of life. The likelihood of an upset is not particularly great, but you may be reminded of your vulnerability in some small way. Keep in mind that nothing is certain. The customary reaction to a philosophical discussion is to just say that everything will work out, but this is not the best way to handle it. On the contrary, you might find it helpful to reflect on all that you hope to accomplish in your life and about its meaning and purpose. Be sure to let loved ones know your feelings. Express appreciation for all that they do for you rather than complaining about what is not done.

12. THURSDAY. Frustrating. You will have to deal with love or romance in some way. Very few people feel truly fulfilled in a personal relationship. Often there is an uneasy compromise between what a person wants and what is being freely given. Most people manage to live with this, but there can be some measure of frustration and discontent just below the surface. Some of these discomforts could be especially noticeable today. Your longings may turn toward someone attractive but out of reach, perhaps a friend or someone's spouse you encounter at a party. This may lead you to ponder your own desires and how they can be more satisfyingly met without exposing yourself to shame or blame.

13. FRIDAY. Mixed. You will probably become somewhat impatient with details as the ordinary tasks of life seem frankly boring. You may find yourself glancing at the clock every few minutes, wondering how soon you can finish routine work so that you can go and do something more enjoyable. Very likely it will not be as soon as you hope. The best approach is to set clear limits on what you want to accomplish today. Achieve these goals, then set them aside so you can have some fun and recreation. You may want to spend some time daydreaming or just quietly watching television. Find something that relaxes your mind and inspires you at the same time. Your mate or partner may want to join you, but company is not necessary in order for you to feel contented.

14. SATURDAY. Happy. The general atmosphere of the day is extremely bright. Your thoughts may be drawn to travel. If you have been toying with the idea of taking a trip, circumstances could be lining up in your favor. You might go through your financial records and realize that you have a little extra money that would allow you and a loved one to go on a vacation somewhere. The ideas and enthusiasm you feel now should be running very high. Just do not go overboard in spending or planning to spend. There is some chance of getting in over your head financially. Be realistic and you have some real opportunities to see the world and not go deep into debt in the process.

15. SUNDAY. Misleading. Your reactions are apt to be somewhat out of the ordinary. Someone you know may be very eager to talk to you in private. If you actually have the conversation, it is likely to be pleasant and to go quite well at the time. However, when it is all over, you may go away wondering what exactly was said or meant. The actual messages exchanged may be vague or contradictory. If you try to sort them out through ordinary conversation, you could find that you are getting nowhere. It may be necessary simply to do nothing about this for the next day or two. Eventually you are likely to be able to ferret out the truth through all the conflicting signals and offer some helpful suggestions for solving the problem.

16. MONDAY. Buoyant. You may notice some important shift taking place in your basic reasoning. As a Leo you have always held certain ideals, but you may never have been able to integrate them fully into your everyday life. You could also sense that they are not completely in harmony with one another. On the other hand, it may be that your values have seemed at odds with those of people close to you and the world at large. Resolving such differences might have seemed impossible at one time. Now, however, you have the opportunity to bring more order and harmony into these areas. On a practical level, you should have a clear sense of how to take what you value most and make it happen as soon as possible.

17. TUESDAY. Contradictory. Some questions are likely to arise about who you really are. You may see that your true nature has been shaped by conflict with authority, perhaps an institution or your parents or other family members. You are likely to be very aware of any difficulties you have in these areas, and they could provoke a sense of rebellion in you. Having to adhere to conventional standards in any form is probably not going to appeal, particularly if doing so seems to stand in the way of personal fulfillment. Instead you will probably take the position of the maverick or the rebel. You could decide that there is something you want that can only be realized if you act as your own person despite society's norms and standards.

18. WEDNESDAY. Fortunate. This day could reveal some very fortunate influences. These are likely to involve personal authority and willpower and how you make your mark in the world. The most probable outcome is that you will have a much stronger sense of how to get your message across, and without ever raising your voice. The key will lie in some mixture of charm and geniality on the one hand and personal dynamism on the other. You will not see these changes all at once. They are likely to make themselves known gradually over the course of the next few months. In future years you will probably look back on this as a time in which you matured a great deal.

19. THURSDAY. Variable. Focus your attention on the ins and outs of your social circle. Your emotions and interests will probably be centered there. You may be drawn to some kind of public activity, even if it is just a cocktail party or a holiday meeting of an organization you have belonged to for a long time. You have the chance not only to enjoy yourself but to circulate and become better known. The situation is not entirely sunny, however. You could encounter some limitations because you are not quite as compatible with a certain group of people as you like to think. You could be made aware of this through some small slight or catty remark that leaves you wondering who your friends really are.

20. FRIDAY. Challenging. You will probably have more than your customary share of vim and vigor at this point. However, you may not be totally enthusiastic about displaying it in public. Most likely you will feel comfortable working behind the scenes, either at home or in some area where you are not exposed to the spotlight. There could also be a strong pull toward secrecy and what is hidden. You might become interested in solving a puzzle or mystery, whether large or small. It could even be fun to play detective in an amateur fashion. With your good Leo intuition you will be able to figure out what is going on once you have a clear sense of the motives involved.

21. SATURDAY. Fair. Your sense of passion could be heightened, causing you to feel more loving than usual. The only drawback is that these passions could be difficult to express. You might want to deliver some kind of speech about how much a certain person means to you, only to find that you become tongue-tied and you blurt out a mass of silly details. If this happens, do not take it too seriously. When all has been said and done, the strength of your relationship is far deeper than the words you use. That special person in your life will understand what you are trying to say regardless of how well you manage to express it. In fact, the best communication between you may involve no words at all.

22. SUNDAY. Mixed. Your attention is likely to shift toward fulfilling a personal ambition. The natural place for this to happen is at work and with your career. Even if you are not on the job today, you could find that you are thinking about it. Look at your goals for the new year to see how well what you are now doing fits in with what you would like to be doing. It is all very well to speak of resolutions. However, rather than think of commitments you are not likely to keep, devote some thought to long-term positive goals. Your reasoning may not be crystal clear, so do not jump to hasty conclusions about what to do next. Explore possibilities, and keep all of your options open.

23. MONDAY. Enjoyable. Your spirits could turn toward holiday festivities. Today finds you in a jovial mood, ready for partying and socializing. You will also want to indulge the more generous side of your nature at this season. There is some chance, though, that your physical energy may not be quite up to par. As a result you could want to go out to shop and socialize but find that you are just too tired. Allow yourself some rest and quiet relaxation sometime during the day. This will help you avoid any possibilities that you may become sick. Some extra rest now will help keep your energy high so that you do not have to take time to recuperate from an illness later on.

24. TUESDAY. Good. This is a good day to finish up all those last-minute holiday chores. You will be generally quite productive and able to get through a long list of errands without a great deal of effort. Be careful, though, of any tendency to rush. There is a chance of an accident or a mishap if you are not careful. Pay attention to all safety precautions, and be sure to drive especially carefully. You do not have to hide out in the house, however. This evening go out somewhere and shine, whether it is at a large party or in a cozy family circle. Warm feelings of love and affection are present in abundance, and these are the best gift you can ever receive or bestow.

25. WEDNESDAY. Merry Christmas! You can expect to get some especially nice presents. More important, though, is the sense that you are loved and appreciated by those close to you. This feeling should shine through. There is always a certain risk during the holidays that old family conflicts could come to the surface and spoil a good time for loved ones. There is the possibility that this could happen this Christmas. You know all your family's weak and sensitive spots, so take special pains to avoid bringing them up. If someone is becoming quarrelsome or just ungenerous, do what you can to smooth over the tension by playing the role of peacemaker.

26. THURSDAY. Slow. Post-Christmas laziness is the dominant mood today. You may be so tired from the holiday whirl that nothing pleases you so much as the thought of getting away from it. At this point you are probably likely to enjoy people only at a distance. You may have to devote some of the day to sending belated Christmas cards or calling friends and relatives you did not get to see yesterday. You may not find social gatherings the most ideal form of recreation. There is no harm in going, but there is a chance that any gathering will seem stodgy and boring. An early exit may be the best option, but come up with a good excuse as you get ready to leave.

27. FRIDAY. Useful. If you need to run some errands or exchange some gifts, today is a good day. You can put in enough effort to deal with them all in quick order, leaving you free for leisure pursuits. Be careful not to become bogged down in useless details. Catch up on your thank-you cards and phone or e-mail messages. You could add an extra artistic touch to some of them. Also take some time to reflect on the spiritual meaning of the season, which may have been swallowed up in the usual hustle and bustle of preparing for the big day. The quiet winter season does make it possible to cultivate serenity. Make some contact with your inner self, seeking the stillness that allows you to be rejuvenated.

28. SATURDAY. Difficult. Guard against the temptation to eat or drink too much. You and those around you could be inclined to overdo. If you attend any seasonal party, be very attentive to when you have had enough to eat or drink. If you indulge more than you should, it could cause some physical upset. This is not a day when you can count on your usual stamina to carry you through. Pay close attention to your health. The stresses of the season may have weakened your system, so be sure to get enough rest. Refuse invitations and excuse yourself from company if you need to. Now that the holiday social season is over, make sure to give yourself the extra rest and the physical recreation you need to be in the best of shape.

29. SUNDAY. Demanding. You should find it easy enough to fulfill routine tasks and requirements. However, the larger dimension of life may seem closed to you today. The spiritual side of life, and a sense of larger purpose, may be strangely absent. You could become trapped in petty details that take over your day to the point where you forget what you planned to do. When you got up in the morning you may have been a bit overly ambitious, attempting to take on too much and being completely unrealistic about what you can reasonably be expected to accomplish. If you limit yourself to modest, routine tasks, you will probably encounter no particular difficulties.

30. MONDAY. Pleasant. If holiday plans make it possible to stay home and spend time with your family, by all means do so. Venturing out into the world will not be as pleasant or satisfying as being with loved ones. Some small scrape or narrow miss could suggest to you that the world is a dangerous place. You do not need to respond by hiding under the bed. You almost certainly are in no real danger, but overall you will enjoy yourself more in a domestic setting. Do your best to be cozy. Prepare some comforting food and curl up with a good book. Or rent a movie that you have been meaning to see. Invite some friends over if you are in the mood for company, but do not turn the gathering into a formal party.

31. TUESDAY. Challenging. There is a sense this New Year's Eve that the world somehow includes unseen dimensions. A subtle shift in the atmosphere signals a movement from one phase to another that consists of more than just turning the page of a calendar. You may notice this quality today. By all means enjoy yourself this evening. However, try to keep alert for what is unseen and mysterious. There is a special message waiting for you at this very moment. It will not come with a loud voice, however, so keep your eyes and ears open. You are sure to find out what it is and how it will affect your life next year if you just watch and listen.

LEO
NOVEMBER–DECEMBER 2001

November 2001

1. THURSDAY. Excellent. You should wake up feeling bright and full of ideas. If a desire to make more friends is nagging at the edges of your mind, one way of doing so is to join a local club. It would not hurt to diversify your leisure interests at the same time. All that is needed to revive a long-term relationship is a little extra effort to show that you really care. Consider reserving a table at a restaurant you often frequented in your early days together. This is a good time to sign a contract. Just make sure you read it carefully, and do not hesitate to speak up if there are any terms that do not sound right. Try not to bring work home this evening; it is more important to relax.

2. FRIDAY. Troublesome. If you have made mistakes at work, there is no point thinking they will go unnoticed. Rather than hope to get away with them, own up to the errors and work to rectify them without delay. It is not kind to suddenly withdraw your attention from someone after you have been providing a lot of support and encouragement. This person has probably come to depend on you quite a lot, and you should honor this need. Romantic affairs may seem to be almost more trouble than they are worth. Actually, however, this is a period when you and that special person in your life can learn a great deal about relating. To do so, you need to put aside selfish concerns and focus intently on each other.

3. SATURDAY. Variable. A more hopeful atmosphere pervades much of this day. You should be able to cheer up a brother or sister who is down in the dumps, and they will be very grateful. Shopping for special gifts promises to be extremely pleasurable. Do not worry too much if you do not have any particular items in mind: you will know what is right as you see them. A social occasion is apt to be more in the line of a duty than a delight. That does not excuse you, however, from making your best effort to get along with people even if they are not your sort. There is special enjoyment waiting for you if you spend time with your nearest and dearest at home this evening.

4. SUNDAY. Deceptive. It is very important not to push yourself too hard. Even though you feel full of energy and pep, that could easily evaporate at a moment's notice. You should be conserving your energy, no matter what demands might be made. The only way to learn about someone is by getting close to them, which takes time. For this reason it is not unusual to be well into a relationship before the truth about the other person begins to emerge. If you do not like what is beginning to be clear, take time to reconsider your options. Your strong ideals could make you vulnerable to a ruthless businessperson. Try to avoid making any major decisions.

5. MONDAY. Favorable. There is no need to imagine you are not as skilled or as talented as your colleagues. This morning offers ample opportunity to prove your abilities. It should be possible to organize other workers in a most efficient manner, so that jobs get done faster. Attending court is not likely to be a favorite way for you to pass the time. However, you are bound to be entranced by the dramatic elements of the proceedings. In addition, there is much to be learned about human nature. Friendship can develop into love in gentle stages, as a warm and supportive relationship evolves almost without you noticing what is happening.

6. TUESDAY. Good. Focus on matters that are close to home. It is time to give more attention to your living conditions, resolving to make them as comfortable and attractive as possible. This will have a very positive effect not only on you but on your loved ones as well. It would be ideal if you could shut out the world and concentrate on your own inner reality. If that does not seem possible, at least set aside an hour or two for quiet reflection on your life and its purpose. This is a suitable day to invite friends to drop by. There is no need to prepare an elaborate meal. Instead, concentrate on creating a soothing atmosphere, with soft music and candlelight to put everyone in a relaxed mood.

7. WEDNESDAY. Confusing. Children may have to be kept home from school because of nasty viruses that are going around. This may mean that for much of your day you must find ways to keep them quietly amused. Where love is concerned, you may not even know what your own heart is telling you. Forget conventional expectations. When you look within, the way ahead in your present relationship should be clear. If you are driving, expect to be frustrated by delays for no apparent reason. The local roads, in particular, may be clogged with traffic. One result of this could be that someone who was going to do work in your house misses the appointment.

8. THURSDAY. Useful. Your family willingly rallies around with assistance when changes are occurring in your life. Even when all you need is emotional support, there is someone you can rely on. Do not be too proud to ask for a shoulder to lean on. The focus is not so much on getting your own work done as on lending a hand to colleagues. Just do so in an unobtrusive manner so that they do not feel they owe you a favor in return. Love does not always have to be exciting. Sometimes you just feel so comfortable with a certain person that there is no question of being apart. It is as if you completely understand each other without many words being spoken.

9. FRIDAY. Pleasant. This slightly more relaxed day allows you to give some thought to your individual self-development. There are two areas to focus on: relating to people at large and communicating with them. It is very important to have some means of self-expression. To better relate, it is important to develop greater empathy and compassion. Youngsters seem very eager to learn about the world around them. You will probably enjoy answering their questions, and there should be opportunities to guide their thoughts along lines you think most suitable. Consider treating yourself to a luxurious sauna or a day at a beauty spa where you are sure to feel special.

10. SATURDAY. Changeable. The morning is likely to be quite demanding. Tasks may have piled up to the extent they can no longer be ignored. You can usually rely on friends to give you a sense of security and support. Expecting this help, however, can make it quite hard when there are issues that you and you alone must cope with. It can be immensely strengthening to work out problems on your own and, what is more, you will be developing greater self-confidence in your ability to cope with difficulties. Happily, you have some cash available for pleasurable spending. It certainly will not hurt to be frivolous for once.

11. SUNDAY. Tricky. Since honesty is a vital part of every close relationship, it can be very difficult when you have a valid reason to keep information from your mate or partner. In fact, the only excuse for doing so should be to protect them from pain. Even then, the truth has to be revealed sooner or later. You may not feel like going out. Family members will be equally happy to stay home. Just make sure children do not decide to get creative in the bathroom, or there may be a flood to contend with. Find a quiet hour or two to review your finances and perhaps update your savings plan. You may also need to revise your insurance coverage for the contents of your home.

12. MONDAY. Fair. All extra efforts to get physically fit should prove very beneficial. You may want to consider jogging or running regularly. That can also be a good way of meeting other people who are using local roads and paths for the same reason. A business deal can be closed with outstanding results, although you may have to put up a fight to get the terms you want. Brace yourself; determination will help you win the day. Friends are good sources of information on all kinds of topics. The larger your social circle, the wider range of subjects probably covered. All you have to do is ask the right question. Some important dreams may come to you as you sleep tonight.

13. TUESDAY. Unsettling. When youngsters leave home, it can be very difficult to let them go without worrying. Naturally your protective instincts are aroused, but the time does come for them to achieve their independence. Sometimes working from home can be more stressful than being in an office. At home you are more vulnerable to interruptions, so it is vital to get in the right frame of mind. All domestic matters and personal calls must be ignored while you are on the job. Arrangements for a wedding or other family occasion should be going well. All the same, step back and allow other family members to do their fair share.

14. WEDNESDAY. Mixed. It is one thing to have an idealized image of the person you love, but quite another to live together. If you manage to get past the waning of absolute romance, it will prove far more deeply satisfying to relate to a real human being. If youngsters are showing early signs of artistic or musical talent, foster these to the best of your ability. It might help to get some advice from a teacher or a professional. All matters concerning property look quite challenging. You should be able to get the price you want, but not without a struggle. It is important not to be persuaded into a deal you are not wholly comfortable with.

15. THURSDAY. Disconcerting. Changes are afoot. If you do not willingly go along with them, life will be difficult. The dynamics of family relationships may cause you to have a falling out with some loved ones, but that is likely to be only a temporary problem. There is no reason to end a business partnership just because you are not getting your own way all the time. If that is nevertheless the course on which you have decided, realize that you may be throwing out the baby with the bathwater. On the positive side, you have a great deal of determination to achieve a personal ideal, and you can count on your mate or partner to back you up in your attempts.

16. FRIDAY. Difficult. Words spoken in anger may not be meant but they are rarely forgotten. If you lash out at a loved one, you may do far more damage to the relationship than you realize or intend. With youngsters so full of energy, they may show a tendency to be quite destructive around the house. Even though this is not deliberate, they need an eye kept on them. A few words concerning proper behavior would also be useful. If a romantic affair is teetering on the brink of dissolving, it is probably because you sense that closer involvement could become very demanding. You must decide if you want to make a commitment or end the relationship.

17. SATURDAY. Buoyant. Dynamic energy frees you up to accomplish whatever you set your mind to do. There is something unstoppable about you today, so focus your mind on creative or idealistic enterprises and go for it. A loving relationship may seem to be quite profoundly changing the way you look at the world. Do not resist this. A deeper understanding of what human beings want and need will serve you well in all kinds of situations. This is a great day for hosting a party. Pull out all the stops to create a memorable evening, and remember that success depends primarily on an interesting mix of guests.

18. SUNDAY. Quiet. You will probably be glad to spend an extra hour in bed this morning. Recent stresses have taken a toll on you, but happily there is a good chance to recuperate today. Ideally you should pursue a favorite hobby, allowing the comfortable familiarity of what you are doing to soothe away the cares of the outside world. Love is in the air, but there is no urgency to begin a new relationship. It would be more suitable to review romantic experiences you have enjoyed so far. Everyone with whom you are ever involved has something to teach you, and you may be amazed to realize how rich your experience has been.

19. MONDAY. Variable. The morning should be quietly enjoyable, with the chance for Leos to concentrate on undemanding tasks. This enables you to ease gently into the workweek, conserving your energy for more challenging work later on. If you have been feeling slightly under the weather, do not just ignore the symptoms and try to carry on as usual. It would be far more sensible to grant yourself some time off, or even to make an appointment to see a doctor. A general checkup might be a good idea, so that you can get yourself in peak condition for the months ahead. This is a good time to expand your cooking skills by trying some new recipes that you dream up yourself.

20. TUESDAY. Exciting. You may well have had a secret admirer for some time, without even realizing it. Now that you are becoming aware of this admiration, a lot of past behavior will begin to make sense. The question is whether to return the affection. Leo people who enjoy buying special items for the house should have a great time poking around in antique shops and home supply stores. Even if you have nothing specific in mind, there is bound to be a vase or bowl or other ornament that virtually jumps into your hands. Since you are apt to be in a rather dreamy and unfocused state, be extra careful when dealing with financial matters.

21. WEDNESDAY. Disquieting. There is little that is more upsetting than having to listen to criticism from the person you love best. When it is unleashed on you out of the blue, the immediate temptation is often to lash out in angry defense. Try to exercise some restraint, however, so that you have time to consider what is being said. Negotiations for property sales may appear to be going well, but you should expect hitches somewhere along the way. Since these can crop up at any time, it is best to be prepared. Mixed messages are the order of the day in romance. It is unclear whether you should pursue a relationship in greater depth or break free from it altogether.

22. THURSDAY. Difficult. Not all is smooth sailing in a legal matter that has been on your mind recently. Possibly the best course of action is to discuss it with a your lawyer, frankly expressing your doubts. You are unlikely to want to be separated from your mate or partner for long, but a necessary journey might make an overnight stay inevitable. Unfortunately this may come at quite a crucial time in the relationship, so you will need to do some sensitive negotiating. A more creative period is about to begin, with self-expression being vital for your happiness. This can be achieved through quite ordinary activities, such as cooking.

23. FRIDAY. Frustrating. Although love may not be the first thing on your mind when you are trying to complete an important piece of business, it could intrude unexpectedly. An attraction to someone you are working with can prove quite disastrous; the best thing to do is to keep it to yourself or your work is apt to suffer. You and a close relative may have your wires crossed. A quarrel could erupt unless both of you make an effort to keep the peace. Do not expect to be thrilled after an evening out with friends; it could be a bit of a downer. However, once you get home there is quiet pleasure in the company of those who are closest to you.

24. SATURDAY. Fair. As long as you control a tendency to dominate loved ones, today should be pleasurable. There is some danger that you will feel people are ganging up on you, which probably is far from the case. You should be able to have some fun planning what to do with a small financial windfall. It will probably be spent ten times over in your mind before you actually get around to seeing what it will realistically buy. This is an excellent time to gather materials for redecorating your home. Take care with your choices since you will have to live with the result for a long time. Seek professional advice on complicated color or pattern decisions.

25. SUNDAY. Good. Sometimes the best and most valuable support is given in silence. There is much to be said for sympathy that goes beyond the superficial help of words. Emotionally you should be better able than usual to express yourself. Do not miss this chance to clear up issues with loved ones that they previously were not able to understand. Youngsters may want to stay close to home, giving you the opportunity to spend some quality time with them. They may confide very revealing secrets which allow you to help them all the more. Romance is highlighted, with the focus on shared pleasure through a mutual hobby.

26. MONDAY. Cautious. More haste definitely means less speed where work is concerned. Try too hard to beat a competitor and you will probably end up having to backtrack to correct mistakes. There is bound to be a problem during the day with a computer system, and getting angry will not solve it. If this system crash means not being able to get to important data for a while, you will just have to focus your energy elsewhere. This should be a positive day for creative writers. Putting your thoughts down in words may release emotions that have had no other outlet until now. You may want to try writing a love poem dedicated to that special person in your life.

27. TUESDAY. Favorable. Training courses can teach you a lot, including how to handle people in awkward situations. In addition, you may meet people who could advise you on ways to develop your career. If the thought of a winter break is quite tempting, review your bank account and see if you can spare enough cash to treat yourself. Discontent with some aspects of life can actually be a positive, motivating force. At least this means that you can see where changes for the better need to be made. Listen carefully if your mate or partner is bursting with excitement about a new idea for making money; there could be something to it after all.

28. WEDNESDAY. Enjoyable. This promises to be a highly romantic day. Leo singles who have been hesitating on the brink of
a proposal should pluck up the courage needed to go ahead. Since
this is a once-in-a-lifetime moment, make sure it is as memorable
an occasion as you can manage. All artistic work is favored. There
is even a chance of making an impact on someone who can sell
your work for a reasonable profit. For once, risking money is not
entirely out of the question. Take a chance if you feel the urge;
just do not gamble away your entire week's earnings. Your dreams
almost certainly have a meaningful message; let your good Leo
intuition be your guide.

29. THURSDAY. Sensitive. Although you are probably feeling
fine, the same cannot be said for a certain loved one. This makes
it all the more essential that you tread carefully, moderating your
manner with someone who is clearly a bit depressed. Trouble with
a senior staff member at work is all but inevitable. Fur will fly if
a project is not completed to their liking, which is bad news if you
have been hoping for a promotion on the strength of recent work.
All is not lost, however; you can calm them down if you have the
patience to do so. You and your mate or partner will thrive as
long as you allow each other a greater measure of independence
and freedom.

30. FRIDAY. Uncertain. It may not be exactly clear where you
stand with romance. Talking about it may just confuse the issue
all the more. In the end the only thing you can truly trust is your
own instinct which is bound to be right on target. If you have
been waiting for examination results, you are likely to be getting
impatient. However, making inquiries may not get you very far.
There may have been a mixup somewhere in the marking process
that has slowed down release of the results. This is an ideal evening for shutting out the world and forgetting your worries by
losing yourself in a good movie or a favorite book.

December 2001

1. SATURDAY. Slow. Since a planned social occasion may be canceled or postponed, you can afford not to rush around. Instead, fill the extra time by calling some old friends or writing them cards with letters. Romance is likely to be a sore subject at the moment. If an argument has made both you and your mate or steady date miserable, keep out of each other's hair for a day or two. This is not the best time to try a new sport, no matter how persuasive friends might try to be. Be content with observing them instead; then you will get a better idea of whether the activity truly appeals to you. Close family members would appreciate some special attention this evening.

2. SUNDAY. Productive. This is an excellent day to call in favors owed by friends, especially true if you want help achieving a long-term aim. After all, everyone needs support at one time or another. There is a change of focus where romance is concerned. The first blissful days of a relationship seem to be over, and now it is time to settle into ordinary life. Take a critical look around your home and decide what you would most like improved. Perhaps you long for a new kitchen or a new bathroom. Whatever your choice, now is the time to begin saving for it. Dinner with friends this evening promises to be lively and stimulating.

3. MONDAY. Difficult. The workweek is apt to get off to a less than perfect start. A work meeting may arouse more problems than it solves. Basically it is a question of people getting along together. If you feel that it is timely and appropriate, point out that personal matters should not be allowed to intrude on work. Getting involved with an older person can have great benefits, but there are some serious drawbacks, too. With this person you cannot take a shared cultural background for granted, which means there is a greater need to strive to understand each other. Happily, you will gain much pleasure and relaxation from a quiet evening spent at home.

4. TUESDAY. Buoyant. It is now or never for a romantic affair. Unless you declare yourself, the relationship is never likely to get off the ground, so be bold. All artistic activity should be encouraged where youngsters are concerned. It is never too early to promote signs of talent, but do not be so serious that it ceases to be fun. If you are taking a test, it should be comparatively easy to breeze through. Quick reactions are important, as are clear answers to all of the questions. Sometimes there are issues between friends which should not be commented upon. Let them sort these out themselves, and do not risk getting caught in any cross-fire.

5. WEDNESDAY. Challenging. Waking out of a deep sleep to find you have missed the alarm is certainly not the best way to start the day. Just make sure you are properly alert before leaving the house. This is a promising day to go on a job interview. As long as you put yourself across as a responsible person, you should make an excellent impression. Be sure to dress in a smart, businesslike fashion. A face across a crowded room could haunt your dreams. Instead of letting this torment you, figure out some way of getting in touch with that person. You might want to start the search by contacting other people who were there at the time; someone is bound to know who the person is.

6. THURSDAY. Sensitive. Leo parents of young children are bound to be aware that they have fears and fancies which are difficult to dislodge. Right now you need to shower as much affection on them as you can in order to make them feel secure. Bad dreams and fantasies will fade with time. A romantic partner may be all too ready to pick holes in everything you say. Rather than lose your temper, try to find out what is at the bottom of their negative mood. Unless you are very careful you could be taken in by a so-called expert who claims to be able to make you a lot of money quickly. Unfortunately such promises are not likely to be fulfilled; in fact, you could lose all that you invest.

7. FRIDAY. Cautious. Your personal power is heightened to such an extent that you could sway anyone to do your bidding with comparative ease. It would not be a good idea to do so, however. Instead, focus your considerable energy on a creative outlet. There is danger of love fading into oblivion unless you do something to rescue it quickly. It is not just that your mate or partner is disillusioned, but that you seem to be almost deliberately trying to draw away. You need to stop this self-destructive behavior immediately, for their sake and your own. A slight cash-flow problem may mean that you cannot socialize as much as you would like, but it will not do you any harm to stay home.

8. SATURDAY. Calm. This relatively laid-back day should entice you to catch up with work that needs to be done. It would be a good idea to stock up on household goods that are currently in short supply in your kitchen. Even though money is tight, with careful management you can make it go quite far. It would be a good idea to cut down on magazine subscriptions and other similar luxuries that you would not mind doing without. Deep emotions can be stirred by a loss in the family, even if you were not close to the person. It is far better to face these feelings than to try to be brave and suppress them.

9. SUNDAY. Fair. Consider taking your mate or partner out for a special treat. Lunch at a local restaurant would be enjoyable for both of you. Forget the time; just relax and let the day drift by. Leisure activities promise to be especially enjoyable. At last you should be mastering the intricacies of a sport or hobby that once seemed all but impossible, so give yourself a pat on the back. It is not always a good idea to throw away old letters and photographs since you are almost bound to regret doing so later. Even love letters from a past admirer will have an increasingly poignant value as time passes; by no means should you consider them irrelevant.

10. MONDAY. Challenging. A work matter may seem to be almost like a game since you enjoy a challenge to your wits so much. You certainly should be well able to rise to the occasion, with unusual problem-solving ideas springing to mind. Although children are likely to be restless and easily bored, they should also be great fun to be with. It will not hurt you to be kept on the go thanks to their astute comments. A declaration of love could come out of the blue, making you stumped for an immediate response. Actually, it would probably be better not to give one yet. If your car is out of commission, consider getting some exercise by walking or cycling to your local destination.

11. TUESDAY. Disappointing. Some love affairs are not destined to succeed. Naturally you are bound to feel upset when a relationship fizzles, but comfort yourself with the thought that a far more satisfying one lies just around the corner. Risking money now would be foolish. Nor can you really afford to make a large loan to a friend, since you would probably have to wait a long time for it to be repaid. An item of antique jewelry or one with family connections could be lost. If it came off while you were at a social function, it may be gone for good. However, it is still worth asking friends if they have seen it and perhaps putting a notice in the newspaper.

12. WEDNESDAY. Disquieting. If it seems that something is going on behind your back at work, you have to get at the truth somehow. Rumors could be circulating that you need to know about, and possibly stop without delay. All is not as well as it could be between you and your mate or partner; much depends on your ability to face up to that fact. Honest discussion is worth a great deal more in the long run than keeping a stiff upper lip. Problems with electricity at home should not be ignored. Get them fixed now before matters worsen. It is important to relax this evening so that you can get a good night's sleep.

13. THURSDAY. Unsettling. Most people are happiest in an established routine, and that is true for you as a Leo. For this reason it can be quite upsetting to be forced to cope with special circumstances, especially when there is no clear indication of when life will get back to normal. All you can do is make the most of it, keeping a positive outlook and recognizing that there is much to be learned from the experience. A love affair with someone who would not normally capture your interest is foreseen. You might even enter into it simply because the other person refuses to stop pestering you for a date. It would be unwise to make a big financial decision; postpone it at least until tomorrow.

14. FRIDAY. Rosy. The love you have always wanted is within reach, but strangely you might almost be tempted to hold back. Realizing a dream can be quite scary, although in this case you should be brave and plunge right in. There is a good possibility of a stroke of luck if you enter a competition, especially a prize drawing for which you do not even need to prove your talent or skill in any way. You can make a fresh start with youngsters who have been rather negative lately. Now something is causing them to turn over a new leaf, and it does not much matter what that catalyst was. It is only important that you now begin to build a new and a firmer relationship.

15. SATURDAY. Favorable. Act on an urge to write or draw this morning; the inspiration will evaporate if you do not heed it. The quality of what you produce is not as important as the personal satisfaction it gives you. As a Leo you have a delightfully playful side, so it is natural for you to enjoy the company of children. Today is a starred time to organize a party for youngsters, even if it is on the spur of the moment. Later in the day a more serious mood leads you to take stock of your overall health. There is room for improvement to your diet, so focus on that for now. If you go out to eat, opt for a salad rather than meat and potatoes.

16. SUNDAY. Changeable. There is no need to go overboard with exercise, no matter how negligent you may have been lately. Suddenly putting your muscles to hard use will only result in strain or other injury. Pets should receive some extra attention, especially one that may wander off and get lost if not kept indoors. Otherwise you could spend an uncomfortable and worrying day scouring the neighborhood. Plans to go through closets and bureau drawers could come to nothing. For one thing, you are bound to get distracted by nostalgia when you come across old mementos, making it impossible to throw a lot away.

17. MONDAY. Quiet. Make a good start to the workweek by settling down to routine tasks. This can be a very satisfying way of passing a morning that some people might find boring. There may be opportunities to help a colleague, especially if they are new to the job, and you might even make a new friend in this way. Find time to stock up on cooking ingredients such as herbs and spices. If you have plenty of exotic food on hand, you can try out a new and unusual recipe. A dentist's appointment should find you without much needing to be done, which proves how silly it is to get nervous beforehand.

18. TUESDAY. Mixed. It may seem almost impossible to keep your mind on work. All kinds of concerns will keep cropping up from the depths of your mind, none of them relevant to what you are supposed to be doing. If possible, avoid practical tasks and any important decision-making. After you have been with a partner for a while, it becomes second nature to expect them to be there for you. However, you need to guard against taking your closest relationship for granted. Express your love and appreciation with a little gift or with a surprise outing, this evening. This is a good time to try to achieve an ideal. Hard work that you do now will pay off handsomely in time.

19. WEDNESDAY. Profitable. Romance could take you by surprise, especially because the other person is apt to be quite unconventional and even shocking in their behavior. That does not matter, however, compared with the affection they give to you. Dare to be different, and see how good it makes you feel. Social events are highlighted; your calendar is probably filled up as the holiday season draws to a climax. It may be necessary to discriminate among what events you actually want to attend so that you do not get worn out. A last-minute business decision could mean that you end the day running around trying to get organized before it is time to close up shop and go home.

20. THURSDAY. Fair. The chance of making some extra money by selling crafts or art could be a one-time-only occurrence, but it is not to be sneezed at for that reason. Make the most of this opportunity. Sometimes it is not wise to insist on having your own way in a relationship. However, when you can see that things will go wrong if you do not make your wishes known, then there is nothing to do but firmly put your foot down. An intensely practical atmosphere this afternoon favors hard work. You might even get so absorbed that you do not hear the phone ring or notice when darkness descends. It would be good to do as much research as possible, checking first with primary sources.

21. FRIDAY. Successful. If this is the last day at work before the holidays for you, there is certain to be a scramble to get urgent tasks finished. Happily you should be able to look at ordinary jobs and see clearly which are most important in the long run. Your health could benefit from some gentle alternative remedy. Just make sure that anything you take is recommended by experts, since it is easy to be misled in this regard. Old friends may seem rather touchy; you have to be extra careful not to upset them in any way. Clearly there is something going on in their life, but they may not be ready to tell you what it is.

22. SATURDAY. Frustrating. Hard work is the order of the day. You should be prepared to be frustrated from achieving all that you set out to do. It is possible that you will have to be available for a friend who needs some moral support; this has to take precedence over less important matters. Although it can be difficult preparing for the holiday season when cash is in short supply, your Leo ingenuity can save the day. The main ingredient for success is warm emotion, not lavish gifts. A romantic relationship may seems to be invading your freedom. There is no doubt that you need to balance closeness with trust in your ability to survive alone if necessary.

23. SUNDAY. Demanding. What is likely to exhaust you is not so much household chores but conversation. There is so much to organize at the moment, and everyone is apt to have their own ideas about what would work best. It may be necessary to put your foot down. Be sure to look after pets with special care, since there is some danger of them being forgotten or at least neglected. This could be a task that children would enjoy doing. If you are feeling a little under the weather, it is probably because you have not been eating properly recently. Get your mate or partner to cook for you or take you out; the rest will do you good.

24. MONDAY. Satisfactory. Even this quite emotional time should not prevent you from doing some serious cleaning around the house. There may be interesting discoveries to be made in the process, probably hidden in the back of drawers that have been stuffed full of papers for years. This is a time to mull over your long-term goals. Even half an hour of seclusion can make a big difference to your level of serenity. Try to let go of past unhappiness and to make your peace with those who once upset you. A long-distance phone call could lead to a surprising but delightful conversation. It is clear that someone loves you, even if you cannot physically be together at the moment.

25. TUESDAY. Merry Christmas! Today should be truly memorable. You should feel as if you are with the one you love for the first time, being swept off your feet all over again. Try to make time to call relatives and friends who live far away. This is a day for good fellowship to be spread far and wide. Nothing could be more romantic than a proposal on this special day of the year. The circumstances are just right; all it takes is courage and commitment. Leos with young children will naturally structure the day around their pleasure. The sight of their faces lit up with joy should be sufficient reward for all your expense and hard work.

26. WEDNESDAY. Fortunate. Even though there is a fair amount of clearing up to do, you should be in a relaxed mood and able to take it in stride. Housework can become a kind of meditation, performed slowly and with positive pleasure. Improving your health can also have a very good effect on your looks, which is a bonus. If you have been working out or following a more healthy diet for some time, take a critical look at yourself. The difference should be noticeable, encouraging you to stick to it. While you are not involved in your day job, it is possible to think about it more clearly and consider whether you need to make a change.

27. THURSDAY. Stressful. Enjoying the company of your mate or partner is one thing, but being cooped up together for too long is another. Do not get annoyed at yourself if you are beginning to get a little irritable. Arrange to spend some hours apart, then see how much better you both feel. Quite an introspective mood may be making you feel that you have not achieved the goals you would like. Consider whether you are being too hard on yourself. Nothing is to be gained by impatience; aims that are worth reaching take time. It would be good to get some fresh air and brisk exercise. Guard against making any promises to a relative.

28. FRIDAY. Tricky. You are not likely to be in the most sociable of moods, so it can be quite an effort to put on a cheerful face in company. This must be done, however, for the sake of friends who have gone to a great deal of trouble to make an occasion special. Although it is always a bit difficult asking for a loan to be repaid, especially when it is long overdue, the last thing you should do is write it off. Make sure the borrower understands that you are getting impatient; set a deadline for final repayment. Falling in love with someone who is outside your usual social circle can be very stimulating, but getting your friends to accept them may be a little awkward at first.

29. SATURDAY. Exciting. This is a good day to go out on a whim. Spur-of-the-moment decisions will be far more fun than an organized trip. You and your mate or partner can renew your relationship, so that life becomes almost as magical and exciting as when you first met. Just make sure you spend time together without getting distracted by routine household tasks and practical topics of conversation such as bill paying. Although Leos are usually strong individualists, it is not always possible to act with the freedom you would like. Today, however, you should give your creativity free rein and regain the sense of being a truly special person.

30. SUNDAY. Difficult. Emotions may be rumbling away in the background of a love affair, even though neither of you is yet willing to admit that anything is wrong. This is a period when you can both develop a deeper trust in the strength of the relationship by honestly facing up to the fears and doubts that you both feel. Although you might be enthusiastic to play a sport, some caution is needed. The physical action may be too hard for your level of experience, so that you have to back off. Resolve to look after your health better and today could be a real turning point. It is a matter of moderation and balance in all things and at all times.

31. MONDAY. Calm. As the year draws to an end you naturally dwell on and think about the past. Just do not get so caught up in reminiscing that you no longer value the present. Instead, resolve to make your future bright and happy. It can give you a good feeling to clean up your home and get everything spic-and-span, so that you start the new year in good order. Youngsters may be quite secretive about what they are doing. It would be a good plan to spend more time with them in the weeks ahead in order to check on their intentions. You may not favor partying; a quiet evening at home with loved ones might be better.

WHAT DOES YOUR FUTURE HOLD...?

DISCOVER IT IN *ASTROANALYSIS*—

COMPLETELY REVISED TO THE YEAR 2015, THESE GUIDES INCLUDE
COLOR-CODED CHARTS FOR TOTAL ASTROLOGICAL EVALUATION,
PLANET TABLES AND CUSP CHARTS, AND STREAMLINED INFORMA-
TION FOR ANYONE WHO HAS EVER LOOKED TO THE STARS AND
WONDERED....

__ARIES	0-425-17558-8/$12.95
__TAURUS	0-425-17559-6/$12.95
__GEMINI	0-425-17560-X/$12.95
__CANCER	0-425-17561-8/$12.95
__LEO	0-425-17562-6/$12.95
__VIRGO	0-425-17563-4/$12.95
__LIBRA	0-425-17564-2/$12.95
__SCORPIO	0-425-17565-0/$12.95
__SAGITTARIUS	0-425-17566-9/$12.95
__CAPRICORN	0-425-17567-7/$12.95
__AQUARIUS	0-425-17568-5/$12.95
__PISCES	0-425-17569-3/$12.95

Prices slightly higher in Canada

Payable by Visa, MC or AMEX only ($10.00 min.), No cash, checks or COD. Shipping & handling:
US/Can. $2.75 for one book, $1.00 for each add'l book; Int'l $5.00 for one book, $1.00 for each
add'l. Call (800) 788-6262 or (201) 933-9292, fax (201) 896-8569 or mail your orders to:

Penguin Putnam Inc.   Bill my: ❑ Visa ❑ MasterCard ❑ Amex _____(expires)
P.O. Box 12289, Dept. B
Newark, NJ 07101-5289   Card# _____
Please allow 4-6 weeks for delivery.   Signature _____
Foreign and Canadian delivery 6-8 weeks.

Bill to:
Name _____
Address _____City _____
State/ZIP _____Daytime Phone # _____
Ship to:
Name _____Book Total $ _____
Address _____Applicable Sales Tax $ _____
City _____Postage & Handling $ _____
State/ZIP _____Total Amount Due $ _____

This offer subject to change without notice.   Ad # 893 (3/00)

Advertisement

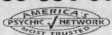

Advertisement

Advertisement

Advertisement